If We Can Keep It

OTHER BOOKS BY

Michael Tomasky

Yeah! Yeah! Yeah!

Hillary's Turn

Left for Dead

Bill Clinton

Supporters of George W. Bush and Al Gore confront each other awaiting the Supreme Court's ruling in Bush v. Gore, *December 11, 2000.*

GETTY / PHOTO BY MARK WILSON / NEWSMAKERS.

If We Can Keep It

HOW THE REPUBLIC COLLAPSED

and

HOW IT MIGHT BE SAVED

MICHAEL TOMASKY

LIVERIGHT PUBLISHING
CORPORATION
A Division of W. W. Norton & Company
Independent Publishers Since 1923
NEW YORK   LONDON

For information about permission to reproduce selections from this book, write to
Permissions, Liveright Publishing Corporation, a division of
W. W. Norton & Company, Inc., 500 Fifth Avenue, New York, NY 10110

For information about special discounts for bulk purchases, please contact
W. W. Norton Special Sales at specialsales@wwnorton.com or 800-233-4830

Manufacturing by Lake Book Manufacturing
Book design by Barbara Bachman
Production manager: Lauren Abbate

Library of Congress Cataloging-in-Publication Data

Names: Tomasky, Michael, 1960– author.
Title: If we can keep it : how the republic collapsed and how it might
be saved / Michael Tomasky.
Description: First edition. | New York : Liveright Publishing, 2019. | Includes
bibliographical references and index.
Identifiers: LCCN 2018043229 | ISBN 9781631494086 (hardcover)
Subjects: LCSH: Political culture—United States. | Polarization (Social sciences)—
Political aspects—United States. | Political participation—United States. | United States—
Politics and government—21st century.
Classification: LCC JK1726 .T66 2019 | DDC 320.973—dc23
LC record available at https://lccn.loc.gov/2018043229

Liveright Publishing Corporation, 500 Fifth Avenue, New York, N.Y. 10110
www.wwnorton.com

W. W. Norton & Company Ltd., 15 Carlisle Street, London W1D 3BS

1 2 3 4 5 6 7 8 9 0

To the memory of
my dear friend and political mentor

RUSSELL D. HEMENWAY

1925–2014

Adviser to Eleanor Roosevelt;
Member of Nixon's Enemies List.
"Would ya write it, Mikey? Please!"

CONTENTS

★

A CHRONOLOGY OF POLARIZATION

★

A LIST OF FIFTY-FIVE
EVENTS, EPISODES, AND TRENDS
THAT EXPLAIN OUR HISTORY
OF NOT GETTING ALONG
WITH EACH OTHER

I.
THE AGE OF CREATION, 1787–1865

1. *July 1787:* The Constitutional Convention passes the Connecticut Compromise by one vote, 5–4–1, creating the inherently unrepresentative United States Senate.

2. *September 1787:* On their last day, convention delegates pass a resolution setting 30,000 as the number of people each congressional district should contain, a number that would increase with each census and require the drawing of new, fair district lines—a process that most states resolutely ignored until the 1960s.

3. *Early 1790s:* Despite the founders' wishes to the contrary, the first political parties are formed, the Federalists and the Democratic-Republicans. They begin fighting immediately over the size and scope of the federal government.

4. *November 1800 to February 1801:* The rancorous 1800 presidential

election is held, and finally settled by the House of Representatives on the thirty-sixth ballot on February 17, when Thomas Jefferson defeats Aaron Burr.

5.   *December 1814 to January 1815:* Federalists meet in Hartford, Connecticut, at the so-called Hartford Convention, drawing up a list of grievances and restating their opposition to the War of 1812—just as Andrew Jackson was defeating the British in New Orleans. Shortly, the Federalists dissolve.

6.   *1820:* The Missouri Compromise brings Missouri into the union as a slave state and Maine as a free state. They become the sixth and seventh states added over the prior decade. Afterward, no new state was added for fifteen years.

7.   *1825:* Martin Van Buren, the father of the modern American political party, starts to pull together the forces that would make up the Democratic Party.

8.   *November 1828:* Andrew Jackson wins the presidency as a Democrat; he is the first president of the "common man," though he is denounced as "King Andrew" by his foes for his quasi-dictatorial tendencies.

9.   *Early 1830s:* The Whig Party takes shape, formed initially by anti-Jackson Northerners who then add slaveholding Jackson foes in the South to their ranks.

10. *1832:* The Nullification Crisis hits, as South Carolina announces it will not obey a federal tariff law.

11. *June 1842:* Congress passes and President John Tyler signs the Apportionment Act, which for the first time mandates single-member congressional districts. Four states, three of them slave, disobey the new law.

12. *1850:* Congress passes and President Millard Fillmore signs the Compromise of 1850, which admits California to the union as a free state but includes much more stringent laws pertaining to the capture and return of fugitive slaves.

13. *March 20, 1854:* A group meets in Ripon, Wisconsin, to form a new party, which would become the Republican Party—at first wholly Northern and antislavery.

14. *1854:* The Kansas-Nebraska Act passes, allowing for popular sovereignty on the slave question in all new states.

15. *1854:* The Whig Party collapses over its internal divisions on the slavery question.

16. *November 1860:* Abraham Lincoln wins the presidency in a four-way race, taking every Northern state plus California and Oregon.

17. *December 1860:* South Carolina secedes; within a few months, ten other states follow suit and form the Confederate States of America.

18. *April 1861:* Confederate forces open fire on Union troops at Fort Sumter, South Carolina; the Civil War begins.

19. *April 1865:* The South surrenders, and five days later, President Lincoln is assassinated by John Wilkes Booth.

II.

THE AGE OF POWER, 1865-1929

20. *1865 to 1877:* The Reconstruction Era arrives, as the country engages in a bitterly contested series of debates over how and under what terms the Southern states can rejoin the Union, and over the rights of freed slaves under the newly passed 13th, 14th, and 15th amendments.

21. *1876 and 1877:* Republican Rutherford B. Hayes wins the presidential election despite losing the popular vote to Democrat Samuel Tilden; Hayes is made president as part of a deal whereby he agrees to end Reconstruction.

22. *1880s:* Republicans split between the Half-Breeds, who back civil-service reform, and the Stalwarts, who do not. Also, Democrats of this era are basically two parties, the racist Southern party and the immigrant-friendly (but corrupt) big-city Northern party.

23. *1912:* Teddy Roosevelt, enraged at his successor William Howard Taft's backing away from trust-busting, decides to enter the 1912 race as a third candidate on the Bull-Moose ballot line and thus helps elect Democrat Woodrow Wilson.

24. *1924:* The Johnson-Reed immigration bill dramatically reduces immigration to the United States over time.

25. *1924:* In a sign of their intense internal divisions, Democrats need 103 ballots to nominate for president John W. Davis of West Virginia.

26. *October 1929:* The stock market crashes, sparking the Great Depression, taking unemployment to 24 percent and raising real questions about whether the American free-enterprise system will survive.

III.
THE AGE OF CONSENSUS, 1933–1980

27. *1933:* The New Deal begins under Franklin Roosevelt, realigning American politics, creating the outlines of the modern Democratic Party.

28. *1933 to 1941:* Tremendous fights take place over the New Deal, which is attacked by the Liberty League and other probusiness groups, as Roosevelt expands government, raises taxes, and tries to pack the Supreme Court with supporters.

29. *December 1941:* The United States enters World War II, commencing a period of shared sacrifice and unity.

30. *Late 1940s:* After the war victory, prominent Americans in business, labor, show business, and other realms work to promote tolerance and diversity; it is also a time of race riots and much labor unrest.

31. *Late 1940s:* The beginning of the era economists call the "Great Compression," a period of high wages and low inequality (it lasted until the mid-1970s).

32. *Early 1950s:* The Red Scare and the McCarthy Era heighten the Cold War. McCarthy is censured by the Senate in 1954.

33. *1964:* President Lyndon Johnson signs the Civil Rights Act; Republicans nominate anticivil-rights crusader Barry Goldwater for president; Johnson wins in a huge landslide, but Goldwater carries five states in the formerly "Solid South," which had been anti-Republican ever since Lincoln freed the slaves.

34. *1965:* The Immigration and Nationality Act passes, undoing the

1924 restrictions and emphasizing family reunification; it is not controversial, and no one expects much change.

35. *1968:* Public opinion turns against the Vietnam War; Johnson announces he will not seek reelection in March; student antiwar protests escalate; Richard Nixon wins a narrow victory.

36. *1971:* The U.S. Chamber of Commerce asks Richmond lawyer and future Supreme Court associate justice Lewis Powell to write a memo suggesting ways for the chamber to combat what it sees as relentless attacks on the free-enterprise system.

37. *1973:* Supreme Court decides *Roe v. Wade,* finding, by a 7–2 vote with three conservatives joining the majority, that the 14th Amendment protects a woman's right to have an abortion.

38. *1973:* The wage-productivity link ends, and middle-class wages begin to stagnate; the OPEC oil embargo of America results in the quadrupling of the price of oil in a few months.

39. *August 1974:* Richard Nixon resigns over the Watergate crisis.

40. *Mid-to-late 1970s:* The battle over ratification of the Equal Rights Amendment ensues, as the ERA falls short of being added to the Constitution; also, the religious right emerges as a force.

41. *Late 1970s and early 1980s:* The country experiences rampant, double-digit inflation, something that had never happened in the postwar era.

42. *Beginning in the 1970s:* The two parties, once ideological amalgams of interests with a tremendous amount of crossover, start to become more ideologically coherent.

IV.

THE AGE OF FRACTURE, 1980-PRESENT

43. *August 1981:* President Ronald Reagan fires the striking air-traffic controllers, forever changing labor-management relations; union membership, already in decline, begins to fall off steeply.

44. *August 1987:* The Federal Communications Commission repeals the Fairness Doctrine; within a year or two, radio is dominated by conservative political talk.

45.   *September 1987:* The Senate holds hearings on the confirmation of Robert Bork, nominated by President Reagan to the Supreme Court; they become the first intensely politicized nomination hearings in American history. Bork is defeated, with fifty-two Democrats and six Republicans voting no.

46.   *Throughout the 1980s and 1990s:* Money comes to dominate politics, both in terms of the amount spent by corporate America on lobbying and the fund-raising demands on candidates.

47.   *September 1990:* George H. W. Bush agrees in a budget deal to raise taxes; House Republicans vote against their president 163–10.

48.   *November 1992:* Bill Clinton is elected president with 43 percent of the vote, and he and First Lady Hillary Clinton immediately become cultural Rorschach tests.

49.   *November 1994:* The Republicans capture control of the House of Representatives for the first time in forty years in the "Gingrich Revolution"; Newt Gingrich becomes speaker.

50.   *Throughout the 1990s:* The two congressional parties become still more ideological, with less and less crossover.

51.   *January 1998:* The Monica Lewinsky saga unfolds; by December, the House votes four articles of impeachment against President Clinton, but the next February, the Senate fails to convict.

52.   *December 2000:* The Supreme Court, in *Bush v. Gore*, halts the presidential election recount in Florida, in essence declaring George W. Bush the president by a divided 5–4 margin.

53.   *Throughout the 2000s:* The country divides into "red" (Republican/conservative) and "blue" (Democratic/liberal) states and regions; Congress grows more and more divided. Much new scholarship is devoted to studying this phenomenon.

54.   *2010:* President Barack Obama and the Democrats pass the Patient Protection and Affordable Care Act—Obamacare; during the next seven years, Republicans try to repeal the law more than seventy times, and fail.

55.   *2016:* Donald Trump is elected president, winning the Electoral College handily, while Hillary Clinton wins 2.8 million more votes.

A FOURTEEN-POINT
AGENDA TO REDUCE
POLARIZATION

★

Political Fixes

1. *End Partisan Gerrymandering.*

2. *Bring Back At-Large Congressional Elections.*

3. *Introduce Ranked-Choice Voting to Congressional Elections.*

4. *Expand the House of Representatives to 500 Members.*

5. *Eliminate the Senate Filibuster.*

6. *Get Rid of the Electoral College (or Make It Obey the Popular Vote).*

7. *Revive Moderate Republicanism.*

Social and Cultural Fixes

8. *Establish "Foreign" Interstate College-Student Exchange Programs Between Blue and Red States.*

9. *Reduce College to Three Years and Make Year Four a Service Year.*

INTRODUCTION

★

Dr. Franklin's Challenge

*I*F WE CAN KEEP IT IS MY ATTEMPT TO ANSWER TWO SIMPLE QUES-
tions:

1. Why and how did the American political system fall into this
   state of horrible dysfunction?
2. Can it ever be fixed?

I do answer them, but spoiler alert: The answers aren't simple or satis-
fying. Neither, however, are my answers to question two entirely bereft
of hope. In this book's closing chapter, you'll read the fuller and more
fleshed-out version of my fourteen suggestions (see above) of things that I
think can start to fix our problems. But this isn't a Hollywood movie. It's
life. It's complicated. For example, if you look at the evidence—evidence
I'll present to you shortly—you'll learn that our system has functioned
properly only sporadically. And you will learn that division and rancor,
often ferocious, are normal for us, historically speaking. The red-blue
enmities that exist today—again, as you'll read shortly—existed at the
dawn of the republic in almost the precise form we see them in our time.

   This book is about polarization. And, since fate directed that I would
write it during the first year of Donald Trump's presidency, it's also
about something more: It's about what we need to do to ensure that we

survive as a democratic republic. Chapter for chapter, most of this book could have appeared just as it now stands no matter who became president. This is because I don't think of polarization as a merely *political* problem. It's a historical problem. It's a social problem. And a cultural problem, and an economic problem. All of these forces have pressed— for years, decades, centuries—on the political system as gravity presses on rock, changing its structure and its density and eventually its very essence. So most of what's in the pages that follow describes problems that long predate the current situation. But having Trump in the White House makes these questions, and the search for answers to them, far more urgent. So I hope to persuade you to think of this problem more broadly than you instinctively might.

I hope also to have some measure of influence in changing some of the ways people think about polarization. There are two broadly held misconceptions I'd like to play a role in correcting. The first is this: People think this problem is relatively new, that it dates back to the 1990s. Newt Gingrich, the Clintons, all that. No. Polarization—simply defined, political division along ideological, regional, or other pertinent fault lines—is our normal state. It is true that before the nineties, when people born in the fifties and sixties were becoming adults and beginning to assume their first positions of responsibility in the world, the political system wasn't so polarized. Therefore, people of a certain age think that the earlier, more civil time was "normal." That's what our eyes and ears told us.

But the reality is—and this is a really important point to understand and to accept—that that time was *ab*normal. What's normal, as a longer look at history amply shows, is, indeed, polarization. That period of low polarization from roughly 1945 to 1980 or thereabouts happened for a very specific set of historical reasons that cannot be repeated. It was an aberration.

However, there is something about today's polarization that *is* new, and that makes it worse than it was in earlier polarized eras. Back then, we had *inter*party polarization—disagreements between the parties. But we also had a lot of *intra*party polarization—disagreements within the parties. For example, the Democratic Party of the 1940s and 1950s was the party of both very liberal integrationists and Southern racist segregationists. Going back in time, the Whigs had passionately antislavery Northerners and proslave, states' rights Southerners. These anomalies developed for reasons that I'll explain. For now, just accept that they existed.

What that meant was that in earlier times, cross-party coalitions were often needed to pass bills, for ill or for good—the Southern Democrats and Southern Whigs uniting to form the core of support for the hideous Fugitive Slave Act of 1850, or, a century-plus later, non-Southern Democrats and liberal and moderate Republicans uniting to pass civil rights. This is the norm in our political history.

Now, it's different. Today, in this time of very little party crossover, these kinds of coalitions are rare—or actually, nonexistent. This is a worse kind of polarization than the old kind.

Think about it this way. Suppose you have twenty people, ten white and ten black, and they need to take a vote on an issue. And suppose they're deadlocked ten-ten, but that six whites voted with four blacks in favor of the matter at hand, while four whites and six blacks voted against. That's a deadlock. But at least on top of everything else, it's not a racial deadlock.

Now suppose that the vote was strictly racial: The ten whites supported the thing, and the ten blacks opposed it. That's a deadlock, too. But it's a far worse one than the first deadlock because now it's racial. Or take race out of it. Say it's ten men and ten women, or ten Catholics and ten Jews, or ten homeowners and ten renters, or ten Kiwanis and ten Rotarians. If the ten-ten deadlocks involve crossovers, people can negotiate, cajole their friends toward compromise, find a meeting point of interests. But if the deadlock is along group lines, forget it. Suddenly, it's tribal.

That's what we have today, with our near-total absence of intraparty polarization. Those cross-party coalitions were crucial, first for passing a bill, but especially *after* a bill became law, because the coalitions meant that however many years later, when the bill needed fine-tuning, members of both parties, having voted to pass it, felt obliged to fix it—together. No such obligations exist now. Now, we have party tribalism. More and more Americans are turned off by parties. But those who are still loyal are intensely loyal. And the loyalty to party—and even more so, the loathing of the other party, which the political scientists call "negative partisanship"—makes today's polarization worse than the old variant because the lack of party crossover leads to a more general breakdown in trust, makes it easier to demonize the other side.

The second broad misconception I'd love for this book to play a part in correcting is this: We are not divided because of some lack of will or maturity on the part of politicians. A lot of pundits talk like this on television, huffing and puffing about why these people can't just get along. It makes regular people like you think that ending polarization is simply a matter of will.

It's not. Will is—by far—the most overrated commodity in politics. Very few things happen because of political will. Sometimes the will of leaders matters—Churchill in the spring of 1940, say. It's understandable why people are drawn to these examples: they are history's most stirring moments! But usually, will is not decisive. Usually, things happen because of historical and social and institutional forces that push on these people. They compromised forty and fifty years ago not because of will, or because they were better human beings. Politicians compromised because those forces, as they were arrayed at the time, beckoned them toward compromise. There were big social forces, like the fact that these men had all fought in the war together and therefore did not, could not, see each other as enemies. And there were more specific institutional forces, like the fact that back then there weren't yet a thousand ideological interest groups judging and scoring these people, threatening them (especially from the right) with a primary challenge if they bolted the party line.

Mike Mansfield and Everett Dirksen were the Democratic and Republican leaders, respectively, of the Senate back in the glory days of compromise in the postwar era. Their counterparts today, Chuck Schumer and Mitch McConnell, compare quite unfavorably to them in terms of working together to get things done (you'll encounter an almost-heartbreaking anecdote along these lines at the end of Chapter Three). But that isn't because Mansfield and Dirksen had more will. It was because the circumstances were different. In fact, I would argue to you that if you put Schumer and McConnell back in the Senate of fifty years ago, they'd have worked together, and if you transported Mansfield and Dirksen up to our time, they'd be presiding over roughly as much dysfunctionality as

Schumer and McConnell. It's all because of historical conditions. Will has little to do with it.

The story I tell here is the story of how and when and why those conditions changed, and whether it's possible to change them back. I'll be honest. I'm not sure it is possible—the political system has changed, the culture has changed, and we as a people have changed (yes, some of this mess is *our* fault, not the politicians'). But I am sure it's worth trying, which is why this book exists.

★

It's been my conviction that I wanted to write this book not for my friends—other journalists, political insiders, politics junkies—but for average concerned citizens. I hope to reach the schoolteacher in Akron, the bank vice president in Chattanooga. They may have different political beliefs, but they surely share a frustration over our present situation and, I hope, a desire to understand it a little more deeply. In that spirit I want to discuss here briefly each chapter and make clear why this book is organized as it is.

In Chapter One, I write about the history of political representation, going back to the early-to-mid 1700s. Most people give no thought these days to these kinds of questions—why, for example, we elect our House of Representatives from what are called single-member districts, and why we have a two-party system when most other democracies have multiparty systems, and how finally dealing with the question of fair representation literally gave one Supreme Court justice a nervous breakdown. These decisions made so long ago contribute to the polarization problem; in Chapter Seven, I circle back around to this question with some suggestions about how we might change this for the better—suggestions that may seem far-fetched right now but deserve to be discussed seriously.

In Chapter Two, I lay out the history of our three different systems of party competition. The first ran from the early 1790s to 1815; the second from the late 1820s or early 1830s (depending on how you measure it) to the mid-1850s; and the third from the late 1850s to today. The point of this chapter is to show that polarization has always existed, and that throughout most of our history our divisions were both inter- and intra-party. You'll learn in this chapter more than you ever thought you needed to know about Martin Van Buren—an inconsequential president, but arguably the most consequential political figure of that era, save perhaps for Andrew Jackson. You'll see how the Republicans became the party of Wall Street, and the Democrats the party of immigrants and workers. Then you'll see how the Republicans, in the person of Theodore Roosevelt, successfully challenged Wall Street's power once, but how they reverted to form through three uninspiring presidencies in the 1920s.

Chapter Three brings in the Depression and the New Deal, World War II, and the postwar period, and it describes how and why the United States in this period found a measure of consensus. From the way Americans accepted rationing during the war to the small but symbolic fact that the freckles on the face of the children's television marionette Howdy Doody intentionally numbered forty-eight—one for every state in the union—this was the one period in our history when Americans by and large felt they were participating in a common civic and historical project.

But, as we know, that project didn't include everyone equally. Chapter Four describes how America entered a new phase of conflict; how the country began to split apart over race, feminism, Vietnam, issues of law and the courts, cultural issues, immigration, and economic stresses like stagnant wages in the 1970s, which postwar America had never experienced. The crucial point here is that this is when the parties began to homogenize, began to divide into two warring ideological camps. On all these issues—civil rights, abortion, and so on—it was bound to be the case that one party would be for those things, and the other against. I call it the great ideological sorting out of the two parties, and I think it's *the* central political fact of the last fifty years.

Chapter Five looks more squarely at economic sources of polarization—how we became two different countries in economic terms, and how the marketplace suffocated the public square. It opens with an account of the years of terrible inflation in the late 1970s, and what that did to our collective psyche. It then moves to a discussion of what can fairly be called the financialization of the broad middle class—the credit-card explosion, for example—and how this made Americans a different people than the people who fought through the Depression:

more acquisitive, more self-interested; frankly, more selfish. It then looks at the Wall Street boom: the huge deals, the staggering salaries at the top, the mergers and layoffs. And it examines the rise of the high-end consumer culture we're so familiar with today in the form of $600 vacuum cleaners and $5,000 propane grills. Too often today in journalistic shorthand, the country changed in the 1980s because a character in a movie (Gordon Gekko in *Wall Street*) said "greed is good." There was a lot more to it than that, involving Supreme Court decisions, acts of Congress, regulatory changes, and new business practices. I discuss them all, and their corrosive impact on our sense of ourselves as citizens.

Chapter Six gets us up to the period that most people think of when they hear the word "polarization"—the 1990s of Newt Gingrich and Bill and Hillary Clinton and the Fox News Channel and the Internet and the ceaseless demands of fund-raising and Monica Lewinsky; and, in the new century, *Bush v. Gore* and the Iraq War and the Obama years and the emergence of Donald Trump. Much of this may be familiar to you, but I think some of it won't be. For example, the story of what happened at Andrews Air Force Base in the fall of 1990 and what conservatives did as a result of that episode is largely unknown by the general public but is central to our current dysfunction; arguably more central than any other single factor.

Finally, Chapter Seven offers my ideas about how we might go about trying to fix things. As emphasized therein, it won't be easy; it took us a long time to make this mess, and it'll take us a long time to correct it. Also, to look to politicians and the political system to lead us out of this quicksand is foolish. Politicians don't lead. They follow. When outside forces demand change, then and only then do politicians get down to the business of making changes. So in Chapter Seven, we see who and what those outside forces are, and what they might do to make the politicians take notice.

★

If We Can Keep It is not about Donald Trump, though I do discuss him in the sixth and (especially) seventh chapters. But there's a level on which no political book released during his presidency *isn't* about Trump. He forms the context in which you will receive this book, read it, consider its arguments. He's like Woody Allen's mother in the movie *New York Stories*, always there, up in the sky, huge, inescapable, hectically coiffed, frantically browbeating.

Except of course that he's more malevolent than that. He makes this book's topic, polarization, much worse than it would be without him because he is the first president since Andrew Johnson, and I'd say only the second of all time alongside Johnson, to so openly thrive on division. Animosity is what elected him. Without it, or with even a recognizable lessening of it, he's gone. There's a lot he doesn't know, but I suspect he knows that.

So we are forced now to ponder the question of the future of the republic. Because we currently have a president who respects no laws, knows nothing of the Constitution, and is capable of doing anything, that future is actually in doubt in a way it hasn't been since before the Civil War. In this book's final chapter, I define four ages of American history. First came the Age of Creation, as the republic was forged; it lasted until the North's victory in the Civil War, because we weren't really a republic until slavery was eradicated. Next came the Age of Power—the Industrial Revolution and the great fortunes it gave life to, the almost wholly unchecked power of capital over labor. Third came the Age of Consensus, which started, tentatively, in the 1930s as campaigns were undertaken to persuade people of the glories of the American Way (although there were plenty of divisions over the New Deal), but then flowered during the war and the postwar period. Finally, to borrow from the title of a recent book I'll quote later, we have the Age of Fracture, the current era, which we can date to the late 1980s and early 1990s.

We won't be in this age forever. Something, someday, will give. We will either enter into an Age of Repair, or . . . well, I'm not sure what the right word is for something that's worse than fracture, but alas, it's no longer unthinkable.

This book takes its title from the famous Ben Franklin quote that we learned as schoolchildren. It was the final day of the Constitutional Convention in Philadelphia, September 17, 1787. Franklin emerged from the hall, and a woman, sometimes recorded as a Mrs. Powell and sometimes just as "a lady," asked him: "Well, doctor, what have we got—a republic or a monarchy?" His reply: "A republic, if you can keep it." Notice he didn't say "congratulations" or "have fun." He issued a challenge. That challenge bears down on us today in a way it rarely has in our history.

If We Can Keep It

A 1965 Herblock cartoon.

ONE

The True History of Our Not-Very-Representative Democracy

★

*Our Odd System of Voting • Building the House and
the Senate • The Sheep Represented in Parliament •
1790–1840: The Crazy-Quilt Congress • John Tyler and the
Apportionment Act of 1842 • How We Finally Got
Fair Representation—175 Years Late*

I F THIS BOOK IS ABOUT TRYING TO UNDERSTAND HOW OUR SYSTEM became so broken, we should first understand how it was built. We all studied this in school, although most of us barely skimmed the surface on these questions. This doesn't mean that we need to go over the entire early history of the republic, or the whole Constitution. Rather, we need to focus on a few more specific and granular matters—questions about how we decided to conduct elections and organize our legislature, and why those decisions were made.

Why is this relevant? Because Congress is where modern-day polarization lives. That is to say: When contemporary scholars discuss polarization, they're mostly talking about Congress. Yes, some literature addresses broader cultural polarization; the most influential book along these lines is probably Bill Bishop's *The Big Sort* from 2008, in which he described how politically like-minded people were segregating themselves geographically, economically, and so on. Social and cultural polarization are fundamentally important developments, often overlooked by scholars because they're a lot harder to quantify than congressional votes, and two chapters of this book, as well as parts of the conclusion, will take up these matters. They're of fundamental importance, and if we have any chance of lessening our divisions, that work will have to start outside the political realm.

But in the main, when we say "polarization," we mean the mess we behold in Congress—the hardening over the past quarter-century or so of the major parties into two warring battalions. And when we say "Congress," what we really mean, at bottom, is the House of Representatives, more than the Senate. Polarization is bad in both houses, but most experts agree it's worse in the House of Representatives than in the Senate.

So let's start by thinking about these institutions—why they exist, and why they exist in the exact form they do. After all, they can, and do, exist in many different forms around the world, a matter we'll touch on below. Why did the founders decide to build our legislative branch the way they did, and why are our elections conducted as they are? Quite often, their decisions weren't the majestic acts of pure genius that we were told they were back in third grade. They were either compromises, often distasteful to everyone involved; or, in one pretty important instance, the outcome was something they barely discussed at all!

The history I'll be going over in this chapter bears directly on our polarization problem today in ways that I'll discuss in more detail in the last chapter, when I offer ideas for reforming the system so that it might produce fewer extreme candidates and officeholders. But before we get to that, it's important to understand that this system that's now being perverted by aggressive gerrymandering—which played a role, for example, in enabling the Republicans to maintain their House majority in 2012 even though Democratic House candidates as a group got more votes[1]— has almost always been distorted by some force or another; has been, in the arresting words of one critic, "deliberately misshapen."

Our Odd System of Voting

Let's think about the different ways that exist to elect a legislature. I imagine most Americans have never given this a moment's thought. Our system is *our* system, and it's worked for nearly 250 years, and we are, at least we're told, the greatest democracy on earth; why should we think about other ways to do it? For starters, the way we do it is unusual. In fact, of the thirty-five "major world democracies" identified by the organization FairVote, a nonprofit group devoted to the study of voting systems, only six use some version of the system we use.[2]

What is our system? It's called "winner take all." It means simply that the candidate who gets the most votes wins, even if she or he got less than 50 percent. Winner-take-all elections are usually though not always, but certainly in the United States, carried out in geographically designated districts, called single-member districts because just one person represents them. This seems as natural to us Americans as the sun rising in the east. We have districts, and whoever gets the most votes wins—whoever, as it is often put, is the "first past the post." What else would people do?

Actually, most countries use a form of what's called proportional representation. Under proportional representation ("PR," among people who speak of such things), a political party wins the number of seats in the legislature in direct proportion to the percentage of votes it received, whether that was 55 percent or 5 percent. You know how other countries have a number of small parties, parties with only a few seats in the legislature? You may have wondered why that is. It's because those countries use some form of proportional representation. Of the fiftyish nations of Europe, all but three use some form of proportional representation. Most use what they call "list" proportional representation, under which there are no geographic districts—parties present their lists, voters vote for the lists, and seats in the legislature are divvied up in precise proportion to the number of votes received. Some, most notably Germany, have mixed systems—some proportional representation, with single-member districts mixed in. But only three use a single-member district, winner-take-all system: Belarus, France, and the United Kingdom.

Does all this rejection mean that there's some problem with single-member districts? To a lot of experts, yes, it means exactly that. In a nutshell, the problem is that single-member districts tend to leave a lot of people feeling like their interests aren't really being represented. Consider the following hypothetical.

Imagine a new republic, and a new district in which six candidates are running for the legislative seat—that is to say, six different groups of interests have organized themselves well enough to become a party and put forward a candidate. In a field of six candidates in a first-past-the-post election, a candidate can win with, say, 27 percent of the vote. So right away, 73 percent of the voters have lost. The supporters of the candidate who finished second—say, with 24 percent—will probably want him to try again. But the voters of the candidates who finished fifth and sixth with 7 and 4 percent will see that they can never win, and in the next election, they'll tend to throw their support toward the plausible candidate to whom they object the least. That takes us down to four parties. In the next election, the voters for the parties that finished third and fourth will probably also throw in the towel, and for the same reason—they'll see that their person can't win. In a proportional representation system, if you're a member of those back-of-the-pack parties, the Greens or the Freedom Party or whatever, you know you'll be getting seats in the legislature in proportion to the actual vote won, no matter how small. This provides more of an incentive to stick with the party you truly like. But in a single-member district system, the smaller parties usually see the writing on the wall and give up.

And so, single-member districts tend to produce two-party systems. There's even a name for this. It's called Duverger's Law, after the French political scientist Maurice Duverger, who first advanced the theory in his enormously influential book from 1951 called simply *Political Parties*. The book surveyed, with a staggering authority and comprehensiveness, the political systems of every democracy in the world at the time, and even some nondemocracies. He seems to have been kind of an odd bird, Duverger; he had decidedly fascist sympathies as a young man but in his later years sat in the European Parliament as a socialist, a mirror image of the path more commonly traveled from left to right as people get older.

Whatever his personal politics, he knew his material. Of the kind of electoral system used in the United States, he wrote: "Its effect can be expressed in the following formula: *the simple-majority single-ballot system favours the two-party system* [italics in original]. Of all the hypotheses that have been defined in this book, this approaches the most nearly perhaps to a true sociological law."[3] Duverger doesn't say this is the only reason we in the United States have a two-party system; his understanding of the ideological and cultural undercurrents of early American society is quite deep. But his research led him to conclude that an "almost complete correlation"[4] exists between what he called the simple-majority single-ballot system and the two-party system. You could build a small library consisting solely of books debating Duverger's Law, but generally speaking it's accepted as valid.

So that's a starting point for us: Our particularly American form of polarization is a two-party polarization. And the fact that we have two parties (in the main; there have always been third parties, but never one capable of gaining enough power to win the White House or control Congress) stems in part from the way we elect our national legislature. So let's turn our attention to how that came to be.

Building the House and the Senate

After the delegates to the Constitutional Convention organized themselves, agreed to rules of debate, and elected officers over what was not yet known in 1787 as Memorial Day weekend, they first resolved that the government of the United States would consist of the three branches we know today. Then, they moved immediately to begin discussion of the branch they considered the most important—the legislative. And by the way, since this chapter is about representation, we might as well stop and ask who decided which people would get to represent the states at this pivotal convention. The answer is the state legislatures. In some cases it was obvious who'd attend: Alexander Hamilton could hardly be left out of the New York delegation, or George Washington and James Madison out of Virginia's (although Thomas Jefferson, interestingly, was not there—he was our minister to France at the time). In other cases, the interests that controlled the legislatures—farming, speculating, etc.—sent men who represented those interests. Also, I should note, the fifty-five men who eventually showed up in Philadelphia did not each have a vote, as we have today in Congress. They decided that each state delegation should have a vote, because the belief in the individual states as the units that would give the federal government its authority and legitimacy was strongly held. If you read through Madison's famous notes, you'll see entries like "Md. ay Va. ay N.J. no N.Y. div," for "divided." If the state's delegation couldn't agree, it went down as an abstention.

The first resolution about the legislature concerned whether representation should be based on population or each state's financial contribution to the treasury. They went with population (imagine if they'd chosen the latter—it would have been ridiculously undemocratic, but it sure would be working out nicely for blue states today!). Then they decided on a bicameral legislature. After that they decided the "first branch"—confusing terminology, since both of these houses together would themselves constitute one of the three branches of government, but that's the word they used—would be elected by the people. There was not universal agreement on this point: Many of the delegates feared direct election would lead to mob rule. They'd read their Machiavelli, on the ease with which the tyrant could manipulate the mob. "The evils we experience flow from the excesses of democracy," argued Elbridge Gerry of Massachusetts, adding, not without prescience given recent events: "The people do not want virtue, but are the dupes of pretended patriots."[5]

But most of them agreed that for better or worse, the house of the people ought to be elected by the people—which meant then, remember, landowning white men—and Gerry failed to carry the day. This, of course, is our modern House of Representatives. They feared that the House would be susceptible to reflecting the hot passions of the moment, so they wanted the Senate to be one step farther away from the people than the House. Therefore, the initial thought about the "second branch," which became the Senate, was that its members would be elected by the first branch, though this resolution was defeated 7–3. They eventually settled on the state legislatures electing senators, which is what we had until the 17th Amendment of 1913—a century and a quarter later!—ordered the direct election of senators by the people.

Through most of June, the delegates talked and talked about how to organize these two "branches." The biggest fight here was between the big states and the small states. Size was—and remains—a fascinating problem, and we'll examine it shortly. But suffice it to say for now that what they came up with, which they debated from late June through mid-July, was what we today call the Connecticut Compromise. Advanced by Connecticut delegates Oliver Ellsworth and Roger Sherman, it called for an upper house in which all states had equal representation, and a lower house based on population—which is to say, the total white population of each state, plus three-fifths of the slave population (the Southerners wanted to be able to call these human beings property for economic purposes, but when it came to determining how much political representation they'd have, by God they wanted them to count for something).

On July 16, 1787, it passed—by one vote, 5-4-1. As Madison records it, Connecticut, New Jersey, Delaware, Maryland, and North Carolina voted aye; Pennsylvania, Vermont, South Carolina, and Georgia voted no; Massachusetts was divided.[6] (Where was New York? Two of its three representatives had left the convention, leaving the state without a quorum of its delegation and thus without a vote.) So one of the most fateful decisions these men made—a decision that today gives Wyoming's 586,000 people an equal voice in our upper house to California's 39.1 million, and that has had untold ramifications over the course of the country's history—passed by one vote. The next morning, the delegates of the large states met to see what they could do about stopping this madness, but as Madison wrote, "It appeared indeed that the opinions of the members who disliked equality of votes differed so much as to the importance of that point, and as to the policy of risking a failure of any general act of the Convention, by inflexibly opposing it."[7] In other words, they had no Plan B, so they punted.

They talked about a lot of things, these delegates. But there's one matter that, surprisingly, they barely seem to have talked about at all—the manner by which representatives would be elected to the lower house. That is to say, by individual districts, or by some other method? This would appear to be a pretty fundamental question—as I showed above, it's one of the most basic building blocks of any political system. But this was thought the kind of detail that was best left to the states. And sure enough, all the Constitution says on the matter is this, in Article I, Section 2: "The House of Representatives shall be chosen every second Year by the People of the several States, and the Electors in each State shall have the Qualifications requisite for Electors of the most numerous Branch of the State Legislature." The word "Electors" here simply means eligible voters, and that second clause just means that if a person was qualified to vote in state elections, then he was also automatically qualified to vote in federal elections (to prevent states from limiting those eligible to vote for House members to a tiny elite).

And that's it—"shall be chosen." Not a word prescribing any particular manner of election. But it was understood at the time that the single-member district would probably hold sway in most places. Why?

The Sheep Represented in Parliament

The main answer is tradition, which dictated that representatives would be elected geographically, to represent a certain town or borough or, later, congressional district. The very first representative legislatures in the world—that is, after the fall of Rome—were medieval parliaments. The word "parliament" comes from the Old French *parlement*, meaning "discussion" or "meeting." Medieval parliaments "were an occasion, rather than a permanent institution, summoned at the king's will and then dismissed once their work was completed,"[8] writes Andy King in his recent short biography of Edward I. He was pretty good about calling parliaments, this Edward, two or sometimes three a year. And to those assemblages, representatives were sent based on geography—two knights of the shire from each county, say. The House of Commons is typically dated back to this era, and it strikes me as fairly progressive considering we're talking about the 1280s.

So it's what we inherited from the British, and it's just what we did. During the colonial period, writes Rosemarie Zagarri in her fascinating work *The Politics of Size*, as regions became more populous, eventually citizens would petition the state legislature to create a new town or parish, and if the legislature chose to act on the request, "it would either create a new political unit or divide an existing community into smaller units."[9] Virginia's House of Burgesses, for example, created an average of five new counties in every decade from 1700 up through the 1760s, and gave each two delegates—the same number as the older, existing counties.

Fair enough. But no one had yet thought about the question of *equality* of representation. That is, of what to do about the fact that these boroughs and counties and shires had wildly varying populations. In England, Surrey County, just south of London, may have had many times the population of Cumbria, way up near Scotland; but each sent the same number of representatives to Parliament. This became known as the "rotten borough" problem, a rotten borough being one that got more representation in Parliament than it deserved. The rottenest borough of them all was Old Sarum, which was (and still is) outside of Salisbury, southwest of London. At one point, according to some sources, it had no human residents at all—only sheep—but nevertheless sent human representatives to the House of Commons (other sources say a few people lived there, but only a few). In fact, Old Sarum sent the same number of representatives to Westminster in the mid-1700s as did Yorkshire, with a million residents! By 1783, writes Zagarri, a Commons committee reported that a majority of the body's members were elected by just 11,075 voters; a staggering 1/170 of the population.[10] England did away with these boroughs in the Reform Act of 1832. Today in America, the finger rests not as heavily on the scale for rural interests as it did then; but as we shall see, the inequity has persisted.

If you read through Madison's notes at the Constitutional Convention, you'll see references to Old Sarum as a problem the delegates should obviously seek to avoid, which means it must have been well known to them. And indeed this question of equal representation is a matter to which the delegates gave considerable study. It was part of a larger debate about the politics of size that vexed the founders and, given the unique geography of the United States, is still with us today.

Think back to colonial times. Travel was very slow and difficult (and dangerous, with huge numbers of brigands and highwaymen staking out all the well-traveled roads). It was an important principle, for example, that to the extent possible state capitals be no more than two days' carriage ride from any point in a given state. And indeed, consider the state capitals, at least in the original thirteen states, and think of how many are more or less centrally located: Albany, New York; Harrisburg, Pennsylvania; Hartford, Connecticut; Trenton, New Jersey; Columbia, South Carolina. All of these locations were subject to intense debate. Not all were agreed upon by 1787, but most were shortly thereafter. Only in Massachusetts did the capital city never move inland, but that was because Maine was part of Massachusetts then, so maybe Boston made sense, as central Massachusetts would have made for an arduous trek for the Mainers.

These debates had their roots in the writings of Montesquieu, the French philosopher of the earlier 1700s whom the founders read avidly. He believed that a republic could survive only as a small entity—that the people's representatives had to know the people. The Anti-Federalists in particular argued for localism. These were the men who were most distrustful of a large state with a powerful central government and were in that sense the forerunners of conservatives today. Anti-Federalist pamphleteers, such as "Brutus" (they got to conceal their real names, just like people do on Twitter), warned "that a consolidation of this extensive continent, under one government . . . cannot succeed, without a sacrifice of your liberties; and therefore that the attempt is not only preposterous, but extremely dangerous."[11] Some delegates to the Constitutional Convention even believed that they should restart the whole business from scratch, redrawing state lines so that all the states were of more or less equal size. "Lay the map of the confederation on the table," said New Jersey's David Brearly, "and extinguish the present boundary lines of the respective state jurisdictions, and make a new division so that each state is equal."[12]

Today, that sounds fanciful or cute, but it might have been a good idea. Over time some states would have grown more than others, but chances are the populations of the states would be closer to equal today, and therefore the basic unfairness of the Senate would be less of a problem for the people who live in states with larger populations. But of course they didn't do it. Interestingly, in the only other country in the world that was debating exactly these same questions at almost exactly the same time, they did precisely that. In France, the revolutionary assembly dissolved the old provinces of the *ancien régime* and created new *départements*. They're small and of roughly the same size; indeed a key organizing principle was that no point in a new *département* be more than one day's carriage ride away from another point. In fact, the French revolutionaries, being more radical than their American counterparts, with centuries of dead-weight history to cast off, even toyed with eliminating all natural boundaries and, to the extent possible, making the *départements* square![13]

In any case, all these questions loomed as the delegates considered the matter of districts. By early July 1787, a committee of the convention chaired by Elbridge Gerry settled on one representative for every 40,000 people (technically, it said the number of representatives "shall not exceed" one per 40,000). They returned to this topic several times, debating the number, and on the very last day of the convention, September 17, as the delegates rose in turn to say whether they could support the finished document—the day Ben Franklin made his famous remark about being now certain that the sun etched into the back of the convention president's chair was a rising and not a setting sun—Nathaniel Gorham of Massachusetts, a speculator and privateer who'd lost his fortune during the Revolutionary War but recently made it back, said he'd feel better about the whole thing if they could change that 40,000 to 30,000. Two delegates seconded Gorham, and the change was made by general assent, by a conclave no doubt anxious to get out of Philadelphia and head home to harvest the crops.

1790–1840: The Crazy-Quilt Congress

But again: The Constitution did not mandate how these representatives would be elected. That was left to the states. The single-member district system was most commonly employed, for the reasons of history and tradition described above. But since it wasn't mandated—in fact, it wasn't fully and finally mandated (for the time being, at least) until 1967—other systems were used, too. The main alternative was the at-large system, which they then called general-ticket voting. General-ticket voting was like proportional representation: There were no congressional districts. One party or faction put up one slate of candidates, and the other party or faction put up another slate. "Electors" voted for those slates, and whichever slate won usually got to seat everybody.

What was the difference between that method and the district method? Potentially big. Let's explain it with a hypothetical. Take a state, say, Vandalia (a proposed and rejected name for my home state of West Virginia). Say Vandalia has eight congressional districts. In district voting, the parties would compete as they do now, with single candidates running on their own in each district. Say the Red Party is strong in the rural areas, and the Blue Party in the urban regions, and the state is roughly balanced in that regard. What would probably happen, *if* districts were drawn fairly, is that it would all come out more or less evenly—maybe 5 to 3 for one party or the other, or possibly even 4 to 4.

Now, however, imagine Vandalia under general-ticket voting in a system in which there are only two parties. The Reds put up a slate of eight candidates, and the Blues put up a slate of eight candidates. Voters vote for each slate. In that case, the state will be represented either by eight members of the Red Party or eight members of the Blue Party. Under some general-ticket systems, a clean sweep might not be inevitable, because there might be provisions that allow voting for candidates individually, which would ensure some minority representation, or other provisions to see to it that some part of the state that got shut out in the voting get some recognition. But the advantage of the winning party would still be clear, at least 6 to 2.

You ought to be able to grasp the difference easily enough. If we used nothing but general-ticket voting today, Republicans might never lose control of the House of Representatives, since they have voting majorities in a majority of states. This would mean that states whose congressional delegations now split something like 6–2 in favor of Republicans would suddenly be 8–0 or 7–1. Of course, the Democrats would control California, New York, and Illinois, which would give them a nice head start, but Republicans would likely make up for that by the sheer number of states where Republican voters predominate. Every election would probably turn on, what else, Florida and Ohio, where Democrats would fight an uphill battle to capture a majority share of the collective House vote.

So, returning to the 1790s: As the Constitutional Convention ended and the ratification debates started in the various states, there was a rough consensus in favor of single-member districts.[14] But after ratification, the consensus collapsed. Generally speaking, the small states preferred the general-ticket system, and the more populous states went with single-member districts (the choice was in the hands of the state legislatures). But the split wasn't that neat. The large states of Pennsylvania and Massachusetts opted for general-ticket voting, or at least they did sometimes. In those two states, the rivalries between Federalists and Anti-Federalists were particularly intense, so each side was intent on shutting out the other. This tension mapped quite cleanly onto geography, too—just as you'd guess, the Anti-Federalists, who had opposed the Constitution and were now wary of big government, were the rural folk from the western parts of both states, while the big-city easterners tended to be Federalists.

I have before me a massive book—I weighed it; it's 12.2 pounds—called *The Historical Atlas of Political Parties in the United States Congress, 1789–1989*, by Kenneth C. Martis, and it is exactly what the title advertises: It has maps showing the districts (or lack thereof) and party makeup of every Congress from the 1st through the 100th. It's great fun to browse through, especially those early Congresses. The 1st Congress was seated before our first two parties had formed, so lacking party labels to use, Martis refers to members as simply "pro-Administration" or "anti-Administration." There were sixty-five House members in that Congress. President Washington had the support of thirty-seven (56 percent) and was opposed by twenty-eight (44 percent). Of the twenty-six senators in the 1st Congress, a hefty eighteen backed Washington, with opposition concentrated in Georgia and, interestingly, the president's own Virginia (mostly on the grounds that Washington had named that big-government Yankee Alexander Hamilton to be his treasury secretary).

The maps show starkly the story of the bitter divisions in Pennsylvania that I alluded to above. Pennsylvania was particularly divided within itself, largely because of the enormous power that reposed in Philadelphia (which, remember, was the national capital at the time, until 1800), so these early elections there were a real chess match between the Philadelphia power and those who fought it. In the 1st Congress, the Keystone State used general-ticket voting and sent six pro-Administration representatives out of eight total to Congress. The six were also from the wealthier eastern part of the state. But the westerners must have gotten together fast, because by the very next Congress just two years later, the state was using the single-member system, and the delegation was evenly split 4 and 4 in terms of support for the administration. Then it went back to general-ticket voting for the 3rd Congress, giving the anti-Washington forces a narrow lead. Then for the 4th Congress, it reverted to districts, and the Anti-Federalists extended their advantage.

But aside from Pennsylvania and Massachusetts, it was mostly the less populous states that used at-large voting: Rhode Island, New Hampshire, Connecticut, New Jersey (incidentally, the five most populous states in 1790, in descending order, were: Virginia, Pennsylvania, North Carolina, Massachusetts, and New York). Georgia, also one of the least populous states then, joined team general-ticket starting with the 3rd Congress. Vermont switched to general-ticket voting in 1813. Generally speaking, the state legislatures of the large states felt that individual districts more fairly represented the diversity within their borders—districts made for an easier compromise, in that sense, between rural and urban interests. The small states, comparatively lacking in such diversity and always fearful of being overpowered by the large states, tended toward at-large systems because it let them speak with one voice.

As more territories became states between 1810 and 1840, most states chose the single-member district system (note: Many new states had small populations that entitled them to only one representative; as such, by definition they elected their lone representative on an at-large basis). By the time of the 26th Congress, seated in 1839, there were twenty-six states; seventeen used districts, according to Zagarri, and nine used an at-large system (three of those nine, I should note, had just one representative, so they were at-large by definition). If anything, the states were drifting away from consensus on how representatives should be elected.

Many people realized that this crazy quilt was becoming untenable, and a rough consensus was starting to develop around the need for uniformity. Remember now that every ten years, under the Constitution, Congress had to reapportion representatives based on the decennial census. These reapportionments had always been the source of intense debate, but by 1840, with tension mounting over other issues, notably slavery, matters reached a boil.

John Tyler and the Apportionment Act of 1842

And so arrived a little moment in American political history that isn't given much thought in broader histories but is a linchpin in the story this chapter is telling. It's called the Apportionment Act of 1842, and under it, Congress finally, for the first time, mandated an election method for the House of Representatives: the single-member district system. You may be wondering: But wait; you wrote a few pages ago that Article I, Section 2 of the Constitution left this to the states. You are correct. But now

I'd like you to meet Article I, Section 4, which says: "The Times, Places and Manner of holding Elections for Senators and Representatives, shall be prescribed in each State by the Legislature thereof; but the Congress may at any time by Law make or alter such Regulations, except as to the Places of chusing [*sic*] Senators." So it was up to the states, but, if Congress didn't like what the states were doing, not really.

How could they pass such a provision, having said two articles before that it was a matter for the states? Madison's record of the convention points us to August 9 as the day the delegates discussed this section. The argument against the article was led by two South Carolinians, the strongest "leave it to the states" advocates, even then, forty-five years before the Nullification Crisis (when South Carolina decided it could just ignore federal laws it didn't like, in that case a tariff law) and 161 years before Strom Thurmond's States' Rights Party presidential bid in 1948. These were Messrs. Rutledge and Pinckney (although there were two Pinckneys from South Carolina, and Madison doesn't say which one!). But Madison himself, along with Gouverneur Morris of Pennsylvania and Rufus King of Massachusetts, argued for passage of the article. Madison: "The necessity of a general government supposes that the State Legislatures will sometimes fail or refuse to consult the common interest at the expence [*sic*] of their local conveniency or prejudices."[15] By debate's end, the South Carolinians saw they didn't have the votes and yielded, and the language passed, to use the Madisonian argot, "nem. con." (*nemine contradicente*, no one dissenting; i.e., unanimously). As fate would have it, these famous notes of Madison's were first published in 1840, which gave the members of this new 27th Congress lots of material to gnaw on that no prior Congress ever had.

The 1842 law is generally thought of as a Whig Party reform. The party captured the House and the Senate in the 1840 elections, giving them their first-ever majorities in both chambers; and they won the presidency that year as well, as William Henry Harrison beat Democratic incumbent Martin Van Buren. Broadly speaking, many Whigs were the high-minded, educated, reformer types. But they were still pols—the whole apportionment law was on one level an act of petty revenge against the state of Alabama, whose Democratic majority had switched from single-member districts to general-ticket voting in 1840 in an attempt to wipe out the state's Whig presence because they saw the party as too antislavery. In any event, whether high- or low-minded, the bill sparked a debate that was without American precedent: "(F)or the very first time in the history of the United States," writes one scholar, "an extensive discussion in Congress on the merit and consequences of electoral systems was translated into a piece of federal legislation."[16] The legislation featured two elements: Section 1 reduced—for the first and only time in U.S. history—the size of the House of Representatives, from 240 to 223. Section 2 prescribed single-member districts as the sole election method.

Why the House voted to reduce its own size is a matter that remains, after all these years, somewhat opaque. The Whigs were kind of elitist and, like the founders, feared an overlarge body devolving into mob rule. The small states wanted to stick it to the large states. The slave-state representatives were terrified that as the nation expanded into the Northwest, the number of free-state representatives would overwhelm them. In the end, the sectional conflict seems most decisive, as two-thirds of House Southerners voted for the amendment ordering the reduction and 83 percent of Northerners opposed.[17] The final passage tallies of the full bill show us how divisive the issue was, and how the interplay between party loyalty and sectional loyalty produced few clear lines. It passed 110–102 in the House, with Whigs supporting it 80–25 and Democrats opposing it 57–28. Slave-state members backed it 56–30, while free staters opposed it, 72–54. In the Senate, it passed by just 25–22. Whigs were 20–8 in favor, Democrats against 14–5. Slave staters backed it 14–10, free staters opposed it 12–11.

The regional dynamic was especially complex, even psychological. By this time, every Northern state except New Hampshire had moved to single-member voting. But four slave states—Georgia, Alabama, Mississippi, and Missouri—used the general ticket. On the one hand, Southerners liked general-ticket voting because they could vote with one voice on slavery questions. However, at the same time, they feared that Northern states might move to general-ticket voting, allowing *them* to vote with one voice, a voice that would have been louder because they had numbers on their side. So the Southerners, even though they used general-ticket voting, warmed to its elimination because of the fear that the North might start using it. Representative John Campbell—also from South Carolina—said during the debate: "On all the questions peculiar to Southern interests, the Northern states, owing to the district system, were now divided, while the Southern voted in solid phalanx; but let the general-ticket system prevail, and they would overwhelm the South."[18]

The bill went to President John Tyler, a well-born, slaveholding, aristocratic Virginian who was a somewhat accidental Whig and a very accidental president, having moved into the White House after Harrison's death from pneumonia just a month after delivering his inaugural address with no overcoat. Tyler signed it on June 25. But he added a signing statement expressing doubts about the bill's constitutionality—a bill he'd just signed! A little background: By this summer of 1842, Tyler and the congressional Whigs already despised each other for other reasons. Tyler had vetoed two bank bills the Whigs wanted, and the party's congressional wing was aghast—the veto seemed to them an imperious use of executive power and smacked of the kind of thing their nemesis "King Andrew" Jackson would do. In September of the previous year, the congressional Whigs had dramatically ostracized Tyler with a grandiose public statement, in essence throwing him out of the party. So Tyler was clearly getting back at them. John Quincy Adams—the son of the second president, an ex-president himself, a man held in the highest esteem in the party—rose in the well of the House and "spoke at great length on the dangerous precedent that must thus be set"[19] by the president attaching such a message.

Adams's objections aside, Tyler's message was heard and received by the bill's opponents. In the next Congress, in spite of the law, four states—Georgia, Alabama, Missouri, and New Hampshire—continued using at-large systems anyway. Then California joined the Union and did the same. Then Minnesota.

By the mid-1850s, however, general-ticket voting was largely phased out. It disappeared completely in 1869—but not for long. A small number of states resumed its use. Congress kept fiddling with the law. By the time the whole continental map was filled in and we had forty-eight states (62nd Congress, 1911), New Mexico and both Dakotas still used general-ticket voting. Then it disappeared again, until it roared back with a vengeance in 1933 (Virginia, Missouri, Minnesota, Kentucky). And on it went. The last holdout was Hawaii, which used the method to elect its two representatives until the election of 1970, in accordance with a federal law passed three years prior.

So this important matter of the manner of federal elections—indeed of the basic stability of a key element of our system—wasn't settled for 190 years. And it turns out that one other aspect of federal representation, a far more fundamental one, wasn't settled either. And that is the last subject this chapter will address.

How We Finally Got Fair Representation—175 Years Late

Now let's return to Old Sarum and the problem of rural overrepresentation. As noted, the founders understood this and mandated that each congressional district should come as close as possible to containing 30,000 people. In addition to that, they called for a census to be taken every decade, with district populations to be adjusted accordingly—but always equitably. Thus was the Old Sarum problem solved.

Or would have been. But almost no one paid attention to it. Oh, Congress did. Every decade, Congress dutifully changed that 30,000 number: To 33,000 in 1790, 37,000 in 1800, 40,000 in 1810, 45,000 in 1820, and 47,000 in 1830. Also in that time frame, with immigrants beginning to arrive from northern and western Europe and with the tally of states increasing from thirteen to twenty-two, the number of congressional districts swelled from 65 in the 1st Congress to 240 in 1830.[20] But most states made no effort whatsoever to keep faith with the Constitution on the question of equal representation.

The reason? Rural people were terrified that the cities would overrun them politically. Rural suspicion of big-city mores, and fear that the city interests were going to tax them heavily and then push them around, is as old as civilization itself. The taxes collected by the Delian League, an alliance of Greek city-states set up by Athens in the 400's BCE, helped finance the building of the Parthenon, and the folks from the smaller city-states like Sparta didn't like it any more than rural Georgians like paying for new projects in Atlanta. In the United States, the veneration of the small and the rural was raised to new levels. This was largely the work of Thomas Jefferson and his hearty frontiersmen followers. The political scientist Gerald Gamm was quoted in the *New York Times* after the 2016 election explaining the view: "They had this vision of what they called the 'yeoman farmer': this independent, free-standing person who owed nothing to anybody, who didn't receive any payments from the government, who didn't live by a wage, but could support himself and his family on a farm growing everything they needed—and these were the people who were going to be the backbone of democracy."[21]

Alexander Hamilton, the dapper New Yorker, took the opposite view, but Jefferson's party finished off Hamilton's by 1815, and a few years later Andrew Jackson carried this yeomanry to still new heights. Then came the expansion of the frontier. And all of this became a core part of the American creed (or myth) that these were the "real" Americans. By 1893, the historian Frederick Jackson Turner was arguing that American democracy gained its shape and character from the frontier; that "frontier individualism has from the beginning promoted democracy,"[22] as he put it in a famous talk he gave in Chicago that year. His "frontier thesis" was enormously influential for decades and embraced by the politicians elected to represent these new sons and daughters of Jefferson.

The big cities, according to this way of seeing things, were iniquitous Babels. This became more pronounced in the later nineteenth century, with mass immigration, bringing millions of Catholics, Jews, people from strange *mittel*-European kingdoms; to continue the Babel metaphor, a literal confusion of tongues. In state capitals, those centrally placed compromise locations that were generally not big cities, and where comparatively few such people came to settle, enthusiasm for granting these urbanites their full political power was scant indeed. Eventually, of course, race became a big part of this story, too, as black Americans left the fields and moved to the cities, which ratcheted up the fear even further.

And one sure-fire way to limit people's political power is to reduce their voice in representative government. If I live in a district of 10,000 constituents, and you live in a district of 50,000 constituents, my vote has five times the weight of yours, and I have five times the representative strength you have. Also, if there are a bunch of rural districts of 10,000, that arrangement is going to send a disproportionately high number of rural representatives to the legislature, and, in turn, an unfairly reduced number of urban legislators from districts of 50,000.

So that's precisely what states did. Virtually all of them, not just in the South, and for the better part of 180 years. They either simply didn't bother to reapportion based on the latest census count, or they did reapportion but did it in such a way as to maintain the status quo or sometimes even make things worse. How did they get away with it? Because they had the power, and they could; and because the courts in those days wouldn't call them on it. Courts, especially federal courts, would often recognize that this was a problem and was unfair to city-dwellers. But usually on separation-of-powers grounds, courts would say it's not our business to propose a remedy—that these were political matters best left to politicians to settle.

Finally, this changed with the Supreme Court case captioned *Baker v. Carr*, from 1962. In *Baker*, the Court ruled 6–2 for the first time ever that the question of apportionment was a "justiciable" issue—that is, one in which it was appropriate for courts to intervene. Then there were two other cases, *Reynolds v. Sims* and *Wesberry v. Sanders*, from two years later. *Baker* is the most famous, because from the moment the decision was announced, it was clear to all concerned that the ramifications were going to be thunderous; but *Reynolds* and *Wesberry* are the cases in which the Court held that all legislatures at all levels (except of course the United States Senate) had to adhere to the "one person, one vote" standard.

I knew these decisions as a student. But I never knew, or if I did I'd forgotten, the disparities that existed before them. They are staggering. In Tennessee, the state whence *Baker* originated (Charles Baker was a Republican voter; Joe C. Carr, the Democratic secretary of state), "the vote for a representative in the lower house of the state legislature of a citizen living in the smallest district was worth 23 times the vote of the citizen who lived in the largest district."[23] Up to that point, the Volunteer State had not completed a reapportionment since 1901. These kinds of tricks ensured both that there were few African-American or white liberal representatives sitting in state legislatures, and that urban voters were constantly underrepresented.

One tends to think of the South first when it comes to this kind of corruption, and indeed *Reynolds* and *Wesberry* emanate from the region. But it wasn't just the South. In fact, the worst offender was Michigan. It makes sense if you stop and think about it. Michigan has vast rural stretches, almost all Republican and very white, especially back then; and it has one very big—and very black—city, Detroit. In terms of its congressional districts, it had the worst ratio of voting power between those in the smallest districts versus the largest, 4.5:1.[24] And at the state level, the disparities were so extreme that with regard to the state senate, according to J. Douglas Smith in his riveting 2014 book *On Democracy's Doorstep*, the Democrats "would have needed to win 70 percent of the votes to take control of the chamber."[25] And in California, the 6,038,771 residents of Los Angeles County sent one state senator to Sacramento, "as did the 14,294 inhabitants of Inyo, Alpine, and Mono Counties on the eastern side of the Sierra."[26]

You can well imagine, with hideous disparities like that, and with many states having ignored reapportionment for decades, and with race a big part of the apportionment story just as the civil-rights movement was exploding, how enormous the ramifications of the *Baker* and *Reynolds* decisions were. Then–chief justice Earl Warren was asked during his tenure and after his retirement about the most important decision his Court ever made; every time, he answered reapportionment—and it was the Warren Court, remember, that decided *Brown v. Board of Education*, *Miranda v. Arizona*, and many more landmark decisions. These were agonizing decisions for the Court. Two titans of jurisprudence, William O. Douglas and Felix Frankfurter, sat implacably on opposite sides (Douglas for, Frankfurter against; Douglas, appointed by FDR, was so progressive on the matter that in his decision he even wrote "one person, one vote" rather than the more customary at the time "one man, one vote"). Another justice, Charles Evans Whittaker, was so tormented over the issue that he suffered a nervous breakdown during *Baker* deliberations (he recused himself, hence the 6–2 vote) and left the Court not long after.

It's a fascinating story, which also features future Watergate prosecutor Archibald Cox, infamously fired by Richard Nixon in the 1973 Saturday Night Massacre. Cox was President Kennedy's solicitor general, and though a liberal, he kept advising the Kennedy Justice Department not to push too hard for the specific one person, one vote remedy, which he feared the Court would be loath to grant. But Bobby Kennedy overruled Cox and pressed hard for it. After *Reynolds*, conservatives immediately organized to undo this nefarious judicial meddling and pushed for a constitutional convention. Everett Dirksen, the Republican leader of the Senate, championed this movement with gusto—an alliance captured in the Herblock cartoon that appears at this chapter's beginning. It almost won—it came up one state short of the number needed by the time of the legal deadline. And so finally, only after these decisions, this post-decision battle, and finally the 1970 census and reapportionment, did we have a democracy that was not, in Smith's memorable phrase, "a deliberately misshapen enterprise."[27]

★

I wrote at the beginning of this chapter that if we're going to understand how our system became so broken, we should first understand how it was built. Now I hope you understand more than you did. The system that we use to elect our federal legislature—the place where we watch polarization happen on a daily basis today—was never anything close to perfectly functioning. The Senate was a bitter compromise that passed by one vote and that survived challenge because the big-state delegates to the Constitutional Convention couldn't agree on an alternative—or on how big a problem it was. At the time, the population disparity between the largest state and the smallest wasn't so pronounced—Virginia had eighteen times the population of Delaware. But today, as noted earlier, California has sixty-nine times the population of Wyoming. If a disparity factor of eighteen times passed by one vote, do we really think a disparity factor of sixty-nine times would have passed at all? I think it's quite reasonable to suggest that there might not have been a Senate in the first place, or that they surely would have come up with a different way to build it.

The House has been even worse in that it has, for most of its history, betrayed its core promise and reason for being. The chamber that was designed to be the people's voice has almost never represented those people fairly. Only since 1970. Even after that there were problems—underrepresentation of minorities in some states, for example, which Congress didn't fully address until certain amendments to the Voting Rights Act were passed in 1982, which had provisions that served to bring levels of minority representation close to population levels for the first time ever. But then we started going backward, and since the 2000s, aggressive gerrymandering, mostly by Republicans, has perverted representation again. And of course the Supreme Court has now thrown out the key provisions of those 1982 voting rights amendments. So the norm in the House of Representatives has not been equal representation, but its polar opposite.

This history is so often left unexamined. I say we must examine it because we need to have a full and unvarnished understanding of our system. The founders were visionaries. That's a given. But they were human. They made some mistakes. They handed us some very imperfect tools with which to work. And then later generations perverted those tools. We need to know all this today. If we're going to address the current crisis with the full spectrum of possible solutions and fixes, we need to know, for example, that nothing obliges us to rely solely on single-member districts. Knowing this history empowers us to think about our system more critically and makes us more willing to wonder if we can do things a better way.

That's the first of this book's two quick history lessons. The second is how we came to have the parties we have, and the legacy to us today of having had those parties. So let's turn to that.

*A political cartoon criticizing President
Martin Van Buren for his handling of the Panic of 1837.*

TWO

We Were Always Polarized

★

The First Party System: Even Then, the Swells vs. the Rubes •
Jeffersonianism Wins, and the Antiwar Elitists Get Theirs •
Martin Van Buren, More Important Than You Thought •
Democrats and Whigs: The Second Party System Begins •
Chaos and War: The Collapse of the Second System and
the Rise of the Third • The Third Party System: How the
Republicans Became the Republicans • After Lincoln:
The Republicans Become the Conservative Party •
The Pre-FDR Democrats: A Horrible Party

A S MANY AMERICAN SCHOOLCHILDREN KNOW, OUR FOUNDERS didn't want political parties. Yet, we have them, and in spite of the fact that the founders didn't want them, we've had them essentially since the beginning. And most of the time, in fact through almost all of our history as a nation, we've had two dominant parties. They have fought against each other. But—and this is the crucial part—they have also fought among themselves. That is, for most of our history, our political parties have been these giant stew pots of competing interests and factions. This was less true at the very beginning of the republic than in subsequent periods, but overall, an enormous amount of internal division characterized our political parties, whichever parties they were, for nearly two hundred years, up until the period of the 1960s through the 1980s. That's when the Democratic and Republican parties started to become more ideologically homogeneous.

This chapter will provide the historical context for understanding just how dramatic a change it was. It will show how and why political parties formed in the first place; and it will review our history up through the 1920s to demonstrate how the default normal for an American political party was typically to be a huge and ideologically unwieldy beast, at war with itself over both petty questions of patronage and fundamental questions like slavery. These internal divisions deepened as time passed and were quite characteristic of our current Democratic and Republican parties, whose competition began in the late 1850s.

Why did our parties grow like this, rather than as ideologically coherent entities, a conservative choice versus a liberal choice, which is what was happening in the young democracies of Europe? The main reason in the republic's early days was the slavery question—specifically, everyone's attempts to paper over the issue with compromises like the three-fifths clause at the Constitutional Convention. The next generation of leaders, when assembling party coalitions, specifically sought to make North-South alliances, aware that the creation of a Northern party versus a Southern party could lead to ruin (in 1861, ruin came anyway).

Geography also drove much of this ideological incoherence. Think about it: Alone among the world's great powers, the United States of America kept expanding, well into the twentieth century, quadrupling the number of political subdivisions. As the country grew and states were added to the map, new political interests kept appearing—oil, cattle, wheat, gold, silver, you name it—and sources of political power were forever shifting. In turn, the parties were constantly adapting in order to put winning coalitions together, and as they did so, internal disagreements were muted by the parties for the sake of gaining majorities in the Electoral College and Congress. But those disagreements were serious. By the late nineteenth century and into the twentieth, intraparty primary battles, notably for the presidential nomination, could sometimes get uglier than the subsequent general election fights.

That was the norm of American politics until quite recently: We had polarization, but a decent chunk of it was *intra*party polarization. A stroll through that history will help us understand how starkly different things are today.

The First Party System: Even Then, the Swells vs. the Rubes

When speaking of political parties, historians have divided our country's past into three periods. They named them, sensibly enough, the First Party System, the Second Party System, and the Third Party System. Actually, they often speak of six party systems, but the fourth, fifth, and sixth represent shifts in the existing parties' coalitions; when it comes to names, this party versus that one, we've had just the three. We also had one brief period, in between the first and second, that historians called the Era of Good Feelings, which was our only one-party system, and it lasted about a decade until the two-party system returned; but as we'll see, deep divisions existed even during this period within the single dominant party.

Why did we even have political parties? You'll recall that the father of our country, who was also our first and our only president who was not a member of a party, famously warned against them. George Washington's reasons were straightforward, and indeed quite relevant to our times: He feared that excessive partisanship ("faction" was the word they used back then) would threaten small-*r* republican government and liberty itself. He wasn't naïve about any of this and acknowledged that parties would almost inevitably exist, but he hoped that a sense of perspective, a general desire to reason together in pursuit of the common good, and the system of checks and balances he'd just helped build in Philadelphia would temper partisan passions. "The common and continual mischiefs of the spirit of party are sufficient to make it the interest and duty of a wise people to discourage and restrain it," as he put it in his famous farewell address of 1796.[1]

Washington had always avoided being too identified with one faction or another going back to his days in Virginia's House of Burgesses. And generally speaking, he did manage to stay above the fray. A brief side note on Washington: He was one of those rare people in history who really deserves all the glory ladled upon him—not only (or even chiefly) for his military prowess, but for the way he refused to become America's dictator when half the population was begging him to. He could have, easily. But in December 1783, with the redcoats brought to heel and Washington-mania at fever pitch, on his way from New York back to Mount Vernon, he stopped off in Annapolis, Maryland (where the Continental Congress was meeting at the time) to resign his military commission, an act that communicated to people that he would not be seizing power. There are eight paintings in the Rotunda of the Capitol Building; most are much more obvious—the signing of the Declaration of Independence, Cornwallis's surrender, and so forth. But Washington at Annapolis is depicted, and there's a good reason why. I believe it's *the* crucial moment in early American history. He had it in his power to make the United States a military dictatorship—and said no. Observers the world over marveled that Washington could actually refuse power ("If he does that," said King George III upon being told that Washington was about to resign his commission, "he will be the greatest man in the world").[2]

When Washington took the oath of office as the first president on April 30, 1789, there were no formal political parties. But by the very next year, the factions that became our first parties were starting to form. There would be only two—not, initially, because of single-member districts, which weren't used universally. Rather, the reason was more substantive: There was only one really big question, and there were only two sides to it. It's exactly the same question that's at the root of our divisions today—the size and power of the federal government.

On one side were the people who believed that a strong and powerful federal government was a fundamental necessity. They'd drawn lessons from the failure of the Articles of Confederation, the precursor to the Constitution that emphasized the sovereignty of the states to such an extent that under it Congress was denied any powers of taxation. On the other side were those who feared giving a national government such powers. The latter group included both opponents of the Constitution (New York governor George Clinton) and supporters of it like Thomas Jefferson and James Madison; though they may have disagreed on that core question, they concurred that the central government should be as limited as possible.

Then as now, these political disputes reflected other, broader differences—where these people were from, what church they attended, their economic and commercial interests, and more. These divisions will sound familiar. The big-government people, who came to be called the

Federalists, tended to be based in the big cities along the coast. They were the moneyed interests, the cosmopolitans and aristocrats; the educated classes, and the bulk of the Continental army's officer corps; the parishioners of the high Anglican denominations; the fishing, shipping, and commercial barons who sought a sturdy central authority to regulate trade; the speculators in western lands who wanted a government strong enough to bring order to the awarding of land grants and to raise an army to fight the Native Americans whose lands they would be, um, "appropriating." Also included in this group were the interests that believed that the new country's economic destiny would be bound up in promoting what they called then "manufactures."

The forces that became the other party in our First Party System, called the Democratic-Republicans (or by some historians just the Republicans), were the opposites of the above in nearly every way. They were woodsmen, farmers, infantrymen, members of the less established and less wealthy Protestant denominations. The government, to them, was usually just this distant thing that taxed them too highly—yes, all these grievances go back to the very beginning. These "inland pioneers" found a sympathetic chronicler in the historian Wilfred E. Binkley, whose fascinating 1943 book *American Political Parties* contains the following two sentences, which, switching out a few nouns here and there and modernizing the language a bit, could have been written last week, or certainly on November 9, 2016, after the election results came in: "The piedmontese were even chided for having pushed into the wilderness, disturbed the Indians, and interfered with the fur-trading interests of the tidewater planters. The cards seemed always to be stacked against the hapless frontiersmen, and their consequent frustration induced a fierce resentment incomprehensible to the comfortable coastal communities."[3]

These two factions were led by two of the Revolution's towering figures. Alexander Hamilton was the Federalist leader. Born poor in the Caribbean, this orphan came to America, rose to become General Washington's right-hand man during the war, moved to New York City, and married into society (Elizabeth Schuyler, one of the three sisters now well known at least to theatergoing Americans because they feature so prominently in Lin-Manuel Miranda's musical). Jefferson, the Virginia planter born into stability and even distinction on his mother's side (she was a Randolph, one of Virginia's most distinguished families), was early America's most brilliant political philosopher and polymath. They differed sharply in background, in outlook, and even in their personal styles. From the eminent historians Henry Steele Commager and Samuel Eliot Morison, writing in 1930:[4]

> Their appearance was as much a contrast as their habits of mind. Hamilton's neat, lithe, dapper figure, and air of brisk energy, went with his tight, compact, disciplined brain. He could not have composed a classic state paper such as the Declaration of Independence; yet Jefferson's mind in comparison was somewhat untidy, constantly gathering new facts and making fresh syntheses. . . . His sandy complexion, hazel eyes, and much-worn clothes played up this impression of careless ease; whilst Hamilton glowed with vigor and intensity. Women found him irresistible, but they did not care much for Jefferson.

Their different visions for the nation were well known by the late 1780s, and Washington, ever the balancer, gave these men the top two positions in his cabinet—Hamilton ran Treasury, and Jefferson, the State Department. Jefferson accepted reluctantly; Hamilton, enthusiastically. Treasury was by far the more important post then; Hamilton oversaw an actual department, while Jefferson's State Department had a staff of four plus one translator who worked part-time.[5] The two men regarded each other warily, but as the 1st Congress convened, there were two major questions to be settled, and they knew it would be up to them to do the settling.

One was the future and permanent location of the nation's capital, and the other was whether the federal government should assume the debt left from the war. For the moment, the capital was New York, but this sat poorly with the Southerners. As for the debt, Hamilton backed assumption, which would give the federal government more power over the states' fiscal affairs, and Jefferson opposed it. So the two of them—joined by James Madison, a congressman at the time who had been Hamilton's ally while the two were writing *The Federalist Papers* but was now a Jeffersonian—had a fateful dinner on June 20, 1790, which led to some eventual legislative horse trading. Land was set aside on the "Potow-mack" River for a new capital, and an "assumption bill" was introduced in Congress.

Coalitions started to form around these two key questions, especially the debt-assumption one. No one had wanted parties—they all agreed with Washington on that point. These were well-read men, and they all read the same things—Thucydides, Gibbon, and a man named Joseph Addison, who wrote for *The Spectator* in London. And every source they studied warned against factionalism. Jefferson had even written: "If I could not go to heaven but with a party, I would not go there at all."[6]

So how did parties happen, if no one wanted them? Remember, there was no precedent for any of this. The Federalists and the Democratic-Republicans were not just the first political parties in America; because America was the first representative democracy, they were the first truly powerful political parties in the world (England had had Tories and Whigs going back to the late 1600s, and they behaved like political parties, but the power really reposed with the monarch).

Here, we need to shift our framework for a moment from history to political science, because political scientists look at these things differently than historians do. Political scientists are more prone to compare different time periods, and even different countries, to look for patterns and ask questions like "What problem did parties' creation and existence solve?"

This question was comprehensively answered in 1995 by the political scientist John H. Aldrich, who surveyed this history and concluded that the creation of parties was "driven by the consequences of majority instability."[7] Political scientists quantify everything, and Aldrich's book is filled with equations demonstrating various paradoxical legislative outcomes and so on, which are interesting but way too in-the-weeds for our purposes. The long and short of it is straightforward: Early legislators found that forming enduring political parties, as opposed to building ad hoc coalitions of convenience, was the surest way to win legislative battles—and, to some extent, elections, although the political party organized with the express purpose of winning an election came later, as we'll soon see.

Hamilton's eventual victory on the assumption question led him to push next for the big one: a national bank. This was a hugely controversial question at the dawn of the republic—it would be the biggest and most powerful manifestation of the national government, so it cut right to the heart of the greatest division of the day. As he had on the debt question, Hamilton won again, in early 1791. Jefferson thought it unconstitutional. The vote was strongly along regional lines—North for, South opposed. "There is a vast mass of discontent gathered in the South," wrote Jefferson, more ominously than he knew, "and how and when it will break God knows."[8]

By 1793, the two factions had become firm antagonists. Two years later, the 4th Congress was convened, and it's the first one that Kenneth C. Martis, in that colossal atlas of the history of Congress, identifies by party. There were fifty-nine Democratic-Republicans and forty-seven Federalists in that 4th Congress, the former based mainly in the South but also dominant in Pennsylvania and downstate New York. The ferocious fights now extended into global affairs, since, in addition to all their other differences, Hamilton and his people were Anglophiles, and the Jeffersonians, Francophiles (this was at the time of the French Reign of Terror, and, right after it, a decade or so when England and France were at war more often than not). America, in other words, sank instantly into a partisanship at least as intense as ours today—and along strikingly similar lines to our divisions today. Passions were aroused enough, in those tempestuous days, that "a Republican had to take care not to stop at a Federal tavern."[9]

Jeffersonianism Wins, and the Antiwar Elitists Get Theirs

These two duked it out for sixteen years. The Federalists put the first party-identified president in the White House, in the person of John Adams. His single term was riotous. Democratic-Republicans in some states refused to enforce laws the Federalists passed, and there was talk of secession. The Federalists responded with the Alien and Sedition Acts, aimed at Jeffersonian pamphleteers and politicians. Adams lost the 1800 election to Jefferson, who won because he carried Hamilton's own New York, with the help of Aaron Burr's political machine. That election was insane; it's miraculous in some ways that the young republic survived it, that someone didn't just seize power (we owe the founders that: They followed the rules they themselves wrote, which not everyone in history has done). The election was thrown to the House of Representatives and ended up being between Jefferson and Burr (his own vice presidential running mate), not Adams; Hamilton, despite his numerous differences with Jefferson, urged support for the Virginian because he utterly despised Burr ("an unprincipled voluptuary," he thundered).[10] From February 11 to 17, the House took *thirty-six ballots* to choose a president. Imagine if they'd had cable news and Twitter then! On ballot number thirty-six, partly because of Hamilton's strenuous ABB lobbying (Anybody But Burr), some state delegations switched from Burr to abstain, and this put Jefferson over the top.

Jefferson served two terms, cruising to an easy reelection in 1804 (it was smack in the middle of that campaign, incidentally, that Burr killed Hamilton in their famous duel). He was followed by James Madison, another Democratic-Republican, and another Virginian. The Democratic-Republicans held comfortable congressional majorities throughout the 1810s, with the Federalists limited to their New England strongholds; then the Federalists made a bit of a comeback in the 1812 elections. This was because the War of 1812 had broken out against Great Britain. Again, the parties were near-absolute in their division: The Democratic-Republicans were prowar (remember, they preferred France), and the Federalists were against (they liked England). Majority opinion backed the war, but a sizable minority opposed it at first, accepting Federalist arguments that it would damage U.S. trade and trade infrastructure.

But war is war, and whether it's James Madison and Henry Clay or Napoleon Bonaparte and his Consulate or Subutai and the Golden Horde or George W. Bush and Dick Cheney, its supporters always find it awfully easy to whip people into a prowar mood eventually. Again, so little has changed: The "War Hawks" (the first time this phrase came into general usage) were based in the South and in states that we call Southern today but were then considered the West, notably Kentucky and Tennessee; the antiwar forces were rooted in New England. The New Englanders, Federalists all, held a meeting in Hartford, Connecticut, in late 1814–early 1815 to state their reasons for opposition to the war and to issue other minority-party grievances. This was the Hartford Convention, which, upon concluding its business, sent representatives down to the capital to present their list of complaints.

But sadly for these fellows, they arrived in Washington simultaneous with news of Andrew Jackson's smashing victory over the British in New Orleans in January 1815. They looked at best ridiculous and at worst treasonous. It was the beginning of the end of the Federalists. They hung around in Congress for a while, but their 1816 presidential candidate was their last, and Rufus King managed just 34 electoral votes to James Monroe's 183.

Thus began the one period in U.S. history without party competition. The Era of Good Feelings—the term was coined by a Boston newspaper in 1817, and historians have adopted it—is generally defined as having lasted from 1815 to 1825. It's mostly associated with Monroe, the fifth president. He'd been Madison's secretary of war and secretary of state (both at the same time) during the recent skirmish with the Brits, which didn't hurt him in electability terms, but he had no serious competition anyway, since after Hartford the Federalists had wilted away to nothing.

Even still, this Era of Good Feelings was in several senses badly misnamed. First of all, political fights obviously didn't stop happening. They were just contained within the one party, which developed internal factions. No sooner did the Democratic-Republicans vanquish the Federalists than they started acting like them: In 1816, during Madison's last year in the White House, the Democratic-Republicans—the party of Jefferson—passed legislation creating a second national bank. The very thing they'd despised more than any other a quarter-century before. To be sure, there was a radical Jeffersonian faction within the party that considered this sail-trimming a complete betrayal of the great man's vision. But paper currency, distrusted back when even by Washington himself, was now more stable, and what with national expansion (we were up to nineteen states by 1816) and the rapid growth of "manufactures," most Jeffersonians came to accept the reality that maybe this bank thing had something going for it after all. Arthur M. Schlesinger Jr., writing of Madison signing the bill, wryly noted that "the approval of the Second Bank of the United States in 1816 by the man who twenty-five years before had been the ablest opponent of the First Bank was an appropriate commentary on the breakdown of the Jeffersonian idyl"[11] (yes, he spelled it with one *l*).

Another development that produced less-than-good feelings was the Panic of 1819. This was the first major depression in the United States, sparked by a bubble created by the existence of too-easy credit. When demand for American-made goods decreased in Europe because of a downturn there, the Second Bank called its loans, state banks had to do the same, credit instantly dried up, and a stampede of foreclosures commenced.

But the worst feelings of all were brought about by the presidential election of 1824, one of the most tumultuous in our history. Four men ran, all under the Democratic-Republican standard, even though John Quincy Adams, the fastidious New Englander—and Harvard professor, no less—was about as far from being a Jeffersonian as you could be (this, incidentally, was the last presidential election Jefferson himself would live to witness). Andrew Jackson, the war hero, won 43 percent of the popular vote to Adams's 31 percent, and he took more electoral votes than Adams by 99–84. But he lacked a majority, and so a second election in the young republic's history went to the House of Representatives, which ultimately chose Adams when candidate Henry Clay urged his backers to shift to Adams (curiously, Adams soon appointed Clay as secretary of state; anti-Adams forces smelled a backroom deal, which they instantly and famously named the "corrupt bargain").

Jackson quickly made it clear he intended to run again four years thence, and his supporters swore they'd exact their revenge. One Jackson enthusiast in particular commenced laying the groundwork for 1828 immediately. He is the father of the modern political party, and therefore in some sense the man we might call the godfather of polarization.

Martin Van Buren, More Important Than You Thought

There aren't many histories of America in which Martin Van Buren figures centrally. You know that he was a president, one of those guys in that line of people who came somewhere before Lincoln and who are hard to keep straight. You may be conjuring in your mind's eye his portrait; the bald pate, the Bozo-like shocks of white hair on either side, those enormous sideburns that ran out a good two inches from his cheeks. You might even know he has something to do with the origin of the word "okay," or more accurately "O.K.," which comes from "Old Kinderhook," which was one of his nicknames (he was born and raised in Kinderhook, New York, in the upper Hudson Valley). And that's about it.

But in his time, Van Buren was a huge player. He was a United States senator for eight years, then secretary of state, and then vice president, all before becoming president. As a senator, he was the kind who, if he were around today, would be on the Sunday shows all the time, and *Morning Joe* twice a week; the toast of the chattering class. He was suave, well-spoken, socially adroit; able "to ingratiate himself with political friend and enemy alike."[12] He was a New Yorker, which was a good thing to be in the 1820s, the very decade that New York supplanted Virginia as the nation's most populous and richest state (the Erie Canal was completed in 1825). And most of all, he was ideologically "interesting" in the way that today's Washington is such a sucker for: Though a New Yorker, he was a firm anti-Hamiltonian, a posture he inherited from his father, a tavern keeper who ran one of those partisan inns referred to above. It was said to have been visited by none other than the Hamilton-slayer himself, Aaron Burr.[13]

He was called "the Magician," or sometimes "the Little Magician"—a reference to his diminutive stature, and a little piece of snark from his opponents. But snark or not, he ran stuff. In the 1810s, while a state pol in New York, he and a few others established something that came to be called the Albany Regency—a group of men who acted together to influence state affairs, complete with their own newspaper (the importance of having some partisan media on your side was understood way before Fox News came along). There were three other such groups in the country, in Richmond, Nashville, and Concord, New Hampshire. The most famous of these was the Richmond "Junto," a word often used in those days in exactly the way we use "junta" today—an ambitious cabal interested in seizing power. The Regency was a junto in evening clothes.

Far from disdaining parties as the founders had, Van Buren thought they were dandy. Parties, to him, were organizations of principle. He observed in his autobiography (insanely detailed, running to 782 densely packed pages) that the Federalists and the Republicans were at each other's throats for sixteen years; either that was because they were all conniving opportunists, he reasoned, or "there were differences of opinion and principle between them of the greatest character, to which their respective devotion and active service could not be relaxed with safety or abandoned without honor."[14] He saw parties as not only defensible, but necessary to democracy, organized around the principle that the party "was to be more important than the men in it."[15]

He held one further belief: That a party had to be intersectional to keep the slavery issue from becoming too dominant. He was against slavery himself (although he had owned one slave, Tom, who escaped, and whose capture Van Buren did not pursue), but he was no abolitionist, at least not yet. Abolitionism was a radical position in the 1820s, so very few American pols became abolitionists until later, if at all. They all put keeping the republic together ahead of abolishing slavery. Hence, free states and slave states were admitted in equal number, most famously in the case of the 1820 Missouri Compromise, which brought Mizzou in as slave and Maine as free, an appendage of Massachusetts no longer.

The line of his that popped in all the books I read about this era is that Van Buren sought to ally "the plain Republicans of the North with the planters of the South"[16] into a national party that would challenge President Adams, revive the two-party system, and, most of all, win the election. He "envisioned a natural structure, tethered together by speedy communications and tight message control" that would give people "the novel sense that politics was a participatory ritual, gaudy and fun."[17] And he knew it had to be done around a figure, a man, and there was no one better than Jackson, a war hero who arguably got cheated in 1824 anyway. Immediately after Adams was sworn into office, Van Buren started lining up support for Jackson. He did a swing through the South; he visited the three juntos.

The 1828 campaign was a rematch of the 1824 finalists, with one difference: By now, the platform that Adams and his men ran on had strayed so far from the old Jeffersonian principles that they ditched the Democratic-Republican cognomen, and he ran as a National Republican. The race was especially vicious; the Adams men attacked Jackson's wife, Rachel, charging that she had been divorced (bad enough) and that her divorce hadn't been finalized when she and Jackson married. It clearly took a toll on her—she died the month after the election, and Jackson, who loved her dearly, held her lifeless body in his arms, refusing to believe that she was dead. But Old Hickory had won handily. And that was the beginning of today's Democratic Party.

In our time, Jackson's stock has tumbled, especially among liberals: He slaughtered and relocated Indians, he owned upwards of 100 slaves, and Donald Trump has invoked him as a role model. But for more than a century, Democrats revered or at least admired him, enough that the party's annual confabs are still called in most states Jefferson-Jackson Day dinners. Why? Because this was the first party of the "common man." This narrative was widely accepted from the start (his inaugural was an unruly affair as thousands of backwoods people swarmed the capital) and was given a renewed push in 1945 by Arthur Schlesinger in his epic, Pulitzer Prize–winning book *The Age of Jackson*. In it Schlesinger connects Jackson to FDR's New Deal. He hits on the common-man theme consistently and praises the refinement and restraint of a man some other authors have found to be uncouth and hotheaded ("though accustomed to maintain his own position with pertinacity, he yielded gracefully when convinced of his error").[18]

So there he was, the first Democratic Party president (although confusingly, these men all tended more often to refer to themselves as Republicans at first, as reflected in the Van Buren quote above; "Democrat" replaced "Republican" over the course of the 1830s). The Little Magician's reward was the secretary of state position, although he advised Jackson more generally. And his advice didn't always end up being so wise. But whose was? The union was starting to fall apart, and with the rise in those tensions, intraparty factionalism reached the boiling point.

Democrats and Whigs: The Second Party System Begins

Up to this point, we've seen very deep cultural and political divisions, and one party driven to its grave in relatively short order. But we haven't yet seen two strong parties vie for power over an extended period of time. Now, though, we enter a phase of prolonged and intense polarization that was both inter- and intraparty, a period that would outlast one of the two parties involved and carry on for more than a century.

Andrew Jackson's presidency thus became a deeply polarized time, exactly the sort of fight over issues of "the greatest character" that Van Buren yearned for. The great battle of his first term concerned tariffs. Generally, Northerners, who had most of the money and did most of the international trading, supported them, and Southerners, who produced the cotton that Europe craved, opposed them. It led to the Nullification Crisis of 1832 and 1833, regarded by many experts as the first step toward the Civil War. South Carolina, led by John C. Calhoun, who along with Henry Clay was one of the most respected senators of his day, was the first state to declare its right not to abide by—that is, to nullify—a tariff or for that matter any law passed by Congress that it deemed detrimental to its interests. Jackson believed in states' rights, but not to the point of threatening the union.

The interesting wrinkle here is that Calhoun, a leading Jackson critic, was also his vice president, having been nominated by the convention (presidential candidates didn't usually choose their running mates then; the conventions did). Jackson accepted Calhoun as his running mate, but he despised him, partly over their principled disagreement on states' rights, and partly over a personal matter—Calhoun had supported a motion of censure of Jackson for his 1818 Florida campaign, when Jackson illegally (but with President Monroe's tacit assent) invaded Spanish Florida and ordered the executions of two British subjects allied with the Seminoles. The bad blood between the two had flowed ever since.

It all came to a head on April 13, 1830, when the Democrats decided to hold a dinner to honor the recently departed (1826) Jefferson—the first Jefferson Day dinner. Jackson gave a toast to "our federal union; it must be preserved!"[19] His vice president rose to give his toast, and he chose to note that the union "can only be preserved by respecting the rights of the states and distributing equally the benefit and burden of union."[20] So insiders got a little preview that night of the divide that would tear the Democratic Party in two for the next thirty years; partly because, like many a senator we observe today, Calhoun, as one historian put it, "never knew when to stop talking."[21]

The United States was changing demonstrably in the 1830s and was no longer the country of its birth. It had expanded to twenty-four states by 1821, although no state had been added since that year because agreement couldn't be reached on the free-state/slave-state question. In addition to that, states were expanding the franchise. In 1821, New York granted suffrage to every male age twenty-one or older who owned or rented property, served in the military, or met some other public labor qualification (say, digging the Erie Canal). And yes, *every* male—black men were included, although the property qualifications were so strict as to disqualify many. In 1825, Jews, though there were few as yet in the United States, won the right to vote in Maryland. In 1830, Virginia enfranchised men owning or renting property of at least $25 in value. And so on. The result? Well, in 1824, about 350,000 male citizens voted. By 1828, with the same twenty-four states voting, that number ballooned to 1.15 million. This is a crucial part of the story of how those Jacksonian mobs were conjured into being.

Other important social forces were transforming society, politics, and the parties. The Second Great Awakening was well underway, the first major religious revival to happen here since the country was founded. Church membership, especially among Baptists and Methodists, exploded in the 1820s, and women's religious societies became prominent. These groups weren't directly involved in politics, but to the extent that they tried to influence debate, they constituted a sort of religious left, exhorting in behalf of women's suffrage, abolition, and temperance (alcoholism—and wife-beating—were *massive* scourges in nineteenth-century America).

Another big change, though not nearly as big as it would become later, was taking place in the realm of immigration. Although the 1845 Potato Famine is generally thought of as when Irish immigration "began," in fact Irish arrivals began coming to the United States in large-ish numbers in the 1820s—more than 250,000, in a country of 13-to-17 million people (the 1830 and 1840 censuses, respectively).[22] Germans began arriving as well, settling mainly in Pennsylvania and Ohio. These new citizens were primarily Catholics, against whom a backlash started with distressing immediacy. And from the start, the Democrats welcomed them. The nineteenth-century Democratic Party has much to be ashamed of, as we'll see; but at least it got this right.

So this was the country that Jackson's Democrats governed (and the one, incidentally, that Alexis de Tocqueville famously visited in 1831).

I mention these larger social trends because they helped give shape to the Second Party System, which describes the competition between the Democrats and the Whig Party from the early-to-mid 1830s until the middle 1850s.

The Whigs grew out of the ashes of John Quincy Adams's National Republican Party, whose men (I use this antiquated language for now, since it was all men) formed the nucleus of the country's anti-Jackson forces. But they were based mainly in New England, and they were well aware that there weren't enough of them to win a national election. So they decided they'd need to make common cause with people with whom they had some serious disagreements but were united by their hatred of the man they sneeringly called "King Andrew." Indeed, the party name was taken from that old, antimonarchical British party of the late 1600s mentioned previously (originally, "Whigs" was short for "Whiggamores," a group of 1648 Scottish insurgents who marched on Edinburgh to oppose the king; in the Scots language, a whiggamore was a mare driver). Our founders had sometimes called themselves Whigs to convey their own antimonarchy stance, and that echo on the part of these new Whigs was of course intentional.

So the Adams forces, in an effort to become a competitive national party, set about casting for allies. They first made common cause with the Anti-Masons. The fraternal organization of Freemasons, in fact, remains with us today. You and I don't give it much thought, but back in those days, a secret society was considered by many to be downright un-American. In 1826, an ex-Mason from upstate New York named William Morgan announced that he was going to write a book dishing all the Freemason dirt he had. But before he could get around to writing it, he was abducted and killed. It was a lurid scandal, as Anti-Masons charged that the Masons had snuffed him. Since the majority of Masons were Jackson supporters, the Anti-Masons organized themselves as anti-Jackson men under the leadership of the exquisitely named New Yorker Thurlow Weed, who had led the opposition to Van Buren's Albany Regency. They made for an awkward pairing: The National Republicans were modernizers, and the Anti-Masons by and large thought modernization and commercialization were grave threats to republican virtue. Their sole glue was what they were both against: Jackson.

Still, they were concentrated in the North and didn't have enough appeal as a party to win nationally. So they took on a second ally that was even more problematic: Many of the most hard-core states' rightists—and of course proslavers—of the South. Northern Whigs were antislavery, many vehemently so. In fact, according to one of their most thorough chroniclers, Michael F. Holt, "Southern Whigs took a more pro-slavery position than Southern Democrats, while Northern Whigs took a decidedly more anti-slavery stance than Northern Democrats."[23] So it was a horrible fit. But they all hated Jackson. And they needed the votes. To a considerable extent, the fact that the Whigs were all over the place ideologically was intentional. Because Jackson was seen as enforcing a strict party discipline, the Whigs "prided themselves on being independents rather than submissionists, on thinking for themselves rather than sheepishly obeying instructions."[24]

Jackson may have enforced discipline, but his departure from the White House revealed the Democrats to be quite fractured themselves. The Little Magician, who had stepped in as vice president during Jackson's second term after the president split with Calhoun, won the 1836 election but didn't possess much magic once he got to the White House. The economy was in the dumps when he took office and only got worse as his term continued. After Van Buren lost his 1840 reelection bid to Whig William Henry Harrison—who wasn't really much of a Whig at heart, but like Jackson was a war hero, which made him good enough—the Democrats spiraled into disarray.

Chaos and War: The Collapse of the Second System and the Rise of the Third

Now we enter what was the most polarized period in our history, even more—I *think*—than our own: the fifteen or so years leading up to the Civil War. By this time, most of the polarization was intraparty. The Democrats, for their part, had ferocious nomination battles for the next few elections that reflected the growing divide in their ranks over what Northern Democrats now called "the Slavepower." Annexation of Texas was a deeply contentious issue; ditto attempts to abolish slavery in the District of Columbia. The 1844 convention deadlocked for eight ballots before settling on compromise candidate James K. Polk, a Tennessean and a Jackson ally who became the country's first dark-horse presidential nominee and who advocated the spread of slavery into the territories taken from Mexico. By 1848 there were three clear factions, writes Jules Witcover in his riveting history of the party:[25] antislavery, led by Van Buren, who had not retired after his 1840 reelection defeat; proslavery, led by Calhoun; and "popular sovereignty," meaning let each new state decide for itself, led by Lewis Cass, a former territorial governor of Michigan. There were subfactions in the party with exotic names: The Barnburners, who were said to be willing to burn down their own barn to rid it of proslavery rats; the Hunkers, who "hunkered" (hungered) so greatly for victory at any cost that they'd do anything to accommodate Southerners; the doughfaces, who were Northerners with Southern sympathies; and best of all, the Locofocos, who were named for a kind of match that existed in the day, and who had flourished in the 1830s and were also said to be willing to torch things, in their case to get the government out of the banking business. It's not something today's Democratic Party would boast about, but its first national chairman, Benjamin Franklin Hallett of Massachusetts, was a Hunker.[26]

The Whigs were in no better shape. The congressional Whigs despised John Tyler, their own president, who had taken over after William Henry Harrison died. But their biggest fight wasn't over the apportionment bill. It was over a bank bill, which had been central to their 1840 platform. The Whigs in Congress, after many internal fights, finally passed a bill, and Tyler vetoed it. Then they listened to Tyler's objections and passed another one—and Tyler vetoed it again. They had gained control of not only the White House in 1840, but of both houses of Congress, an amazing accomplishment for a young party. But they couldn't govern, and they kicked Tyler out of the party. Then they got wiped out in the 1842 by-elections. They denied Tyler renomination in 1844 and went with Kentucky's revered senator Henry Clay. For a while, things were looking up. If there was anyone who could be called "Mr. Whig" in the way that Ohio's Robert Taft was once called "Mr. Republican," it was Clay. The party was briefly unified, even though he was a slaveholder. But he lost narrowly to Polk. The recriminations started immediately, and the Whigs were back to being a normal, divided American political party.

By the 1850s, the battles within the parties were constant. Sometimes internal dissension was so great that a few folks went off and formed their own small parties. There was an Antimasonic Party that flourished briefly in upstate New York; a Nullification Party that at one point held six of South Carolina's eight House seats; a Liberty Party, formed by the so-called Conscience Whigs who couldn't in good conscience compromise with the Slavepower; a Know-Nothing Party, which was America's first anti-immigrant party, so named because like Sergeant Schultz of *Hogan's Heroes,* they said when asked about their party's activities that they knew nothing; a Conservative Party, an Independent Party, a Law and Order Party, various Democratic and Whig offshoots . . . Duverger's Law brought a pretty swift end to all of them, but their mere appearance was proof of how unruly life was under those two big tents.

The breaking point came in the early 1850s, over a series of moves that were as controversial as any in the country's history. The Compromise of 1850 had some components that Northerners liked, such as admission to the Union of California as a free state and the outlawing of slave trading, though not slaveholding, in the District of Columbia. But the pill they swallowed to get that was bitter indeed: An old Fugitive Slave Act was toughened to stipulate that federal justice officials in all states and territories, even free ones, had to assist in the return of runaway slaves to their owners. Northern public opinion had never been so outraged. Harriet Beecher Stowe wrote *Uncle Tom's Cabin* partly in response to it. But still, some Northern Whigs tried to defend their party's appeasement. One young Whig congressman gave a speech in 1852 that unconvincingly tried to assail Democratic presidential nominee Franklin Pierce as a secret abolitionist. But in his heart, according to biographer Sidney Blumenthal, Abraham Lincoln was much more antislavery than the speech let on, and "it was the last speech of its kind he would ever give on behalf of a party that would never again field a presidential candidate."[27]

The Kansas-Nebraska Act of 1854 was even worse than the 1850 Compromise. It revoked the 1820 Missouri Compromise, which had stipulated that no territory north of latitude 36°30' (basically, the Kentucky-Tennessee border) could be admitted as slave. But Illinois Democrat Stephen Douglas, who wrote the bill originally because he wanted to make sure that the main railroad to the rapidly opening West ran through Chicago rather than Texas, agreed to add language letting the Kansas and Nebraska territories, both north of that line, decide the slavery question via popular sovereignty. He did this in order to secure the votes of the Southerners who now dominated the Democratic Party. The bill passed; it divided the Whigs much more deeply than the Democrats, as the Northern Whigs by now were passionately antislavery.

Even before the passage of that bill, Ohio Senator Salmon P. Chase wrote a pamphlet assailing Douglas and warning that the West now looked to become "a dreary region of despotism, inhabited by masters and slaves."[28] Around the same time—on March 20, 1854, to be precise—a group of Conscience Whigs, Northern Democrats, and men associated with the new Free Soil Party, an antislavery group led by Van Buren (the man had survival instincts!), met in Ripon, Wisconsin, to join forces under a new name, or an old but newly revived one: Republicans.

The Whigs were now in tatters. The Northerners just couldn't abide their Southern counterparts' votes for the Kansas-Nebraska bill. Some left the party seeking alliances with antislavery Northern Democrats. Others joined the Know-Nothings; one of the not-so-admirable traits of the Whigs is that they had always been the anti-immigrant party, chiefly because the Democrats had welcomed them (the Democrats of the 1840s and '50s were thus something that could not exist today—a party of the white frontiersman hoi polloi *and* the proimmigrant party, which one suspects may have been possible because at least those immigrants had white skin). In any case, writes Holt, "[B]y the end of 1854 the Northern Whig Party itself was so decimated that neither Northern conservatives nor Southerners who had hoped to preserve the Whig organization for the 1856 presidential campaign believed it was any longer worth the effort."[29] American political parties may have been amalgams of warring factions, but the Whigs proved that there was, in fact, a breaking point.

The Third Party System: How the Republicans Became the Republicans

It sounds awfully strange today, but when the Third Party System—the competition between Republicans and Democrats—started in 1856, the Democrats were the conservative party, and the Republicans the liberals (actually it would be fair to call the Democrats the reactionary and racist party). I return us to the Martis atlas and its maps. The 35th Congress, which was seated in 1857 and was the first to feature mostly members of those two parties, had 132 Democrats and 90 Republicans. The South was completely Democratic, and it would stay that way for the better part of a century; also Democratic were California, Oregon, and Minnesota. The Republicans controlled New England, upstate New York, the northern parts of Pennsylvania, Michigan, Wisconsin, Iowa, Ohio, Illinois, and Indiana (the last three were important Underground Railroad states). They were a Yankee party all the way, at first.

They were also the big government party. Lincoln, who had joined the party in 1856 and become a steadfast opponent of the Slavepower, believed that it was government that could best bring opportunity to the frontier, and most Republicans agreed. Consider this one interesting fact. In July 1862, just after the brutal Seven Days Battles in Richmond when both armies combined for some 35,000 casualties, Lincoln turned his attention away from the war and signed into law the Morrill Land-Grant College Act and the Pacific Railroad Act—on the same day, no less. The former created state universities, and the latter, a railway to the Pacific. The railway act was especially "activist," to use a word that's part of our vernacular today, because it allowed the federal government for the first time to charter a corporation. This was Lincoln's Republican Party.

Of course, the Republicans' first job was to prosecute the war, and on that question, they were internally united for the most part. But on other matters they were divided into two factions, the so-called Radical Republicans and the regulars or moderates. When discussion turned to what would happen after the war—after the North won—these two groups fought energetic battles. Over the breadth of civil rights that should be extended to the "freedmen" (ex-slaves); over how to punish Confederate officials; and over criteria the seceding states would need to meet before being allowed back into the Union, Radicals and regulars disagreed sharply.

The tragedy of Lincoln's assassination gave the party grounds for some all-too-rare unity, mainly because they all hated Andrew Johnson, the new president. Johnson was a Southerner and a Democrat, whom Lincoln had chosen as his running mate in the interest of creating a National Union ticket. As Southerners went, Johnson was somewhat moderate—he'd opposed secession. But he was personally as racist as they came, and a rather nasty and petty fellow besides. As president, he tried to get things back to the way they'd been in 1860 as quickly as possible. He pardoned thousands of Confederate soldiers. He vetoed the 1867 Reconstruction Act, which defined the terms of the Northern military presence in the South. Republicans united to override him. In fact, Johnson vetoed more bills than any president before him—and he also had more vetoes overridden than any other president. Eventually, Republican animus toward Johnson led to his impeachment; not because Johnson had committed any high crime or misdemeanor as most people think of that phrase today, but because he fired his Republican secretary of war. The Senate came up one vote short of conviction; it's said that Johnson's insurance policy was Radical Reconstructionist Ohio senator Benjamin Wade, who would have become president in the event of Johnson's removal, and who was too much even for many of his fellow Republicans.[30]

Johnson aside, internal Republican disagreements continued through the Reconstruction Period, which lasted until 1877. The most important Radical was Charles Sumner, the Massachusetts senator remembered in textbooks as the senator who was beaten nearly to death on the Senate floor by Southern congressman Preston Brooks in 1856. Sumner had calumniated a South Carolina senator who was Brooks's cousin, and Brooks came after Sumner with a cane, striking him repeatedly as other Southerners prevented anyone from coming to Sumner's aid. It was one of the most polarizing events of the 1850s. Southern newspapers mocked Sumner and doubted that his injuries were real (fake news, you might say).

After Lincoln's death, the Radicals had power in Congress, but they never managed to nominate a president. In 1868, the party chose Ulysses Grant—once again, when all else fails, go with a war hero—and he won. But the faction that wanted to end Reconstruction more quickly bolted the party in 1872. They went so far as to share their presidential nominee with the Democrats: newspaperman Horace Greeley, of "Go West, Young Man!" fame. Greeley had the columnist's affliction of having had and expressed too many opinions, some at odds with the people who nominated him (tariffs), some just plain odd (advocacy of the use of human manure in agriculture).[31] Grant, nominated for reelection, won easily.

The proper pace of Reconstruction continued to split the Republicans up through 1876, when Republican Ohio governor Rutherford B. Hayes became president—in another disputed and corrupt election, maybe the worst ever—partly on the strength of his promise to end Reconstruction and pull the last federal troops out of the South. To white Southerners, Reconstruction was an occupation, and indeed, the South was divided into five military districts presided over by Northern generals. To Northern slavery opponents, it represented long-overdue justice for black men, who could finally vote, serve in office (and so many did), sit on a jury, and even testify in court against a white man; the promise of the Constitution finally fulfilled in the 13th, 14th, and 15th amendments (outlawing slavery, extending due process, extending voting rights to black men, respectively). A war of histories ensued, a war that historians sympathetic to the South largely won for the next half century, defining the way the broader culture looked at Reconstruction for the next half century after that, to quite horrific effect.

After Lincoln: The Republicans Become the Conservative Party

So far, I've described a quite liberal Republican Party and a very conservative Democratic Party—roles completely reversed from today. In fact, in her excellent history of the GOP, Heather Cox Richardson writes that Johnson, the Democrat, suspected that Republicans "were planning to get taxpayers across the country to pay for a growing bureaucracy that catered to lazy African Americans"[32]—the kind of thing Republicans would say, if not quite so bluntly, today of Democrats. So how and when did the parties change places? That process started happening in this time period, and it produced new sets of internal frictions on both sides.

Some other currents were swirling around this same time that forced the parties into a choosing of sides on a few important matters. The first was immigration, which had been an increasingly contentious issue since well before the war. By the 1870s, the few hundred thousand arrivals per decade of the Jackson era was up to 2.7 million and would soon be much higher. These immigrants found a home mostly in the Northern cities, which were ruled by Democrats who welcomed these new voters, whose loyalty could be purchased fairly cheaply, with ample room for graft to boot (Boss Tweed ruled the roost in New York City at the time).

The immigrants needed work, which was to be found in the factories then multiplying across the landscape at this beginning of the Industrial Revolution, and in the laying of railroad track, and in the extraction of fossil fuels to power it all. And this meant, in turn, that the American labor movement was waking up. Unions were a source of electric division, instantly. This was the decade of the Molly Maguires in Pennsylvania, the Anthracite Coal Strike, and the Great Railroad Strike of 1877. American capitalists had watched with intense nervousness the events unfolding in Paris in 1871, when the far-left Paris Commune briefly imposed a revolutionary government over the City of Light. They wanted no such nonsense on these shores.

The American Revolution had demanded a choosing of sides ninety years before over the central question of the power and scope of the federal government. And the Industrial Revolution, another world-historical event, made a similar demand—one party was bound to become the party of the immigrants and workers, and the other of the capitalists. It was with the 1872 election that big business first moved dramatically to the Republican column, fearful of the potential power of the Democratic–Radical Republican alliance that coalesced around Horace Greeley. So big business courted the Republicans, but the party sought out big business, too. This was partly ideological, but it was mainly for an electoral reason. Because the Democrats controlled every Southern state and most border ones, the Democratic advantage in the Electoral College was huge. The Republican base was limited to New England and the Great Lakes. Therefore, Republicans knew that "it was impossible to retain control of the national government without controlling New York, and . . . it was impossible to hold New York without having the support of Wall Street."[33] New York had thirty-five electoral votes then, by far the most. And so 1872 is when Republicans first became the party of Wall Street.

Republicans—who started calling their party the Grand Old Party around this time—agreed on that. But there was still plenty of room for disagreement. The factions now were the Half-Breeds, who supported civil-service and other reforms, and the Stalwarts, who opposed all that. James A. Garfield, who won the White House in 1880, was a Half-Breed; his vice president, Chester A. Arthur, was a Stalwart (that was one important way that nineteenth-century parties made peace—the faction that lost the presidential nomination often got the vice presidential one). Garfield was assassinated in 1881 by Charles Guiteau, usually referred to in history books as a "disgruntled office-seeker." But the motive may have been more ideological: "I am a Stalwart, and now Arthur is president!" he is alleged to have shouted as the president collapsed.[34] After that, both sides realized they'd better lower the temperature. But no sooner did they unite after the tragedy than yet another party faction, the Mugwumps, bolted the GOP in 1884 because they felt that nominee James G. Blaine, that "continental liar from the state of Maine," as the satirical poem had it, was too corrupt. (Actually, Lewis L. Gould, in a recent history of the party, argues persuasively that Blaine has been cheated by history and writes that "more than any other Republican of his time, Blaine shaped the destiny of the party for two decades,"[35] making him sort of the Republican Van Buren, except that he never reached the White House.)

After that, matters within the GOP evened out for a while. They were the probusiness, antiunion, pro–gold standard, and high-tariff party—remember, this was before the income tax existed, and tariffs were the main source of government revenue by far. In fact, it's worth noting, this was before the federal government actually did much of anything. Federal spending, these days 15 to 20 percent of GDP, was around 2 percent then. The army, the courts, Civil War pensions, diplomatic posts, domestic patronage posts—that's about all the government really got up to. This status quo held in the GOP for around fifteen relatively quiet years, but soon a new internal division arose. A new generation of Republicans, who remembered Lincoln's activism fondly, thought their party had become too cozy with big business and believed government should do more. The leader of this group, of course, was Teddy Roosevelt.

TR began to gain national attention as a young politician in the 1880s. He was a loyal Republican from an early age, but he and a few other younger Republicans looked with unease on their party's probusiness direction. Their reaction to the Gilded Age was the opposite of the older generation's to the Industrial Revolution: They beheld the sweatshops and the child labor and the crushing urban poverty and the concentration of wealth and thought that the federal government had a clear role to play in alleviating them all. This marks the beginning, incidentally, of our modern use of the word "liberal." The word didn't fully take on its current meaning until Franklin Roosevelt's time, but here, it started to change. Going back to the 1700s, "liberal" meant interested in safeguarding the rights of the individual against the state; this was back when most states were monarchies and there were no bills of rights and the state could do to individuals as it pleased. In other words, "liberal," then, was kind of conservative as we would understand it today: rooted in individual liberty. But by the 1880s, liberalism would begin to concern itself not just with impositions of state power but with private-sector power as well. "After Progressive Republicans came to power," writes Richardson, "the word 'liberal' would still refer to the inherent worth of individuals, but now those embracing liberalism believed enabling individuals to succeed required a strong, not a weak, government."[36]

Liberalism was the furthest thing from the minds of most Republicans, though. The 1896 nominee, William McKinley, was probusiness, influenced by his top adviser, Ohio industrialist Mark Hanna. The platform was strongly pro–Wall Street, especially on the question of the gold standard, which was backed by industrialists and corporatists but opposed by rural interests that supported "free silver" or "bimetallism" to expand the money supply and lead to higher prices for their crops. McKinley was for gold all the way, and the convention's platform plank "was everything gold-standard Republicans could have wished."[37]

McKinley defeated Democrat William Jennings Bryan, about whom we'll learn more in the next section. When he sought reelection four years later, McKinley put Roosevelt—now a genuine celebrity because of his famous charge up Kettle (not, technically, San Juan) Hill in the Spanish-American War in 1898—on his ticket, partly to placate the party's antsy progressive wing. TR was at first so bored as vice president he thought about going back to law school at age forty-two. Then, six months into his second term, McKinley was assassinated.

TR's presidency opened up a new and intense period of intra-Republican contest that would last twelve years. His record of trust-busting and environmental activism would move the GOP dramatically away from its posture of the previous quarter-century. He had many opponents within the party, but such was his popularity and the force of his personality (and ego) that there wasn't much they could do. The election in 1908 resulted in the victory of TR's chosen successor, William

Howard Taft, a taciturn and lawyerly man whose girth ensured that no one would think of him as a dashing hero but who upheld TR's legacy and kept going after trusts—at first.

But Progressive Republicans soon felt betrayed by Taft when he signed the high-tariff Payne-Aldrich bill in 1909; it rubbed salt in their wound that the bill carried the name of patrician Rhode Island Senator Nelson Aldrich, the most influential (and despised) of the old-line Senate Wall Street conservatives. Roosevelt was in Africa on a hunting trip at the time, but shortly after his return, he began plotting to run against the now-hated Taft in 1912. He did so under the banner of the Progressive Party, splitting the GOP vote and ensuring, as he well knew, the election of Democrat Woodrow Wilson, whom he also hated, but evidently a little less than he hated Taft.

Now the GOP was in an unfamiliar position: opposition. Wilson was the first Democratic president in sixteen years, and he won with sizable House and Senate majorities. That meant recriminations time on the GOP side—and also a time when "the Republicans turned away from the moderate progressive reform impulses of Theodore Roosevelt and emerged as the conservative party it would remain for the rest of the twentieth century and beyond."[38] Wilson was quite progressive for his time, on everything except race, on which his views were essentially evil. He lowered tariffs. Republicans disliked that. He created the Federal Reserve Bank, the Federal Trade Commission, and other entities that helped spawn the age of oversight and regulation. Republicans *hated* that. In 1916, contemplating reelection and with an eye toward picking off progressive-minded voters disillusioned by the Republicans, he put Louis Brandeis on the Supreme Court (its first Jew) and beat the GOP to the punch in coming out for women's suffrage. In response to most of these moves (not suffrage; Republicans endorsed that), the GOP swerved rightward. It did the same on foreign policy, when ferocious Republican resistance to Wilson's League of Nations inaugurated the isolationist streak still strong within the party today.

Republicans by now wanted strict conservatism; a progressive at the 1920 convention called for relief for farmers and workers, and "delegates laughed at him, heckled him, threatened to throw him out, and called him a socialist."[39] The country wanted calm, and it got that in three successive conservative presidents who believed the less government did, the less *they* did, the better. Warren Harding preferred playing cards and drinking with his friends ("I am not fit for this office and should never have been here,"[40] he once confided to a friend). Calvin Coolidge, who shot to party stardom by breaking a strike as governor of New Hampshire, said that "the business of America is business." Herbert Hoover was the smartest and most accomplished of the three, but his worldview, and his party's, prevented him from responding to the stock market crash of October 1929 on anything approaching the needed scale. After a tempestuous sixty-five years following the death of their greatest leader, during which they'd started out as the liberal party and then feuded about Reconstruction and tariffs and big business and trusts, the Republican Party had, for better or worse, become roughly the party we recognize today.

The Pre-FDR Democrats: A Horrible Party

The Democrats of the era made Republicans look like a prayer group, again demonstrating that polarization was strongest within the parties. In spirit if not in name, the Democrats remained two parties for the entire period from Lincoln to Franklin Roosevelt, and even beyond. It was the Southern racist party and the Northern immigrant party. Sometimes it was even a third party, the party of the plains farmer. All three had different impulses and priorities. As such, it's a party that didn't accomplish much at all for the country for the entire sixty-eight-year period from the end of the Civil War to the start of the New Deal.

And it's a party that was largely out of power. Consider the following. From 1860 all the way until Woodrow Wilson's victory in 1912, the Democrats won just two out of thirteen presidential elections, in 1884 and 1892, both by Grover Cleveland. In that 1884 election, Cleveland won by just a whisker; he took the Electoral College because he carried New York—by 1,149 votes. But for this entire fifty-two-year period, there was an elected Democratic president for exactly eight years. At the congressional level, the picture remained just as bleak. Over those same fifty-two years, the Democrats were the minority in the House roughly two-thirds of the time, or thirty-four years. They ran the Senate for just four of those fifty-two years; usually, the Republican margin was huge.

How did this come to pass? I'd offer three main reasons. First, once the Republicans became the party of business, they typically had more money. McKinley and Hanna ran what is generally considered to be the first big-money presidential campaign (by the way: because of a precedent set by George Washington, who thought campaigning kind of tacky, presidential candidates did not personally hit the road to campaign in those days; McKinley and a few others conducted "front-porch campaigns" from their homes, and crowds came to see their speeches, but the first presidential candidate to really hit the hustings in the way we see today was Wilson in 1912).

Second, the Democrats adapted less well to the expansion of the country than the Republicans did. Kansas, Nebraska, Minnesota, Iowa, and Wisconsin sent Republican representatives to Washington more often than not during this period, as did Colorado and the other Rocky Mountain and Big Sky states as they were added to the Union. Those states also voted Republican at the presidential level. In addition, these states were also fertile grounds for the Populist Party, which might be the most successful third party in our history. It arose because neither of the major parties was giving real voice to the agrarian populist impulse that gained tremendous strength in the plains states at the turn of the century. It was spiritually closer to the Teddy Roosevelt wing of the GOP, although the most famous midwestern populist of all was a Democrat, as we shall soon see.

The third reason for the Democrats' weakness then was that the party's two factions didn't really care very much about national politics and possessed, shall we say, limited appeal beyond their regions. The Northern Democratic Party was built around its urban machines that were staggeringly corrupt. The rise and spectacular fall of the Tweed Ring, which in just under three years from 1868 to 1871 managed to steal $45 million (close to $1 billion in today's dollars),[41] was sensational national news. Other urban machines, though working on a less operatic scale, were similarly crooked. These Northern Democratic fiefdoms were far more focused on streetlight and paving contracts than on a vision for the country.

As for the Southern Democratic Party, it had a vision all right, if not for the country then for the South: to keep the "Negro" down. Many Democratic politicians were Klan members. Once Reconstruction ended, it was Democrats who put in place the Jim Crow laws. The infamous Mississippi state constitution of 1890 was written—by Democrats—for the express purpose of codifying discrimination against freed slaves and their progeny. Trigger warning for this quote: "There is no use to equivocate or lie about the matter," boasted James Vardaman, a Democrat elected to Congress in 1890. "Mississippi's constitutional convention of 1890 was held for no other purpose than to eliminate the nigger from politics."[42]

That was the Democratic Party. You've heard the phrase "Solid South," to refer to the lock the Democrats had on Dixie until after Lyndon Johnson passed civil rights. A look at Mr. Martis's atlas of Congress shows just how solid it was. From Reconstruction to the New Deal, only rarely did Alabama, Arkansas, Georgia, Louisiana, Mississippi, South Carolina, or Texas send a single Republican to the House of Representatives, and then for just a brief spell; and from 1882 to 1932, a full half-century, those seven states never elected one Republican senator. There were a few interesting exceptions in the mid-South. Eastern Kentucky sometimes went Republican. And fascinatingly, the two easternmost congressional districts of Tennessee, near Johnson City, were *always* Republican. These counties were mountainous, and thus not dependent on the slave economy, and were antislavery from the dawn of the republic. In fact, the nation's first abolitionist newspaper, *The Emancipator*, was founded not in Boston or New York but in Jonesborough, Tennessee, by a man named Elihu Embree, back in 1820.[43]

So the Democratic Party of the late nineteenth century wasn't a national party at all. Of course, every four years, Democrats had to nominate a president, and since New York was so electorally important, the job tended to go to New Yorkers. Cleveland, a former mayor of Buffalo, was the party's only winner during this period, but he hardly unified the party; speakers attacked him at his own nominating convention, including one Tammany Hall man who declared himself "too warm a friend of [Cleveland's] to desire his promotion to an office for which I do not believe he has the mental qualifications."[44] He won narrowly, in no small part because the Stalwart v. Half-Breed infighting on the other side was worse.

Cleveland wasn't a bad president: He favored civil-service reform and resisted imperialist adventure in Hawaii. But he lost reelection. He won the White House back in 1892. But a severe depression hit the next year, and Cleveland simply didn't have the force of personality to quiet the party's factionalism. Jules Witcover is good on the context of the times:[45]

> Within the party, the split now was not between North and South but between Northeast on one side, South and West on the other, the farms against the factory, debtors against creditors, silver Democrats against gold.

Cleveland was a gold man. He decided not to run in 1896, and, given the state of the economy, no one mourned the decision. The Republicans had committed themselves to a hard gold platform plank at their convention. As it happened, a rising Democratic star who was also a newspaperman watched it all go down from the press gallery. Already strongly prosilver, as was his state of Nebraska, he sensed that what the Democrats would need at their convention three weeks later was to nominate a firmly antigold candidate, and William Jennings Bryan, all of thirty-six, decided he was that man.

When liberals hear Bryan's name today, they think of the Bible-thumping reactionary of the 1920s who was sliced to ribbons on the witness stand at the Scopes Trial by Clarence Darrow and mocked in print by the sneering sophisticate H. L. Mencken. But the Bryan of the 1890s was quite progressive for his day. One might wonder why he was a Democrat in the first place, since his brand of prairie populism was more associated with the Republican Party. But Bryan's father was a Virginian originally, devoted to Andrew Jackson, and Bryan himself worshiped Thomas Jefferson and, according to the historian Michael Kazin, "yoked the legitimacy of nearly every major reform for which he campaigned"[46] to the great man. He was acceptable to every faction in the party (though not particularly racist himself by the standards of the day, he didn't push the South on the issue). But most of all he was a mesmerizing orator, so when he stood up at that convention dais and asked "upon which side will the Democratic Party fight; upon the side of the idle holders of capital or upon the side of the struggling masses?"; and when he thundered, "You shall not press down upon the brow of labor this crown of thorns; you shall not crucify mankind upon a cross of gold"; the Democratic Party finally had a unifying star.

A uniter—but not a winner. He lost to McKinley by about 52–48 percent, and by almost 100 electoral votes. But so enamored of Bryan were these Democrats, and so thin of bench, that they nominated him two more times. He lost both races, shedding states from his 1896 high point both times. And Republicans controlled both houses of Congress for the entire first decade of the new century.

In Woodrow Wilson, the Democrats finally found a man who (a) embodied their hideous divisions with gusto and (b) could win. As a native of Georgia, with the racial views aforementioned, he was fine to the South; as an egghead professor and then president of an Ivy League university, Princeton, he was okay by the Yankees. And win he did: a gaudy 435 electoral votes, to Teddy Roosevelt's 88, and poor Taft's mere 8.

For all his success, Wilson didn't really unite the party; he never changed the basic fact that the Democrats were two (or three) regional parties, and after his tenure, the party fell back into even worse disarray than before. Social tensions grew in the 1920s that amplified the party's divisions. On the one hand, the decade saw a Klan revival that led to the infamous 1925 march in Washington, with 25,000 Klansmen in white robes and hoods marching up Pennsylvania Avenue; the effective closing of the borders in the 1924 Johnson-Reed immigration bill; and Prohibition. On the other, the growth of the cities (this was the decade when the urban population first outgrew the rural), the rise of the country's first real professional managerial class as more people went to college, the arrival of the wireless, the first intimations of a distinctly American—and very urban—"culture," with jazz and Fitzgerald and the Harlem Renaissance. These divisions played themselves out within the Democratic Party. The 1924 campaign brought the infamous convention in which 103 ballots were needed to nominate a man none of them really liked, John W. Davis of West Virginia (to his credit, he denounced the Klan, though he still carried the South—but only the South—because he was the Democrat). Then in 1928, New York put forward the first major-party Catholic nominee, Al Smith. It was historic, but it was suicide, as everyone knew. Such was anti-Catholic sentiment at the time that he won only eight states—six in the Deep South, because, again, he was the Democrat.

★

Our parties were, until quite recently, unique among the parties of the advanced industrial world. In England, there were the Liberals and the Conservatives (Labour came later). In continental Europe, the social democrats versus the Christian democrats. They went by different names, but they amounted to essentially the same thing. A party of the right, and a party of the left—all ideologically coherent. In the United States, we didn't have anywhere near that clean a split. Our parties, especially the Democratic Party, made no ideological sense. They became what they became for peculiar historical reasons: the desire of the founders and of later figures like Van Buren to paper over the slavery issue, because they knew how divisive trying to settle it would prove to be; and the need of parties as the nation expanded to form coalitions with factions they had little in common with to try to win presidential and congressional majorities.

You may have read this chapter thinking, "Well, there are internal arguments within the parties today, between Hillary and Bernie, between Trump and the Never-Trumpers." And it's true, there are such divides. But Hillary and Bernie, for all the *sturm und drang*, were arguing about whether the minimum wage should be $12 or $15, and whether college should be affordable or free. The Democrats of the 1800s were arguing about whether slavery should exist. The divisions on the Republican side today are largely about Trump's respect for our norms and the rule of law; they're not about big policy questions, with the partial exception of trade. And while many conservative writers and intellectuals have become eloquent Trump critics, precious few elected Republicans have been openly critical of Trump. The old intraparty differences—over slavery, Reconstruction, civil service, gold, and populism—were much bigger.

But next came two of the most defining events in our history—the Depression and World War II. They changed the country, its politics, and, eventually, its parties, producing the one brief period when our politicians more or less got along.

A Word War II–era poster. Everybody pitched in.

THREE

America in the Age of Consensus

Life During the Depression • Life During Wartime •
Life During the Cold War • The Bipartisan Era Arrives

W E OFTEN WRITE AND TALK ABOUT POLITICS FORGETTING THAT all around it, life goes on. Ordinary life: People go to their jobs, pay their bills, raise their kids, take their vacations. And extraordinary: New economic forces arise, technology alters the way we live, society undergoes imperceptible but certain change, the culture is upended by some unexpected event or product or artistic creation that gives voice to a sentiment or feeling that hadn't yet been articulated. These forces invariably shape politics. In fact, they shape politics more than politics shapes them—certainly they shape politics *before* politics shapes them, because politics, after all, is the process by which society responds to and tries to manage these forces.

To take a couple of obvious examples from our time of how events shape politics: First, the economic meltdown of 2008 clearly had an enormous effect on our politics. It helped elect Barack Obama, the Democrat, since it happened on the watch of a Republican president who had low approval ratings even before the collapse. Then, when Obama didn't fix everything in two years (!), the meltdown's aftershocks helped give rise to the Tea Party movement. The Great Recession continued to hover over Washington, providing the context, for at least five or six years, in which nearly every other decision was interpreted. Such forces need not be merely economic: It can be plausibly argued that Donald Trump would never have been elected president if he hadn't starred in a primetime television series for a dozen years. His role on *The Apprentice* brought him fame and exposure far greater than he'd known and gave some Americans the impression of a can-do executive who wrapped everything up by the hour's end and could do the same in real life. And while on the subject of popular culture, one could also argue that Obama would have been impossible without certain cultural markers and shifts that increased white acceptance of the idea of black people being in positions of authority: without Dr. Huxtable, without Oprah, without Jay-Z.

It's a central argument of this book that some of these broader cultural shifts beyond the political realm in the past century of this country's history have played a crucial role in polarization—first in lessening it for a time, and later in making it worse. The chapters after this one will address some of these larger currents that in more recent times have played a role in exacerbating polarization. Here, we'll look at the social forces of an earlier era that combined to reduce polarization, at least for a while. I'm referring, of course, to the Great Depression and World War II.

My contention is that those two events were unique in American history, and they produced an era of cultural unity that the country had never seen before and is about 99 percent likely never to see again. When a people have lived through poverty and world war, they've gained a certain sense of perspective about life—they have learned about hardship and sacrifice, and they probably weren't very likely to care whether their neighbor whose children were hungry was a Republican or a Democrat. When men who fought in trenches in Italy or Bataan or liberated concentration camps came back home and got elected to the House of Representatives or the Senate, they had a pretty strong sense of who and what an enemy was, and they understood that the fellow across the aisle who voted differently than they did was not he. Thus, those experiences, and the understandings that arose from them, gave rise to an era of more bipartisanship than the United States had ever known. It lasted for about thirty-five years, from the end of the war to around 1980.

And this part is crucial: This era of comparative national consensus *didn't just happen.* Yes, a unique mixture of historical and social forces helped conjure it into being. But on top of that, people *worked* to make it happen. Business and corporate leaders; their counterparts in labor unions; heads of nonprofit groups and civic organizations; presidents of major universities; religious leaders—all participated in projects to promote unity and a sense of a shared American identity. They may have defined it differently, but they believed broadly that a shared civic faith had to be created and encouraged.

This view about this era as one of consensus is hardly original to me; many writers and scholars have expressed it over the years. Where I think I may be adding something to the conversation, because most people don't want to say it, is in the depressing second part, about how that era is almost surely never coming back. By which I mean the following.

When you read political columnists lamenting polarization, they often express a wish like "if only these people in Congress could behave responsibly as they did in the old days." One heard and read this frequently in the 1990s and early aughts, when the men (and by this time a few path-breaking women, like Mary McGrory and Elizabeth Drew) who had cut their teeth as reporters back in the days of bipartisan cooperation had grown to become prominent columnists and television commentators. The late David Broder of the *Washington Post* springs to mind first here; he must have written dozens of columns along exactly these lines.

But Broder and his contemporaries who issued similar lamentations were making two errors. First, they seemed to believe, or seemed to *want* to believe, that because bipartisan consensus was what they'd witnessed early in their careers, it must therefore have been the default normal for American politics. But it was not. As I hope I demonstrated amply in the previous chapter, the default normal for most of our history has been intense polarization and partisanship. Or perhaps they thought it was the new normal. But this postwar period of consensus turns out to have been an aberration. Second, they tended to write about the problem as if fixing it were a mere matter of will on the parts of Washington politicians. But it's not. As I've already noted, polarization decreased in the mid twentieth century because of large structural forces that made it decrease, and it has increased since the late twentieth century because of other large structural forces that made it increase. Will had little to do with it.

Most people don't want to accept this. I experience this when I talk to, say, old friends from my hometown, who ask me why these bozos can't just get along. I try to answer along the lines I'm describing here, and I can see on their crestfallen faces that this just isn't the explanation they wanted to hear. They want me to roll my eyes and curse the bozos in the usual way. But my structural argument, unfortunately, is true.

So now let's examine how that brief shining moment of bipartisan consensus took shape. We start with a picture of what life was like in this country in the 1930s.

Life During the Depression

When the stock market collapsed in October 1929 and the Depression set in, the country's elites were terrified. The 1920s had been the first broadly prosperous decade, arguably, in the country's history; or put another way, the decade when a significant percentage of Americans experienced a kind of prosperity that had never existed before. Most Americans bought radios, meaning they could listen to news and entertainment for the first time. Many had cars, which of course revolutionized the country in a way few inventions have. The fortunate few even started to have refrigerators, and even for those who couldn't have that, earlier advances in commercial refrigeration, aided by the increasing urbanization of the country, had led to dramatic improvements in the way people could shop for meat and produce. They saw moving pictures, even in the era before talkies. They went to baseball games. And Prohibition aside, those who wanted to could drink easily enough. After World War I ended, there was a little more than a decade of this.

And then—boom. In four days, 40 percent of the value of all paper stock was wiped out. The Hoover administration's response proved totally inadequate, and the disaster that unfolded over those four days on Wall Street in October 1929 led to compounding misery for the next four years. The gross domestic product shrank from $103.6 billion in 1929 to just $56.4 billion in 1933.[1] Unemployment in that same period shot from 3.2 percent to an unheard of 24.9 percent.[2] For a sense of how dramatic that was, consider that during the Great Recession of 2009–2010, the number of unemployed was never higher than 15 million; a quarter of the 2010 workforce would have been close to 40 million people out of work. The misery produced unprecedented social upheaval: There were food riots and hunger marches, shantytowns of the homeless and destitute called "Hoovervilles," and mobs parading down city streets singing "The Internationale," the left-wing anthem.

Many people—business and corporate leaders, prominent religious figures, intellectuals—feared that the country might collapse. The very notion of democracy as the preferred system of government came under question. By the time Franklin Roosevelt took office in March 1933, the presence in the world of two dictatorships of the far left and right—Stalin's in the Soviet Union, and Hitler's emerging one in Germany—reminded America's elites that revolution was something that could actually happen (Hitler was not yet Führer, but Americans saw the newsreels of his SA marching through Berlin). Columbia University economist and Roosevelt "brains truster" Rexford Tugwell wrote in his diary about his sense of things on the day FDR was inaugurated: "I do not think it is too much to say that . . . we were confronted with a choice between an orderly revolution—a peaceful and rapid departure from the past concepts—and a violent and disorderly overthrow of the whole capitalist structure."[3]

It's not the point of this section to discuss the political response. Many excellent histories of the New Deal exist, and they do a marvelous job of describing the frantic Hundred Days, the success and ultimate failure of the National Recovery Administration, FDR's battles with the Supreme Court that led to the Court-packing scheme, and all the rest. Suffice it to say, however, that on the subject of political polarization, the 1930s featured divisions as stark as those of any other decade in our history, save the 1850s. Conservative senators and representatives inveighed against the New Deal as socialism from the very start (even as the actual socialists, the ones who wanted Roosevelt to seize factories and end private enterprise, fumed that the president was a stooge of capital). Business groups like the American Liberty League, organized by the du Pont family, sort of the Koch brothers of their day, rose up to try to persuade the public of the "ravenous madness" of the New Deal: "Businessmen are denounced officially as 'organized greed,' 'unscrupulous money changers' who 'gang up' on the liberties of the people . . . the dragon teeth of class warfare are being sown with a vengeance.'[4] It was the usual political tumult, but worse, what with a quarter of the country out of work.

Yet at the same time that all these political battles were playing out, something very much the opposite was taking place. Precisely for the purpose of trying to counteract these great divisions and reassure a suffering people that revolution was not the answer, the nation's corporate, labor, civic, and religious leaders were starting for the first time ever to promote something called "the American Way." The phrase had rarely been used before, as the historian Wendy L. Wall shows in her gripping book *Inventing the "American Way."* Prior to 1933, she notes, she found only two books that used the phrase in its title, and one of those was *The American Way of Playing Ukulele Solos.*[5]

But from 1933 on, the phrase became ubiquitous. It wasn't an accident; it was an orchestrated effort undertaken by the country's elites to sell Americans on their way of life and the values that gave it oxygen. In P.R. terms it's a great phrase, simple and immediately seductive. The problem—although of course, this was also its genius—was that it wasn't necessarily clear precisely what the phrase meant for the simple reason that it meant different things depending on who invoked it. Corporate interests, led by the National Association of Manufacturers (NAM), sought to identify the phrase with the free-enterprise system; to labor unions, it meant what Wall calls "industrial democracy," which was basically the idea that the American conception of rights should be not just political but economic as well, with workers sharing decision-making authority. Civic and religious leaders tried to invest the phrase with an added sense of mutual tolerance and respect for the nation's diverse immigrant groups. This ever so occasionally included black people, though the effort could be fraught. One attempt to present America as a "Festival of Nations" at a St. Paul exposition in 1939 was built around the idea that members of the various immigrant groups participating should "don the costumes that their ancestors might have worn around 1850,"[6] an idea that was fine by the Italians and Swedes but that, for the obvious reasons, the African-American participants greeted rather icily.

Nevertheless, conscious public-relations efforts were undertaken during the Depression to convince Americans that our system was the greatest yet devised by the mind of man and that, despite it all, they had it better than most. Billboards sprang up, mostly paid for by NAM, with tag lines like "I'm glad to be an American" and "There's no way like the American way." The images are ones that today we might more quickly associate with the 1950s, but in fact they date to the '30s. The most famous one, pitch-perfect, is of a (white) American family smiling in their car as Dad steers them toward a bountiful future.

For many millions, though, such slogans would have been a pretty tough sell. Consider a few household economic statistics. In 1935, according to a 2006 Department of Labor study, the average household income, in that country of around 122 million, was $1,524.[7] Adjusted for inflation to 2017, that's $27,430. Compare to today: In September 2017, the median household income—not exactly the same as average, but it'll have to do; the government didn't measure median household income yet in the 1930s—was $59,039, as reported by the Census Bureau.[8] The official poverty level for a family of four in 2017, meanwhile, was $24,600. In other words, the *average* family of 1935 was living in near-poverty by today's standards. That family, by the way, while bringing in $1,524, was spending $1,512, according to the same study, leaving them a whopping $12 to salt away against the advent of emergency.

If said emergency was medical, good luck. The health-care industry as we know it began to take shape in the 1930s. Blue Cross and Blue Shield, originally different organizations (the former dealt with hospital stays, the latter, doctor's visits), were formed that decade. Big health insurance plans as we now know them didn't emerge until the war, when the country had near full employment and employers, trying to avoid wage increases, started offering fringe benefits like health coverage. In the 1930s, the general trend was toward state or local systems of prepaid plans, both for hospitalization and physician's care. But not many people could afford the $50 or $60 (around $900 in today's dollars) prepayment that was typically required. As a result, on the eve of World War II, just 9 percent of Americans had health insurance.[9]

Also, people just didn't have *things* in remotely the way we have them today. In the mid-1930s, 75 percent of households had radios,[10] which is a large majority; but on the other hand, just imagine one in four households not even owning a radio! Around 70 percent had electricity, although rural areas lagged behind. Roughly 50 percent had a car. Just 38 percent had a stove. Only one-third of households had a telephone. About 22 percent owned a refrigerator, and 20 percent a clothes washer, although in the 1930s a "clothes washer" was not what we call a washing machine today; it was a cylindrical tub with two rollers on top through which the housewife pressed the clothes to rinse them out; the 1930s equivalent of today's spin cycle was the housewife standing there, cranking the rollers by hand. This was considered very modern at the time, and only one in five housewives enjoyed even this luxury.

Today, most of us, whether we like to admit it or not, are consumers first, citizens second. In the 1930s, most people didn't see themselves this way. The concept of the consumer did, in fact, exist; the 1920s, with general prosperity and motorcars and mass-market magazines (*Time* appeared in 1923) and advertising, had seen to that. There was even a Ralph Nader of the 1930s, a man named Arthur Kallet, who wrote (with fellow engineer F. J. Schlink) an enormously influential 1933 book called *100,000,000 Guinea Pigs: Dangers in Everyday Foods, Drugs, and Cosmetics* (by "Ralph Nader," I mean the early, admirable consumer-rights advocate, not the latter-day ego-driven presidential candidate). But the whole experience of consumption was laughably crude by our standards. Consider that the garment industry didn't even begin to have standardized clothing sizes until the late 1930s—a project, for those of you who are both inveterate shoppers and unshakable big-government haters, of the Department of Agriculture, which measured the girths of tens of thousands of men, women, and children to produce the results from which the textile and garment industries have benefited ever since (it took nearly two decades, though, to complete the project).[11]

Of course, three-quarters of the people *did* work (women, too—about a quarter of American women worked outside the home throughout the 1930s, a fact many fail to realize), and more as the decade went on and unemployment was chased down into the mid-teens. So all wasn't misery. People went to baseball games and boxing matches and the movies.

The rich went on being rich, as we see from the many 1930s films about swells living in gorgeous Manhattan art-deco apartments, many of them still-hilarious screwball comedies, a genre Hollywood kept alive to give the burdened populace something to dream and laugh about. Speaking of Manhattan, the 1930s was the decade that it really became the great metropolis we know today—the muscular skyscrapers rising up, the Chrysler Building and the Empire State Building, with its twenty-five more floors, topped out eleven months after its neighbor eight blocks north. Also at that time, the awakening of the city as an artistic and intellectual hub, as it welcomed artists and writers fleeing Hitler—the Graduate Faculty of Political and Social Science at the New School for Social Research in Greenwich Village was established in 1933 specifically to welcome intellectuals from Europe.

So all was not bleak. But in general the United States remained a very poor country, nothing like the one we live in today. Even in today's left-behind America, people have cell phones and flat-screen TVs and, unless they live way out in the country, good Internet service. There is a sense now that these items are not luxuries but necessities, and indeed they are, with the arguable exception of flat-screen TVs, although even they are "necessities" if for no other reason than that you can't buy the other kind anymore, and nearly everyone has a television (96 percent of households in 2016). But for most people in Depression America, such basic items as stoves and refrigerators were luxuries.

It was, in other words, a society of want, and a society of sacrifice. It was unsought sacrifice, but sacrifice all the same. And it was a society in which, even as they endured the many hardships of Depression life, people were being constantly told that their way of life was the best way, and their standard of living the greatest in the world. And the times being what they were, the majority of people bought all that American Way talk. People hadn't yet become cynical, ironic, skeptical; all that was a good forty years away. In the 1930s, people for the most part still believed. The next phase of American life, during World War II, would intensify this civic faith.

Life During Wartime

As Europe hurtled toward its second war in twenty-plus years, no consensus existed in the United States about how deeply or indeed whether to get involved. As is well known now, the isolationist impulse, embodied by Charles Lindbergh and the America First organization, was somewhere between strong and overpowering in 1940 America. Most Americans were fine with us arming England after Hitler's invasion of Poland in September 1939, but they wanted nothing further done that might draw the United States into the war. The Republican Party was overwhelmingly isolationist, from its leaders—Senators Robert Taft and Arthur Vandenberg—on down to young comers like a Yale law student who'd helped form that campus's America First chapter named Gerald R. Ford (other founders of that storied chapter: the son of the Quaker Oats fortune, future Supreme Court justice Potter Stewart, and the first Peace Corps director, Sargent Shriver).[12]

Most of that sentiment found a home in the Republican Party. Yet in spite of that—and here we return quickly to our theme of intraparty division—the GOP in 1940 nominated an interventionist in Wendell Willkie, a native of Indiana who became a corporate lawyer and president of a large utility company and had moved to New York City just in time for the great crash of '29. Why him? Because the party's eastern establishment was interventionist. More invested in international commerce, more global in outlook, and a wee bit more Jewish, it saw the menace in Hitler more clearly than midwestern farm folk for whom Europe might as well have been on the moon. The easterners had the money and the muscle to defeat the plains-state isolationists, and they did. Willkie's support sprang, quipped Alice Roosevelt Longworth, Teddy Roosevelt's daughter, "from the grassroots of a thousand country clubs."[13]

After Japan invaded Pearl Harbor, and Hitler made the world-historic blunder of declaring war on the United States four days later, the isolationist sentiment dissipated quickly. But that doesn't mean political arguments ended. There were those who thought we should concentrate solely on Japan and leave Hitler, his war declaration notwithstanding, to the Europeans. Other Republicans warned Roosevelt that whatever unity the war required, they would remain staunch New Deal foes. I remember after 9/11 being struck by the insistence with which Republicans and conservative media figures pressed the idea that any criticism of President Bush under the circumstances was tantamount to criticism of America itself. I found this preposterous—indeed un-American—so I went back to December 1941 looking for counterexamples of a Republican going after Roosevelt. Sure enough, I found that the aforementioned Senator Taft—not just a Republican, but "Mr. Republican" in those days—gave a speech to the Executive Club of Chicago, in which he said:[14]

> As a matter of general principle, I believe there can be no doubt that criticism in time of war is essential to the maintenance of any kind of democratic government . . . too many people desire to suppress criticism simply because they think that it will give some comfort to the enemy to know that there is such criticism. If that comfort makes the enemy feel better for a few moments, they are welcome to it as far as I am concerned, because the maintenance of the right of criticism in the long run will do the country maintaining it a great deal more good than it will do the enemy, and will prevent mistakes which might otherwise occur.

Taft spoke these words—and other firm ones, such as warning the president that Republicans would not automatically endorse an expanded draft—on December 19, 1941, just twelve days after Pearl Harbor. And was he attacked as unpatriotic, a person who "hated freedom"? The speech caused hardly a ripple. That kind of political argument was seen as perfectly normal.

But again, while politics and partisanship continued on Capitol Hill, the watchword in the culture at large was "consensus." The elite propaganda about the American Way that had been initiated during the Depression took on much greater urgency during wartime. As was true during the Depression, the consensus promoting the American way exposed fault lines, depending on who was doing the promoting: Liberal and left intellectuals promoted consensus mostly in the name of presenting a broad antifascist front, while corporate interests were keen to defeat fascism in the name of preserving the existing capitalist order. But these distinctions were largely lost on your average American, for whom it was all just about pulling together to win the war.

It seems to me undeniably fair and accurate to say that the United States has never been more united than it was during World War II. The unity was not all-encompassing or perfect because no human thing ever is; but it was about as a close to all-encompassing as 132 million people could get. It happened, first and foremost, naturally. People saw very clearly how and why Nazi Germany and the Axis powers were a threat to democratic values. Black Americans, despite all the discrimination and hatred they faced at home—or perhaps paradoxically, *because* of it, in the sense that they felt that demonstrating their loyalty during the war would win them favor at home after it ended—were patriots and supported the war just about as strongly as whites. The historian Harvey J. Kaye, in his bracing *The Fight for the Four Freedoms*, dug up a March 1943 survey of 7,800 enlisted men—4,800 white and 3,000 black—that asked them whether the United States was fighting for ideals like "free speech for everyone." While more whites said yes (89 percent), the black percentages were high as well, nearly 70 percent.[15]

Regional variations in support were insignificant, first of all because nearly everyone believed in the war, but not incidentally also because the spread of munitions plants and other war factories helped modernize parts of the country, especially the South, that had lagged far behind the industrial Northeast. Italian-American organizations, supportive of Benito Mussolini in the 1920s and '30s, did a quick about-face once the war started. German-American Bund societies were a slightly more complicated story as they were strongly pro-Nazi at first. But that, too, began to change after hostilities commenced; by December 1942, prominent German-Americans—led by none other than Babe Ruth, retired now from baseball but still a household celebrity, and a lifelong political progressive—signed "A Christmas Declaration by Men and Women of German Ancestry" deploring the Nazi regime and urging its overthrow.[16] Even American communists, exercised after Germany invaded Soviet Russia in June 1941, could join the party and sound like patriots. Everyone was in.

And it happened because government, business, labor, and media elites worked very hard at the job of fostering this unity. This started well before Pearl Harbor, and the first moves were economic. FDR first used the phrase "Arsenal of Democracy" just after Christmas in 1940, but going back to the summer of 1939, when the dark clouds gathered over Europe, Roosevelt and others began to speak of what was called the "conversion economy"—quite simply, converting our economic output from normal peacetime ends toward wartime ends, just in case. Merchant shipbuilding moved first. The Roosevelt administration established the U.S. Maritime Commission in 1936 to revive a moribund shipbuilding industry; from 1938 to 1940, the commission's yards turned out 106 ships.[17] The auto industry moved less quickly, but it, too, began to see that converting to war footing would one day be necessary. It was powerful United Auto Workers leader Walter Reuther, one of the most important liberals of the era, who led this charge. On December 28, 1940—the day before, perhaps not coincidentally, FDR gave his "Arsenal of Democracy" speech—Reuther delivered what came to be known as his "500 Planes" speech, in which he argued that Detroit could fairly easily reach the point where it could be cranking out 500 airplanes every day; that it could "in half a year's time turn out planes in unheard of numbers and swamp the Luftwaffe."[18] It didn't happen as fast as Reuther hoped, but by 1942, the auto companies were fully converted to war production. By 1943, nearly every other factory in the country was making something for the war—airplane parts, Jeep parts, ammunition; even broom factories were now selling their brooms to the Pentagon.

Efforts to foster a sense of solidarity weren't just economic, though; they extended far into the realms of public persuasion and propaganda. In 1939, more than one hundred anthropologists, sociologists, psychologists, historians, and journalists formed a group called the Committee for National Morale to apply the techniques of social science toward the end of building national unity. Margaret Mead, already famous for her research into cultures of the South Pacific, was the committee's most celebrated member; in 1942, she published *And Keep Your Powder Dry*, "the first book to apply the revived notion of national character to U.S. society."[19] The committee worked throughout the war to counter Axis propaganda, and Mead's book paved the way for many other wartime studies of the national character. In 1943, Willkie published his book

One World, urging that Americans see this unity as not merely national but global. It became a huge best-seller in the year before his premature death at age fifty-two.

If all that was a bit up in the clouds, other efforts were more concrete. The government created the Office of War Information to deliver propaganda at home and abroad through radio broadcasts, newspaper articles, posters, and films (it was under the auspices of the OWI that Frank Capra's wartime propaganda films were made). Most of OWI's content producers, as we'd call them today, were liberal, leftist, some even communist; eventually, Republican and Southern Democratic members of Congress shut it down, Republicans because they saw it as producing FDR agitprop, the Southerners apoplectic about the office's liberal line on racial matters; but it did much to boost home-front morale until then. On the nongovernment side, Madison Avenue put together a group named the War Advertising Council, which spent the war years promoting patriotism, military recruitment, blood donations; if you've ever seen any of those "loose lips" or "loose talk" posters ("Even in the friendly tavern there may be enemy ears," read one, anchored by a caricature of Hitler with a listening cone to his ear), they were likely produced by the council.

And, yes, there was an Office of Censorship, created shortly after Pearl Harbor. It wasn't really as heavy-handed as that ominous name makes it sound; it concerned itself with a relatively small number of matters, like presidential travel and the weather (because knowledge of things like wind direction would help an enemy planning an attack; after tornadoes in the mid-South killed about 125 people in March 1942 partly because radio stations weren't allowed even to tell citizens of a weather emergency, the rules were relaxed a bit).[20] In any case, the government didn't really need to censor. Given how palpably the free world was imperiled, the press censored itself, and for the most part quite happily. John Steinbeck, after covering the Allied invasions of Sicily and Italy in 1943, said plainly that war correspondents were there to serve the war effort. "We felt responsible to what was called the home front," he said. "There was a general feeling that unless the home front was carefully protected from the whole account of what war was like, it might panic."[21]

This isn't the kind of thing that would go over in today's America. The rules of engagement between the government and the press changed dramatically during Vietnam, when most of the journalists covering the war decided it was wrong or unwinnable or, usually, both. But the America of 1942 wasn't like that at all. It was quite the opposite, and it was quite the opposite because people lived the war every day. First of all, according to the Veterans Administration, more than 16 million Americans (almost all men, with about 400,000 women) served in uniform during the war. That represented an astonishing one-third of all American males age fifteen and older.[22] Everyone knew someone who served, and just about everyone knew someone who'd lost someone. New immigrants vied to join the army. Baseball heroes, including Joe DiMaggio, Ted Williams, and Stan Musial, set their fabled careers aside and went off to war. Actors went—Jimmy Stewart, Henry Fonda, and Clark Gable, who enlisted as a gunner at age forty and took part in many risky combat missions by flying along with them and filming them (it was said at the time that Hermann Goering offered a large cash reward to the German soldier who captured Gable). Bob Hope started his famous USO tours during the war, touring with such megastars as the Andrews Sisters. Most notable of all here, though, was the big-band leader Glenn Miller, who had enlisted in the Army Air Forces and entertained the troops. He attained the rank of major before his plane disappeared over the English Channel on December 15, 1944. He was a massive star; it would be like Kanye West or Drake being killed in a war today.

Even more important, though, was the fact that the war was fought on the home front every single day. Victory required real sacrifice, of everyone and on an ongoing basis. Food and other household items were rationed. Rubber came first, because some of the countries that were the largest exporters of rubber were then under Japanese occupation or assault. But over time, steel, tin, wool, and nylon were added to the mix (to 1940s women's great relief, the war's end meant they could start buying nylons again). Gasoline, kerosene, fuel oil, solid fuels, bicycles, typewriters, shoes, stoves; red meat, bacon, canned fish, butter, sugar, canned goods, processed foods, coffee—all rationed, as recounted by Amy Bentley in her illuminating *Eating for Victory*. Most were rationed from 1942 or 1943 until the fall of 1945, although sugar stayed under quota until 1947. Each rationed food was assigned a point value by the Office of Price Administration—where among the young men assigned to the tire and rubber division toiled one Richard M. Nixon—which was constantly changing goods' values based on supply and demand. Households were issued ration books, and every greengrocer and butcher kept count of the items purchased.

Charged with juggling all this was the American housewife, who became the subject of enormous government and media campaigns in which "the family dinner became a weapon of war, and the kitchen a woman's battlefront."[23] Across the country, housewives engaged in a great act of civic commitment, gathering by the hundreds and thousands in assembly rooms or concert halls to raise their right hands and—right there in front of one another, with their neighbors and friends as witnesses—take the Home Front Pledge: "I will pay no more than top legal prices. I will accept no rationed goods without giving up ration points."[24] Even First Lady Eleanor Roosevelt took it. Housewives were also told in a thousand ways by numerous government boards exactly what their duty was. This language from a National Livestock and Meat Board pamphlet is representative:[25]

> The American homemaker has an important part to play in the war effort. Her uniform is the kitchen apron, and she may wear it proudly; for there is no more important responsibility than hers. . . . This meat recipe book was designed especially for the gallant soldier on the home front. Its purpose is to assist her in making the most of her meat purchases during the present emergency.

The pamphlet goes on to include recipes for such carcass-maximizing delectations as Creole Kidney, Jellied Tongue, and Tripe a la Maryland, served with cherries, bay leaf, and lemon.

The American homemaker's responsibilities hardly ended there. Remember, the army had 16 million stomachs to fill three times a day; consequently, it was buying much of the large farm crop. Hence, canning and "Victory Gardens," the plots that anyone who had a backyard was supposed to plant to grow vegetables, were patriotic requirements. Most victory gardeners were men, but women did a considerable amount of it, plus nearly all the canning, another ubiquitous wartime practice. And on top of all that, 5-to-6 million extra women entered the workforce during the war, to fill war-related jobs vacated by the men who'd joined the armed forces. The term "Rosie the Riveter," applied to all such women, was first used in a popular 1942 song. The question of who was the real Rosie remains a matter of dispute, but one candidate as the real-life inspiration for the song was Rosalind Walter, who, though an Upper East Side heiress to what became Bristol-Myers Squibb, worked the night shift to help build the F4U Corsair.

Lastly, I should say that while all this was going on, taxes were going up. A lot. In 1940, our $1,524 earner from above gave just 4 percent of that to Washington. In 1941, he was paying 10 percent. By 1942, 19 percent. By 1944, 23 percent. A near-sixfold increase in four years. Rich people paid far more. For example, someone who made $22,000 in 1942, about $345,000 in 2017 dollars, paid a top rate of 55 percent (but not on every dollar earned; only on the last $2,000 earned. The way today's media don't understand marginal tax rates and fail to communicate that to the public is insanely irresponsible).[26] The rates were extremely high, but for the most part, these tax increases passed on a strong bipartisan basis. Everyone understood what the money was for: fighting Hitler and Tojo.

If you're looking for one little artifact that expresses the era's ethos, go to YouTube and watch a short, ten-minute film called *The House I Live in*, from 1945, directed by Mervyn LeRoy and starring Frank Sinatra. The then-very-young Blue Eyes is at a recording session and sneaks back to the alley for a smoke break. He sees a gang of boys chasing another boy. He asks them what the trouble is; the gang doesn't like the other boy because of his religion (the word "Jewish" is never spoken, but it's clear). Frankie lectures them, tells them they're behaving like Nazis; then he breaks into the title song, which extols the nation's religious and racial diversity. The song was written by two communists, Earl Robinson (actually an ex-communist by then) and Abel Meeropol, who would go on to adopt Julius and Ethel Rosenberg's two boys after the couple's execution. Nevertheless, it's a lovely celebration of the small town, the churchyard, the flag, and democracy, although one of the song's utopian images was judged to be a little too much: LeRoy and the producers would not let Sinatra sing the second verse, which included a lyric about whites and blacks living as neighbors. The single and vague line about "all races and religions" would have to do.

That was America (actually, with respect to residential segregation, it basically still *is* America, as residential segregation remains rampant). Nevertheless, the pulling together during the war was a concerted effort such as the country never had seen and almost surely will never see again.

Life During the Cold War

After sixteen years of hardship and sacrifice, Americans in 1945 received their reward as the United States entered an era of prosperity greater than any ever known in this or any other country. The broad outlines of this story are familiar to us all. Wages were good, jobs were stable— it's not a coincidence that labor unions were strong—and a huge middle class grew and thrived. Taxes were comparatively high, especially on the well off. Inequality was at the lowest levels the country had ever known (and still has ever known). The economists Claudia Goldin and Robert Margo named this era the Great Compression, meaning that wages were "compressed" (that is, class differences greatly reduced).[27] People bought homes in the suburbs, cars, televisions, washers (now fully automatic) and dryers. Consumer choice exploded in every realm, from household appliances to clothing to breakfast cereals, as American businesses sought to satisfy the needs and wants of the millions of married couples reunited after the war and all those new babies they were now busy making.

There was, of course, a new war, the Cold War, against the Soviet Union. As this war was fought not with bullets but with words (well, and massive defense outlays), the nation's elites determined that it required the same kind of unity and resolve that had helped defeat the Axis powers in the shooting war. Those elites began laying the groundwork for this effort well before the war ended. They foresaw that the transition back to a peacetime economy wouldn't be easy, and time proved many of their fears to be correct. There was some inflation after the war, and social unrest in the form of strikes and race riots; there was also the simple fact of millions of men finding it hard to readjust to civilian life, a trauma captured so poignantly by director William Wyler in his stunning 1946 film *The Best Years of Our Lives*, in which three veterans who all occupy different rungs on the class ladder (Fredric March, Dana Andrews, and Harold Russell, not an actor but an actual veteran who had lost both hands in the war) struggle with disability, drink, marriages on the brink.

As was the case during the Depression and the war, the national-unity effort against communism involved corporate chieftains, labor leaders, religious leaders, heads of major universities and large nonprofit groups, and Madison Avenue. The National Conference of Christians and Jews had been founded in 1928 to fight the anti-Catholic bigotry that arose when the Democrats nominated Al Smith and the anti-Semitism spread by such prominent figures as Henry Ford. Throughout the Depression it had sponsored an American Brotherhood week or day, but they were nothing like the 1946 celebration, which lasted nine full days, during which more than a hundred popular radio shows worked themes of religious and racial tolerance into their broadcasts. Movie theaters showed a three-minute short called *American Creed*, featuring Katharine Hepburn, Jimmy Stewart, Ingrid Bergman, and Shirley Temple; theatergoers were asked to donate a dollar to the cause and to sign a pledge written by the Hollywood producer David O. Selznick, then a towering figure in American culture:[28]

> I pledge allegiance to this basic ideal of my country—fair play for all.
>
> I pledge myself to keep America free from the disease of hate that destroyed Europe.
>
> In good heart I pledge unto my fellow Americans all the rights and dignities I desire for myself.
>
> And to win support for these principles across the land, I join the

American Brotherhood, sponsored by the National Conference of Christians and Jews.

There were many efforts like these, including the fascinating story of Stetson Kennedy, who went undercover in the Ku Klux Klan in 1946 and fed information to the writers of the radio show *The Adventures of Superman*, transforming the Man of Steel for a time from a pursuer of bank robbers and hoods into a racial-justice crusader. A lot of this propaganda was aimed at children: Howdy Doody, the famous puppet who was the star of an enormously popular 1950s TV show with puppeteer "Buffalo Bob" Smith, was consciously painted with forty-eight freckles on his face—one for every state in the union (pre Hawaii and Alaska).

These efforts had their limits, and they obviously didn't end bigotry and racism and hatred. Jim Crow continued in the South, as toxic as ever. In 1948, after Harry Truman had integrated the military and young Minnesota senator Hubert Humphrey had pushed a civil-rights plank through the party convention, some Southerners left the Democratic Party and nominated Strom Thurmond for president. He won the four states of Alabama, Louisiana, Mississippi, and South Carolina, and won them handily (but he got trounced in neighboring Georgia, which Senator Richard Russell, a stone-cold racist but a party institutionalist, held for Truman). And in the North, while African-Americans enjoyed political rights, they couldn't live in those pristine new suburbs sprouting up in Long Island, up Philadelphia's Main Line, or in the western and northern suburbs of Chicago. Off limits also were most good jobs and professions, unless one served one's own people (that is, Howard University would educate black lawyers and doctors who would hang out shingles in black neighborhoods).

So it was a time of a racism both searing and casual in ways that would shock us today. It was also a time when immigration was choked off. The United States of the 1950s remained a very homogenous country. Official statistics are hard to come by as the Census Bureau didn't even start counting Latinos until 1970, but the United States of 1950 was roughly 88 percent white, 10 percent black, and 2 percent other. If we're being honest, we must acknowledge the possibility of a link between all this consensus and all this . . . whiteness. Southern and Eastern Europeans who weren't really seen as white a half-century prior were by this time more fully assimilated. "For a brief moment," wrote the historian Jefferson Cowie in his important 2016 book *The Great Exception*, "a sort of 'Caucasian' unity took place among a historically divided working class, with the heterogeneity of American experience transformed into a rare moment of homogeneity."[29] There is surely more truth to this than many of us would like to admit: social cohesion and hefty government spending were acceptable to a broad majority as long as that broad majority was white.

And, not least, it was also the time of one of the darkest interludes in American history—a time of the Red Scare and Joseph McCarthy. Truman, in that 1948 race, was progressive on race and a number of issues, but he red-baited left-wing Progressive Party nominee Henry Wallace aggressively. The atmosphere of paranoia gave rise to McCarthy, who shot to fame in 1950 waving his lists of names of suspected communists. "No bolder seditionist ever moved among us," wrote Richard Rovere, the *New Yorker* writer who most ably chronicled the senator's rise and fall, "nor any politician with a surer, swifter access to the dark places of the American mind."[30] (I can't help but wonder if it's still McCarthy who holds that distinction.) He flamed out fairly quickly, thanks to CBS's Edward R. Murrow and the lawyer Joseph Welch, who famously asked him at a Senate hearing before a transfixed live television audience, "Have you no sense of decency, sir?"—and, more broadly, to the keepers of consensus who saw in his demagoguery a threat to the American values of presumption of innocence and plain fair play. More insidiously effective for a longer period of time was the House Un-American Activities Committee, whence the Alger Hiss and the Hollywood Blacklist scandals emanated. While McCarthy was censured in 1954, HUAC carried on for about another five years before public opinion turned against it.

Was it a conservative time, or a liberal time? Conventional histories call it conservative, and these histories aren't wrong. Beyond the racism and red-baiting, it was the age of the bomb—of vastly increased peacetime military spending, largely on these terrifying new armaments, and on a sprawling national-security state such as had never existed in the world. It wasn't just the billions of dollars. It was the psychological toll of the bomb—the "duck and cover" exercises at school, the fallout shelters popping up in hospitals and public buildings across the nation, with their tins full of crackers that were supposed to last five years; the existential grappling with the possibility of instant annihilation, so soon after the world had learned of the systematic annihilation of 6 million human beings. "Probably, we will never be able to determine the psychic horror of the concentration camps and the atom bomb upon the unconscious mind of probably everyone alive in these years," wrote Norman Mailer in *Dissent* in 1957.[31]

It was also, as has often been noted, an age of conformity, of tidy front lawns, of fedoras and suits, of June Cleaver vacuuming in high heels (husband Ward never touched a vacuum). It was a time when many issues and problems simply weren't discussed—rape and domestic violence, for instance, weren't "issues" at all; what we call domestic violence now was back then, in a system totally designed and enforced by men, just a hard-working man getting something out of his system, and his wife had to bear it. Simply being a homosexual was illegal and considered a disease; the thinking of the 1950s was that with the right amount of counseling and electroshock therapy, people could be "cured" of having such urges. And this thinking was considered new, enlightened, scientific.

There was, and there's no need to deny it, a downside to all that consensus-building. It meant that certain *other* matters, matters that might chip away at the consensus, weren't discussed. Any news story that cast the military or the police in a negative light would likely never see publication in that America. Cities and towns had local censorship boards, and in the context of the Cold War, they took great care to shield the public from news that might challenge their resolve against the ideological enemy. Today, when a police officer shoots an unarmed black man, the cop most likely will not be convicted, but at least it's likely to become a controversy, to provoke public debate on broader issues. In those days, it simply wasn't discussed. This was true of many matters—it's impossible to know how many military sexual assault scandals, for example, no one ever heard a word about, as the elites cast a sanitizing blanket over the nation to keep the grown-ups strong and to prepare the young people for the solemn responsibility of safe-guarding freedom and maintaining the greatest way of life the world had ever known.

And yet: Was it a liberal time? In some important senses, it surely was. First and foremost, there was no longer much debate over the central historical issue, the one that had divided Hamilton and Jefferson and that tears at us today: Nearly everyone accepted a large and powerful federal government as a given. There is a famous quote from President Dwight Eisenhower, which he wrote in a letter to his brother Edgar on November 8, 1954:[32]

> Should any political party attempt to abolish Social Security, unemployment insurance, and eliminate labor laws and farm programs, you would not hear of that party again in our political history. There is a tiny splinter group of course that believes you can do these things. Among them are H. L. Hunt (you possibly know his background), a few other Texas oil millionaires and an occasional politician or business man from other areas. Their number is negligible and they are stupid.

Not everyone agreed, of course, and we'll hear more from them later. But in the 1950s, a solid majority of Americans, and a solid majority of politicians of both parties, accepted the basic premises of the New Deal.

Labor unions were also accepted. They were by no means universally admired, and there was no small amount of labor strife in that America. Many Republicans fought to roll back their power, most successfully through the Taft-Hartley Act of 1947, which barred some strikes, gave management the ability to campaign against the union in the workplace, and more. And yet, unions were more fully embraced by the public; not so surprising considering that in the 1950s nearly one in every three American workers had a union card. In 1950, Walter Reuther, who had previously pledged his workers so faithfully to the war effort, had negotiated with the Big Three auto companies the famous "Treaty of Detroit," which established pensions, better health-care coverage, paid vacation time, and more for upwards of 500,000 auto workers (in return for five years of labor peace). Reuther's victory established norms and practices that were adopted by other industries.

For the most part, businesses and corporations came to agree that organized labor was part of the consensus, and that they would overcome their reservations and make peace with it. Corporate America's posture in the 1950s was quite different from today's—less slavish devotion to returning value to shareholders and maximizing profits, more social responsibility. Again, this didn't just happen. It was forged. One important group here was the Committee for Economic Development (CED), which had been founded during the war by executives from the Studebaker auto company and Eastman Kodak to plan reconversion to a peacetime economy. The CED got corporate America behind the Marshall Plan; then, it worked to ensure that corporations and businesses thought not just about their bottom lines but about how their decisions would impact society. I have before me a small CED pamphlet called *Social Responsibilities of Business Corporations*. This one was published a good bit later, in 1971, but it was identical in spirit to material the group was publishing in the 1950s and '60s. We need look no further than the names of some chapters to see an ethos at work very different indeed from today's: "Enlightened Self-Interest: The Corporation's Stake in a Good Society"; "Widening Parameters of Social Performance"; "A Government-Business Partnership for Social Progress." The pamphlet is the work of CED's Research and Policy Committee, a group of fifty men drawn from banking, manufacturing, and the academy.

Swirling around all this was a vibrant liberal-left intellectual life. Arthur Schlesinger, John Kenneth Galbraith, Reinhold Niebuhr, Dwight Macdonald, Lionel Trilling, Irving Howe, Richard Hofstadter, Paul Goodman, C. Wright Mills; yes, all white men, as that's how things were in those days, although Mary McCarthy would have given me an argument about that. These and other writers, some liberal and some radical, churned out dazzling critiques of American politics and society, always aware that the United States had accomplished much, always asking why not more.

So: A conservative time, yes, but also one suffused and sustained by a certain liberal civic faith that doesn't exist today. And it was that faith that made the bipartisan era possible.

The Bipartisan Era Arrives

This was the context that produced the politicians who guided us through the bipartisan era. They were children or youngsters during the Depression, and many grew up working-class or poor. Hubert Humphrey's father was a druggist. Bob Dole's ran a creamery. George McGovern's father was a Wesleyan Methodist pastor, and young George and his three siblings often went hungry during the Depression (after his retirement from politics, he dedicated himself to fighting world hunger). Mike Mansfield, the Democrat who led the Senate in the 1960s, was sent by his father from New York City out to distant Montana to live after Mrs. Mansfield died (Mike was three), and he ran away from that home several times. Everett Dirksen, Mansfield's Republican counterpart, saw his father die when he was just nine; his mother bought a small farm to support the family. The father of Tip O'Neill, the longtime Democratic Speaker of the House, was a bricklayer before he got into politics. Tip's GOP counterpart, Robert Michel, was the son of an immigrant factory worker.

There were rich men in Congress, to be sure, as there ever have been and ever shall be. There were patrician New Englanders, and Texas oilmen; and there was one man, George H. W. Bush, who had the good fortune to be both of those things. But something important was going on at that time that allowed these men from modest backgrounds to rise to these positions of great power: After World War I, college became available to far more people than it had been previously (again, mostly white people, and indeed mostly Protestants). It was actually in the 1910s that applications outpaced enrollment for the first time. Then, in the period from World War I to World War II, college attendance increased fivefold, from 250,000 to 1.3 million.[33] Universities met the demand through philanthropy and massive public investment in monumental academic buildings and huge football stadiums, many of them still in use today (the Rose Bowl, 1922, Michigan's "Big House," 1927, to name two famous examples). In the blink of a historic eye, many thousands more Americans of all economic classes were able to realize their potential as lawyers, doctors, nurses, engineers, teachers, senators.

So they grew up in the Depression, these men, and managed to make their way through college. And then came the most important shared experience of all: the war. Nearly everyone served. Mansfield and Dirksen, being older than the others mentioned above, had served in World War I. Mansfield lied about his age to enlist in the Navy (he was just fifteen), and Dirksen dropped out of law school to enlist in the army. O'Neill, born in 1912, was already a rising star in the Massachusetts House of Representatives when the second war hit, so he was out. But the others were all part of the war effort. Only Humphrey was not in uniform; three times he tried to join the army, and three times he was rejected for physical reasons, but he did become the chief of the Minnesota war service program and assistant director of the national War Manpower Commission.

Bob Dole, the sturdy conservative, was fighting in Italy when he was hit by German machine-gun fire, suffering the injury that has prevented him from ever straightening his right arm. McGovern, the bleeding-heart liberal, flew thirty-five bombing missions over Nazi Germany and its occupied territories. Bob Michel was an infantryman who participated in the Normandy invasion and won two Bronze Stars and a Purple Heart.

More senators: Jacob Javits, New York Republican, was nearly forty when the war started but won a place in the Chemical Warfare Department as a lieutenant colonel. Frank Church, Democrat of Idaho (yes, a Democrat, from Idaho), was a military intelligence officer in China and Burma. Daniel Inouye, Democrat of Hawaii, was, first of all, Japanese-American, and thus originally barred from service by the army; when the ban was lifted in 1943, he enlisted, fought in Italy in the storied—and segregated—442nd Infantry Regiment, and lost his right arm to a German grenade. Edward Brooke, Massachusetts Republican and an African-American, enlisted right after Pearl Harbor and won a Bronze Star in Italy. Phil Hart, Democrat of Michigan, helped storm Utah Beach on D-Day and drew some shrapnel in his arm. Paul Douglas, Illinois Democrat, enlisted in the Marines at age fifty (!) and won two Purple

Hearts. John Sherman Cooper, Republican of Kentucky and a big-time inside player in his day, enlisted at age forty-one and was part of a unit that arrived at Buchenwald right after the Third Army liberated it; he was present as the residents of nearby Weimar, under General Patton's orders, were directed to the camp to bear witness to the horrors committed there in their name.

I could go on like this for paragraphs, but you get the idea. Choose virtually any male senator or prominent member of the House from that era, and chances are strong that he did something in the war, and maybe something extraordinary (Inouye nearly lost his right arm while there was still an undetonated grenade in the hand; he pried the grenade out of his useless right hand with his left and threw it into a bunker of German soldiers). Some of them even got to know each other. The most famous story along these lines involves Dole, Inouye, and Hart. Years before they would remeet in the Senate, the three of them recovered from their war wounds on the same floor in the same hospital, the Percy Jones Army Hospital in Battle Creek, Michigan (now called, as one would hope, the Hart-Dole-Inouye Federal Center). Dole and Inouye in particular, who were injured in the same month (April 1945) and not too far away from each other in Italy, and whose wounds were worse than Hart's, drew close. Inouye made it to the House of Representatives in 1959, beating Dole by fifteen months.

Once men have been through experiences like that, politics doesn't seem much like combat. As Ira Shapiro puts it in his masterful *The Last Great Senate*:[34]

> Men who had fought at Normandy or Iwo Jima or the Battle of the Bulge weren't frightened by the need to cast a hard vote now and then. Seeing Paul Douglas or Daniel Inouye or Bob Dole on the Senate floor, living with crippling injuries or pain, and the other veterans fortunate enough to have escaped unscathed, set a standard of courage and character for those who followed them.

In the Senate, and in the House as well, legislators of this time really did have a sense of a national interest. They were far from perfect, of course;

the Southern racists kept doing all they could to block civil rights, the era had its share of bribe-takers and drunks, and the Congresses of the early and mid-1960s got us into Vietnam (yes, I blame Congress practically as much as Lyndon Johnson, because as Johnson told Senator Richard Russell, the only reason he prosecuted that war, which he knew to be unwinnable, was fear of impeachment by war hawks of both parties if he didn't).[35] So they were flawed, as all human beings are. But they had a sense of duty and responsibility, a profound respect for the institution they served, and an understanding that they were all there to do the job of finding a way to work through their disagreements to make the country a better place.

This isn't just corny rhetoric. It's measurable, and political scientists have measured it. Most notable here is the work of Nolan McCarty, Keith T. Poole, and Howard Rosenthal. In their 2006 book *Polarized America*, this trio, which has studied polarization for thirty years now, examined literally every vote cast in the United States Congress from 1877 up through 2004 (excluding unanimous and near-unanimous votes). Sure enough, they found a marked decline in polarization in the postwar period up until about the mid-1970s. They have lots of charts and formulas, and I won't go into all that, but suffice it to say that polarization was extreme from 1877 up through the 1920s; in the 1930s, it began to lessen, then it narrowed more during the war, and it stayed pretty narrow until the mid-seventies and the post-Watergate era. They found considerable overlap between the two parties in this period—there were many liberal Republicans and conservative Democrats. But ever since, the parties have diverged, with the Republicans moving much farther to the right than the Democrats have moved to the left.

That overlap made cross-party coalition-building possible. Let's look at two historic roll-call votes in both houses to illustrate the point. First, the Civil Rights Act of 1964. I should begin discussion of this legislation by noting the importance in the Senate of the "cloture" vote. Cloture is a Senate rule—a terrible rule—that requires a supermajority to vote to end debate on a bill and move toward the final up-or-down vote. Today the magic number is sixty, but in 1964 it was sixty-seven, and Southern Democrats had always seen to it that civil-rights bills almost never cleared a cloture vote. It seemed impossible that the act would clear cloture, but it did, and the sixty-seventh vote was provided by a fairly conservative Republican from Delaware named John Williams.

As for the roll calls, they went like this. The Senate passed the bill 73–27. Democrats supported it 46–21, the 21 in opposition of course being from the South, and the Republicans backed it 27–6 (the six were the Senate's serious, hard-shell conservatives—Barry Goldwater of Arizona and John Tower of Texas, most notably). The House passed the bill 289–126. Democrats backed it 153–91, and Republicans, 136–35. In other words, this historic and controversial bill won solid majorities of both parties in both houses.

Second, let's look at the votes the next year on the bill that created Medicare, known officially as the Social Security Amendments of 1965. It passed the Senate 70–24, with Democrats voting 57–7 in favor and Republicans narrowly opposing it, by 17–13. In the House, the final vote was 307–116. Democrats overwhelmingly supported it, 237–48; but even Republicans backed it by two votes, 70–68.

First of all: What a different Republican Party, eh? One vote short of exactly half of Republicans—83 out of 168—voted for what Ronald Reagan had been warning for years was "socialized medicine" (he actually released a spoken-word album in 1961 called *Ronald Reagan Speaks Out Against Socialized Medicine*, which was part of a campaign launched by the American Medical Association called Operation Coffee Cup, under which housewives were to hold coffees and, once their captive and unsuspecting guests got comfortable, put this record on the stereo console). But to support the McCarty-Poole-Rosenthal point about reduced party polarization of that time, look at the cross-party coalitions that passed both of those historic bills. Amazing. Utterly and totally impossible today.

★

One day back in 2011, I was at the Senate covering an important vote. It was important—and profoundly depressing. It was a vote to raise the debt ceiling, votes that have always been occasions for silly posturing, but during the Obama presidency Republicans for the first time started attaching other conditions, mainly the demand for large spending cuts. On this day, Senate Republican leader Mitch McConnell had demanded that raising the debt limit be subject to a cloture vote, meaning it would need sixty votes, a move with little or no precedent in Senate history.

I ran into Mark Shields, the veteran journalist. We sat in the Senate press gallery and chatted as we did what reporters covering Congress spend a lot of time doing, sitting around and waiting. Inevitably, given the circumstances that brought us both there, on a Sunday afternoon no less, I started asking Mark about the old days, and he told me the following story.

He was a young reporter covering Capitol Hill in 1965, when the Voting Rights Act was being considered. Despite the historic nature of the previous year's civil-rights bill, Southern states had still managed to avoid allowing many black people to register to vote, so Congress circled back with a bill aimed right at the heart of poll taxes and literacy tests and the rest.

As opponents of the bill filibustered it, Shields told me, senators from both parties held briefings for reporters to fill them in on the latest twists and turns in the bill's progress. The briefings were always held, he noticed, outside the office of Minority Leader Everett Dirksen, who did most of the talking. Shields found this odd; after all, it was Democrats who controlled the chamber (and the legislative calendar), and it was mainly Democrats who were pushing the bill. Some Democratic senators thought it was odd, too, and after a while, they complained about Dirksen hogging the spotlight and wanted half the briefings moved to Mansfield's office. Mansfield's chief counsel, Charlie Ferris, was deputized to approach the majority leader in their behalf.

Mansfield was a huge believer in bipartisan comity. He used to make senators from opposite parties carpool to work together, so they'd become friends, get to know about each other's lives and families. Mansfield, Shields told me, answered Ferris thus: "Charlie, last year, the Republican Party drifted far from the mainstream during the presidential election. If the public can see the Republican leader each day reporting on the progress of what will hopefully be the most significant civil-rights legislation ever, it will be very beneficial for the country to grasp that this bill was being drafted by both parties even in an overwhelmingly Democratic Congress."

We paused. We looked down at the Senate floor; the same chamber, of course, where that historic bill was passed, where on this day the GOP minority was putting at risk the nation's good credit standing for the sake of gaining a partisan advantage. We were silent for a good while.

Phyllis Schlafly campaigns against the Equal Rights Amendment in front of the White House, February 1977.

LIBRARY OF CONGRESS.

FOUR

Coming Apart

Coming Apart on Race • Coming Apart on Gender •
Coming Apart on Immigration • Coming Apart on Wages •
The Right Gets in the Game

HISTORICAL ERAS ARE CHARACTERIZED BY A DOMINANT DYNAMIC or urge. But inevitably, the opposite dynamic is churning away as well. There are always some people seeking to change the status quo. So, even during the era of comparative social cohesion I wrote about in the previous chapter, there were dissenters. Underneath the placid surface of 1950s America lived all manner of outcasts and subversives—the beatniks, the jazz cats, the poets like Allen Ginsberg, who published his *Howl* in 1956, the artists like Mark Rothko and Willem de Kooning and Jackson Pollock and Jasper Johns, radically redefining what painting could be. In 1952, in a decision that upheld a New York theater's right to show an Italian film in which a character named St. Joseph impregnates a mentally disturbed woman, the Supreme Court first extended First Amendment protections to motion pictures, which began to chip away at the Hays Code that had kept movies clean and wholesome and redeeming (literature didn't really catch up until the 1960s, because of censorship laws). And perhaps most subversively of all, this new invention, an electrified guitar that you plugged into an amplifier, hit the mass market for the first time; in the hands of men like Chuck Berry, it produced sounds never heard before, wild sounds that brought out the animal instincts in those who heard it. So just below the social cohesion were forces gathering like subterranean gases, mingling, changing, waiting to blow. Every era contains the seeds of the coming era that will drive it into oblivion.

It was an odd thing about the Age of Consensus that, despite the dramatic change represented by the reduction in polarization, one thing didn't change: Our two main political parties were still hodgepodges. There were conservative and liberal Democrats, and conservative and liberal Republicans, having their internal feuds and making their cross-party coalitions as they always had. Some people regarded this as natural and just fine, while others saw it as a problem. The latter camp included Franklin Roosevelt, whose ambitions were often hemmed in by his party's conservative Southerners. So in 1944, as the historian Sam Rosenfeld writes in his valuable 2017 book *The Polarizers*, FDR made secret inquiries into trying to work with Wendell Willkie, his vanquished 1940 foe, to bring together the liberals of both parties into one liberal party, leaving the conservatives of both parties to go form a party of the right. "We ought to have two real parties," he said. "One liberal, and one conservative."[1] This would make the United States more like the democracies of Europe and would, Roosevelt and other proponents believed, rationalize our politics.

That effort went for naught, as FDR had a war to win and was in failing health. But the fight was carried on by some political scientists, notably Elmer Eric Schattschneider, a pioneering political scientist and a towering figure to students of such matters. In 1952, E. E. Schattschneider, as he was known, oversaw the writing by a committee of the American Political Science Association of a paper titled "Toward a More Responsible Two-Party System" that called for exactly what Roosevelt had sought. It was enormously influential and instantly controversial in political science circles. But as Rosenfeld shows, it wasn't popular with the public,[2] and besides that it wasn't as if there was some person or persons who could flip a switch and undo more than a century of history. So the hodgepodges ambled on.

It wasn't just political scientists who weren't happy with the alignment of the parties. And so, even as Democrats and Republicans were working together to pass civil-rights bills and other pieces of Great Society legislation, insurgencies were kicking up that would challenge—and ultimately destroy—this consensus. The first is what has become the modern conservative movement. Its roots date back to the early 1950s, when William F. Buckley Jr. published *God and Man at Yale*, his attack on the liberal

and Keynesian presumptions and biases of his alma mater, in 1951. Two
years later came Russell Kirk's *The Conservative Mind*, an idiosyncratic
text from an idiosyncratic man who lived in rural Michigan yet neither
drove a car ("mechanical Jacobins," he called automobiles, fearing they
would "give the quietus to silence")[3] nor watched television; but the first
serious treatment of conservatism as not just a bunch of tub-thumping
Old Testament preachers or greedy Wall Streeters enforcing their economic order on everyone else, but a set of ideas and principles worthy
of intellectual contemplation. Two years after that, Buckley started the
National Review, still a leading conservative opinion journal today.

In practical political terms, this conservatism started getting off the
ground in places like Orange County, California—wealthy suburbs of
the Southwest and West where an unusually high percentage of the men
worked in the defense industry and where the churches and the newspapers were reliably right-wing. Many rich entrepreneurs began putting
massive amounts of money into conservative politics; men like Walter
Knott of Orange County, whose roadside pie business had morphed into
a successful restaurant and finally into the Knott's Berry Farm amusement park. Another locus of the movement was South Bend, Indiana,
where a former Notre Dame Law School dean named Clarence Manion,
once a New Dealer, moved increasingly to the right over the course of the
1950s. He hosted a radio show, a little fifteen-minute daily syndicated
segment, that at that point was one of the few pieces of national glue holding this nascent movement together.

As their movement grew, they faced a decision, these conservatives,
about what their posture was going to be with respect to the Republican
Party: go outside it and build a new party, or work from within and take it
over. For a time, in the run-up to the 1960 presidential race, Manion had
warmed to the idea of running Orval Faubus as a third-party candidate to
be called the States' Rights Party; Manion believed that the Democratic
Arkansas governor and ardent segregationist could unite "Dixiecrats and
Taft Republicans" and "finally block the major-party candidates from an
electoral college majority,"[4] as Rick Perlstein puts it in *Before the Storm*,
his rich history of the conservative movement's early days.

But while Manion was courting Faubus, Arizona senator Barry Goldwater, who'd just that year published his surprise best-selling *Conscience*

of a Conservative, gave a speech in Greenville, South Carolina, in which he vigorously defended states' rights. It turned him into a sensation, and it transformed Manion into a believer. Goldwater made a modest push for the Republican nomination in 1960, but that was mostly just to prove to America that conservatism existed. In 1964, he would capture the nomination. That he was utterly slaughtered in the general election (by 22.5 percent) seemed hardly to matter to conservatives. Like many nascent movements, they had a Happy Warrior aspect about them; having failed to take Washington, they charged on Sacramento and made Ronald Reagan the governor of the state that was, at that moment, just in the process of overtaking New York as the country's most populous.

Meanwhile, in a related insurgency, Southern Democrats were beginning to revolt against their party. Lyndon Johnson chose, in 1964, to make the Democrats the party of civil rights; the right choice, morally and ethically. But he knew very well that the party would lose the South, as he supposedly put it, "for a generation." There's been a debate lately about whether he really said that. If he did say it, he was wrong; we're now coming up on three generations, and the South has been getting more and more lost to Democrats with nearly every passing election.

All the above, the Manions and Goldwaters and Dixiecrats, attacked the consensus from the right. On the left, other and at first smaller insurgencies were incubating among people who'd felt, quite rightly, marginalized and left out of the consensus. There were African-Americans, mostly younger and more radical, who weren't seeing change come nearly fast enough. As the decade unraveled, there were students outraged that their generation was being asked to fight and die in a war they saw as immoral. There were women who wanted much more than the roles the consensus society had largely assigned them—mother and housewife, maybe schoolteacher, department store clerk, a few other jobs. All these groups and others found intellectual sustenance from new critiques of the consensus society that described it not as a glorious democratic achievement but as a ruse, a subjugation, a deceptively sinister state putting its citizens to sleep under this narcotizing blanket of suburban homes and automatic washing machines. "If the worker and his boss enjoy the same television program and visit the same resort places, if the typist is as attractively made up as the daughter of her employer, if the Negro owns a Cadillac, if they all read the same newspaper, then this assimilation indicates not the disappearance of classes, but the extent to which the needs and satisfactions that serve the preservation of the Establishment are shared by the underlying population,"[5] wrote the German émigré philosopher Herbert Marcuse in *One-Dimensional Man*, one of the 1960s' most celebrated critiques of what had become the Western way of life.

You wonder today why our politicians can't just get along? This is when they, and we, started not getting along. And for good reason—there was a lot to argue about. It would take a long, long time, but E. E. Schattschneider was going to get his wish.

Coming Apart on Race

The Civil Rights Act of 1964 had been two or three decades in the making. All those public-education campaigns going back to the 1930s tried, in the tentative and careful way these things had to be phrased then, to advance racial equality. As time went on, as Americans watched graphic news reports from Birmingham and Selma and elsewhere of church bombings and police riots, more and more people knew that racism was the country's great sin and that the law had to change. A handful of racist senators and congressmen prevented it, held off progress as long as they could. But finally they were overwhelmed by three forces.

The first was Lyndon Johnson. This is one case where presidential will to do the right thing really did make it happen. He knew from the instant he assumed the presidency that he wanted to take a much more aggressive line on civil rights than John Kennedy had. It was a mere five days into his presidency that he was meeting with aides to map out a strategy on passing civil rights; as the aides counseled caution, an exasperated Johnson lashed out at them: "Well, what the hell's the presidency for?"[6] He then set about moving heaven and earth to circumvent or subdue the old Southern racists—one of whom, Georgia senator Richard Russell, had been his mentor—and pass the bill.

Second, it also couldn't have happened without certain structural changes to Congress that began in the 1950s—most notably, the election to both chambers, but especially the starchy, conservative Senate, of a lot more liberals. It's hard to pinpoint exactly why. They may all

have been better candidates than their counterparts. Maybe, also, a sur-
feit of liberals was in some sense the natural product of Depression and
war—intensely communal experiences producing men who promised to
continue that communion, carry it into the civic sphere. Also, more pro-
saically, everything was going fine economically—there were no jitters,
no dislocations, no opioid crises, and therefore no big economic anxieties for demagogues to exploit. Whatever the case, the 1958 elections were
especially pivotal here, bringing to the Senate new liberals like future
presidential candidates Edmund Muskie of Maine and Eugene McCarthy of Minnesota, along with Michigan's Philip Hart and Frank Moss of
Utah (Utah?!). Slowly, the balance within the Democratic Party began
to tip, and by the early 1960s the old Southern segregationists no longer wielded the absolute power they once had. The 1962 elections had
brought in three more committed liberals in South Dakota's George
McGovern, Indiana's Birch Bayh, and Wisconsin's Gaylord Nelson. Ted
Kennedy also won that year, in a special election. By January 1963, the
Democrats held 68 Senate seats, and there were enough liberals that the
"old bulls" of the South could be defeated.

   The third development that helped the civil-rights bill pass was, from
our vantage point today, the most surprising of all. The Republican
Party as a whole was pro–civil rights. President Eisenhower had enforced
the integration of Central High School in Little Rock, and Republican
platforms supported civil rights. Richard Nixon pushed in 1960 to make
the GOP platform language stronger at the convention. Texas senator
John Tower challenged that language but was soundly defeated. Americans saw little difference between the two parties on the question. In
1962, one poll asked Americans which party they saw as more likely "to
see to it that Negroes get fair treatment in jobs and housing"; 23 percent
said Democrats and 21 percent Republicans.[7] The pro–civil rights view
was so deeply inculcated in the Republican worldview of the time that
it wasn't just the moderate GOP senators like Jacob Javits and Margaret
Chase Smith who voted for the bill, but strong conservatives like Nebraska's Roman Hruska and South Dakota's Karl Mundt.

   The bill's passage into law on July 2, 1964, realigned American politics
instantly, at least at the presidential level. The Republicans' 1964 platform
became anti–civil rights, and Goldwater ran aggressively against Johnson's

bill. He carried only Arizona and five states in the Deep South, but did he ever carry those five. He won his own home state by a single percentage point, but he got 69 percent of the vote in Alabama, while Johnson literally got 0 percent ("Unpledged Democratic Electors" got 31 percent). Goldwater took 57 percent in Louisiana, 59 percent in South Carolina—and in Mississippi, an astounding 87 percent. The states just named would vote for Jimmy Carter in 1976, and Louisiana backed Bill Clinton both times, but other than that, they've been Republican ever since—except for 1968, when they went for segregationist cheerleader George Wallace.

Below the presidential level, changes in party affiliation and loyalty took longer to effect. Century-old habits don't die easily, and so at levels below the presidency, the South stayed largely Democratic for a long time, well into the 1990s and even the 2000s in some cases. South Carolina senator Strom Thurmond changed his party registration from Democratic to Republican in September 1964, but none of the others did. The other senators stayed in the party and modulated or in some cases outright changed their racial views. A new breed and generation of Southern Democrats rose up. Some were straight-up liberals, like 1970s Florida governor Reubin Askew, who fought for school desegregation (he even supported busing, in Florida!) and named the first African-American justice to the State Supreme Court. A lot of them weren't exactly liberal, but they made gestures to acknowledge change. William Waller, an early 1970s Mississippi governor, declared a state holiday to honor murdered civil-rights leader Medgar Evers, defunded the Mississippi State Sovereignty Commission—essentially a state intelligence agency that spied on civil-rights advocates—and appointed some blacks to prominent positions. Jimmy Carter was a classic "New South" governor: culturally conservative, fiscally moderate, but progressive on race. It made sense: After all, all these states now had hundreds of thousands of new black voters, and they were voting Democratic. So even as Southerners immediately ditched the Democratic Party at the presidential level over race, in these other ways, the South was finally joining the national consensus in favor of equal political rights (I stress *political* rights because there weren't equal rights in housing, lending, and other realms anywhere in the United States then and essentially still aren't in many places).

Within the GOP, moderates were fighting hard to stay with the consensus, and their position in support of civil rights was a linchpin of their efforts. Before the 1964 election, they had formed an organization, the Ripon Society, named for that town in Wisconsin that was host to the first organizational meeting back in 1854 of what became the Republican Party. Ripon's goals were to advance moderate ideas and philosophy, to block the conservative wave, to back civil rights, and to try to nominate New York governor Nelson Rockefeller as president. They failed at that, but afterward, the Riponites were able to say to conservatives: We just got shellacked, and it's your fault. Moderates took more steps to try to solidify their position in the party. The Republican Governors Association (RGA) had been formed in 1963 and by 1965 became an active force for moderation, since GOP governors as a whole were more centrist than many senators and members of Congress.

This period of 1965 to 1968 was a crucial one for the moderates and for the future direction of the GOP. For a while, it looked as if the moderates would win. In addition to the formation of the RGA, House Republicans elected moderate Gerald Ford their leader, and Republican National Committee members removed a chairman Goldwater had installed in favor of Ray Bliss, a moderate from Ohio. Moderate, pro–civil rights Republicans won some key governorships in 1966; In Massachusetts, voters even elected a moderate Republican African-American, Edward Brooke, as senator. At the same time, conservatives claimed key wins, too, most notably Reagan's victory in the 1966 California governor's race. Even so, "1967," writes the historian Geoffrey Kabaservice, "was the high point of moderate fortunes in the Republican Party in the half-century following Eisenhower's presidency."[8]

A crushing blow arrived for them, however, with the demise of George Romney's presidential candidacy. The moderate Michigan governor (and father of Mitt) was lined up to be the party's nominee in 1968. He was the first Republican elected governor of the state in fourteen years and had built a formidable record, but in September 1967 he criticized the war in Vietnam on Michigan television and said that on a visit there the U.S. generals had been "brainwashing" him into trying to believe we were winning the war ("I would have thought a light rinse would have done it," quipped Gene McCarthy).[9] This finished off Romney. It didn't finish off moderate Republicanism just yet, but Richard Nixon, who ran in 1968 on the famous "Southern Strategy" to pander to Southern white views on racial matters, began to shift the party away from the support for civil rights about which the moderates had been so steadfast.

The backlash that Nixon exploited was real enough. White America had watched the Watts riots in Los Angeles in 1965, as well as the riots in Detroit and Newark in 1967 and others, with at least puzzlement, since laws had just been passed to improve black people's lives, and, for some, with uncomprehending fury. Most whites then (and now, for that matter) couldn't understand the bottled rage that permeated those communities, just waiting to explode at some random provocation (in Detroit, it was a police raid on an unlicensed, after-hours bar, where people were gathered, and how's this for irony, to celebrate the return home of some soldiers from serving their country in Vietnam; five days later, forty-three people were dead). Crime was rising fast—the number of violent crimes in the United States nearly tripled from 1960 to 1970.[10] White people were leaving cities pell-mell for segregated suburbs. Welfare-rights groups sprang up urging people to go on public assistance, and the church-based, nonviolent civil-rights movement now shared marquee space with the much more radical Black Power movement. Nixon had a lot to run against, and he ran against all of it.

The rough consensus on race and civil rights that had existed in the early 1960s had completely disintegrated by 1968. It might have continued, at least for a while, had Rockefeller secured the 1964 nomination (which eluded him in large part because of love—he just couldn't wait to marry his second wife, Happy, a divorcee with four kids, which was scandalous then, particularly to Republican women). But the Republicans—during the very same summer that so many Republicans on Capitol Hill were instrumental in passing civil rights—chose Goldwater and have basically been an anticivil-rights party ever since.

The Democrats skewed in the other direction. The party undertook an admirable effort to include more women and minorities in its official ranks, but many party insiders felt the activists leading this charge were moving way too fast. The emblematic battle here was the fight over which Cook County delegation would be seated at the 1972 convention. Mayor Daley's slate erred in one direction: far too heavy on white ethnics, with few minorities and women. Reformers who were supportive of George McGovern erred in the other, naming a slate that had just three Poles out of fifty-nine delegates (in Chicago!).[11] The McGovern slate won that fight, but the white ethnic vote was already turning Republican then, nearly a half-century before Donald Trump came along.

Civil rights and race are closely tied in the national memory to Vietnam. First, because both were the projects of the same president; all these years later it remains nearly incomprehensible that the same man could undertake such an act of courage in pursuing civil rights, I think the most courageous action by any president in my lifetime, and such an act of tragic cowardice as getting the country deeply involved in such an unnecessary war. And second, because the consensus in support of both collapsed right around the same time. The Vietnam War had the support of a majority of the American public until the fall of 1967, by which time the public was about evenly split. Then, after the Tet Offensive in March 1968, public opinion turned against the war.[12] In just four years, the country had been transformed from a mostly unified nation that was finally addressing its most grievous past wrong with the support of business, labor, churches, and both political parties to a country that was torn apart by conflict over race and war.

Coming Apart on Gender

That year of 1968 was, of course, one of the pivotal years in the country's history. The assassinations of Martin Luther King Jr. and Bobby Kennedy; the riots after King's shooting, which crept to within blocks of the Capitol and Supreme Court buildings, areas that weren't redeveloped for thirty years thereafter; the tumultuous Democratic convention, where police and students clashed violently, as police beat and gassed protesters in the "Battle of Michigan Avenue"; the war becoming so overwhelmingly unpopular that Lyndon Johnson had to announce on national television that he wasn't seeking reelection; the Nixon campaign sabotaging the Paris Peace Talks, an act of outright treason that Nixon always denied but that was recently confirmed by the historian John Aloysius Farrell;[13] a bitter presidential election in which Nixon won the popular vote by around a half a percentage point. There was little escape from it all; the Smothers Brothers smuggled leftish politics into the prime-time television schedule (for the one year that CBS permitted them to do so), and even the Olympics were politicized by the raised, begloved fists of sprinting medalists Tommie Smith and John Carlos.

Some normal rituals continued apace, or tried to, but even they were not immune. So it was that at the Miss America pageant in Atlantic City on September 7, about 400 feminists and other protesters showed up to toss bras, girdles, cosmetics, issues of *Playboy*, and other "instruments of female torture" into a large "Freedom Trash Can" they'd placed on the boardwalk. You've heard feminists called "bra-burners"?[14] That epithet was widely used for years, in spirits both humorous and venomous; it dates to this event, as the participants had originally intended to burn bras and other items, but the police told them that lighting a fire on the wooden boardwalk was impermissible. They duly obeyed, but the handle stuck, even though not a single bra was burned.

The decade had opened with Mamie Eisenhower and Jacqueline Kennedy and Donna Reed (as her sitcom housewife character Donna Stone) as the models of American womanhood, and with the Supreme Court, all men at the time, upholding the idea that women shouldn't serve on juries as it would interfere with their domestic duties (*Hoyt v. Florida*, 1961). Then, change: In 1963, Betty Friedan published *The Feminine Mystique*, which challenged the idea that women should aspire only to be housewives and mothers and sold a million copies, and a young journalist named Gloria Steinem published her account of working undercover as a Playboy Bunny. Congress passed an equal pay law and the civil-rights bill (which had sections applying to women) in 1964, and the next year, the Supreme Court ruled in *Griswold v. Connecticut* that married couples could use contraception. That ruling led to much more widespread use of the birth-control pill, which had been the project of International Harvester heiress Katharine McCormick, who financed the research that led a chemist in Mexico City to discover in the early 1950s that yams, of all things, contained a constituent element that could be chemically converted into a hormone that could block the fertilization of an egg. The clinical trial success rate was 100 percent![15] The FDA approved it in 1960, but *Griswold* really expanded the market. For the first time in history, women could have sex free of consequences (at least biological ones), a revolutionary event in gender history that doesn't quite get the attention it deserves in histories that aren't specifically about feminism.

The next frontier on the march to sexual freedom is the issue that remains probably the single most divisive one we face today. Abortions had always been performed, of course, under some circumstances, and always debated; Aristotle wrote about abortion in *Politics*, albeit in a somewhat unclear way that today has both sides of the debate claiming him. Historically, it was generally legal until "quickening" (when the infant begins to stir in the womb, around seventeen to twenty weeks). Antiabortion statutes began to appear in the 1820s, during the Second Great Awakening. Stricter ones came along in the 1870s. So things basically stood until the late 1950s and early 1960s, when some women began to push for cautious changes to state laws. One of the first states to liberalize abortion laws was California, ironically enough under Governor Ronald Reagan, in 1967. It wouldn't be fair to say Reagan was ever really prochoice; back then it was an issue that he, like a lot of people, hadn't given much thought to. Abortion was something that was acknowledged to exist but never discussed. Very rarely a film dealt in the topic, such as 1963's *Love with the Proper Stranger*, in which Steve McQueen knocks up Natalie Wood, who at first wants him to give her money for an abortion (in the end, of course, it being Hollywood, they decide to get together and have the child). But no politician, certainly no presidential candidate back then of either party, had ever had to take a position on the subject.

Laws liberalizing abortion rights passed in more than a dozen states from the mid-sixties up through 1972. Still, no controversy ensued—the Democrats' 1972 platform doesn't mention the word. Then came January 22, 1973, and the Supreme Court's decision in *Roe v. Wade*, extending the federal right to privacy to abortion rights. The case had taken four years to get to this moment. "Jane Roe" was actually Norma McCorvey, unhappily pregnant with her third child (she later became a vocal abortion opponent, and passed away in 2017). "Wade" was Dallas County District Attorney Henry Wade, representing the State of Texas. Linda Coffee and Sarah Weddington were the two lawyers who pushed the case challenging Texas's abortion law up the legal food chain, with Weddington ultimately arguing the case before the Court.

The Court ruling was 7–2, with only William Rehnquist and Byron White dissenting; it was supported by Chief Justice Warren Burger, a Nixon appointee, and two other Court Republicans, along with the Democrats, but it was instantly controversial. Fate relegated the decision to the second story in the next day's *New York Times*—Lyndon Johnson died that same day. But the front-page editors gave both stories the full six columns, Johnson on top in all caps, with "High Court Rules Abortion Legal the First 3 Months" right below. Interestingly, in the *Times*'s sidebar story that day summarizing reaction, the "against" quotes were not from Southern evangelicals but rather from Northern Catholics— New York's Terence Cardinal Cooke, as cardinals were called back then, and the woman who headed the Bronx Right to Life chapter.[16]

Meanwhile, the Equal Rights Amendment was bubbling to the surface. The ERA had roots going back to the 1920s, when suffragist leader Alice Paul talked it up, trying to build on the momentum created by women winning the right to vote. But it was only after the National Organization for Women (formed in 1966) put its weight behind the measure that it finally got a hearing in Congress. The amendment passed both houses of Congress overwhelmingly. The House by 354–23 in October 1971; a male representative from Mississippi announced that his wife had told him to vote no, after which the Manhattan feminist congresswoman Bella Abzug thundered, "I do not come here under instructions from my husband as to how to vote!"[17] The Senate passed it by 84–8 the next spring.

With those kinds of numbers, who on earth was against it? Ratification by three-fourths of the states seemed assured, and indeed within a year of the Senate's action, thirty states had ratified (with thirty-eight needed). Enter Phyllis Schlafly. A native of St. Louis and an archconservative all her life, who had nevertheless spent a year in the liberal lion's den of Cambridge, Massachusetts, while obtaining a master's degree at Radcliffe, Schlafly had first become famous with her 1964 book *A Choice Not an Echo*, urging the Republican Party to swerve hard to starboard. She ran unsuccessfully for Congress in 1970, but now found her cause: to defeat this insidious "women's lib," as it was called then. She led an effort that got the lower house of the Oklahoma legislature to reject ratification. In July 1972, she assembled a small group of supporters at O'Hare Airport to map out the broader strategy, which over time became aimed at convincing conservative groups that had not previously had a dog in this fight to join their side, and to lobby friendly state legislatures to reject or reverse earlier ratification. She also did a lot of TV, at a time when one almost never saw hard-charging, unapologetic right-wingers on television, especially women. Feminists, writes Marjorie Spruill in her excellent *Divided We Stand*, were "outraged" at first that news shows gave her equal time; to them, "it was like inviting a Klansman to present the 'other side' in a debate about civil rights."[18]

Whatever the feminists thought of her, Schlafly won. Thirty-five states backed ratification, but it fell three short, and the original deadline, in March 1979, came and went. By that time, Schlafly had a good bit more company on the right than she'd had in 1972. In the 1960s, white evangelicals thought getting involved in politics was unseemly. "Preachers are not called to be politicians, but soul winners," said none other than Jerry Falwell in 1964—at the time, rebuking the political activism of Dr. King.[19] But by 1970, that view began to change. It was not, as is commonly believed, the *Roe* decision around which the Christian right first mobilized. The truth is less attractive: It was desegregation.

After *Brown v. Board of Education*, the South refused to integrate for many years, finally starting (in some places) in the later 1960s. As the schools filled with black children, white parents took their kids out, and many private Christian academies were opened around the South. Virtually all of them expressly banned black students. The American Friends Service Committee found that segregated private schools were opened in 31 percent of counties in five Deep South states.[20] Because they were religious academies, they enjoyed a tax exemption. But in 1969, some black parents sued and were granted an injunction, and then in July 1970 the Nixon administration unexpectedly ended the schools' exemption. And that's what originally got the religious right into politics—the fact that they had to start admitting black children to their schools. Some did admit a few black students, but for the most part resistance was fierce. Randall Balmer, a Dartmouth historian who has studied the movement's origins, quotes movement founder Paul Weyrich as recalling at a 1990 conference that he tried to get religious conservatives mobilized around pornography, school prayer, the ERA, and abortion. "I was trying to get these people interested in those issues, and I utterly failed," Weyrich said.[21]

Over the course of the decade, the religious right became more focused on abortion. Republicans started campaigning on their opposition to it; an antiabortion plank was inserted for the first time into the party platform in 1976 (President Gerald Ford was prochoice, but he knew where the votes were and didn't fight the plank). "Pro-life" Republicans won some pivotal Senate races in 1978. By that time, the country was deeply divided. Gallup started polling the issue in 1975, asking respondents if abortion should be legal "under certain circumstances," or always legal or always illegal. A majority of 54 percent said legal under some circumstances, 22 percent said always, and 21 percent said never.[22] The numbers have fluctuated in the succeeding four decades, but not all that dramatically. So a set of conflicts that hadn't even really existed in 1965 had us deeply divided by 1975.

Coming Apart on Immigration

The shorthand history of immigration in this country is as follows. It started with the Irish potato famine of the 1840s; grew enormously during the period of 1880 to 1920, although that period did include the Chinese Exclusion Act of 1882; was cut off completely with the Johnson-Reed Act of 1924 for the next forty years; then all that suddenly changed with the Immigration and Naturalization Act of 1965, after which the doors flew open.

The full story is a bit more complicated. First of all, immigrants started arriving here in large numbers in the 1820s, though the levels did indeed explode in the 1840s and then again in the 1880s. But Johnson-Reed—Johnson was Albert Johnson, a Washington State congressman, and Reed was Pennsylvania senator David Reed; both Republicans—did not immediately slow immigration, as the cliché goes, "to a trickle." In 1923, the number of legal permanent residents entering and living in the United States was 522,919, according to the Migration Policy Institute; in 1924, it was 706,896; in 1925, 294,314.[23] In the five years from 1920 to 1924 (inclusive), the average number was roughly 493,000 per year, and in the five years after the act, the number was around 300,000; so, slowed, but not quite to a trickle. It wasn't until the early 1930s that it dropped below 100,000. Much of that drop was due not to the law but to the Depression, because fewer people wanted to come to a country in the throes of economic crisis, and because most of Europe was feeling the Depression, too, and not as many people could afford to come.

The number of arrivals stayed low, for obvious reasons, through the end of World War II. Then it bounced back up to six figures right after— throughout the 1950s, the number of new legal permanent residents per year (which includes new arrivals and people already here given more secure legal status) averaged about 250,000 a year. I say this not in defense of Johnson-Reed, which was blatantly discriminatory in intent and in effect. It completely excluded all Asians and Arabs, was aimed at dramatically reducing the number of Italians who could come to America, and later blocked Jews desperately fleeing the Holocaust. I'm just noting that the actual history is more complicated than most people think.

In 1942, the nation's farms were experiencing a severe manpower shortage, with so many men fighting the war and others working in the war economy. So the Roosevelt administration and the Mexican government created the *bracero* program that allowed workers to come up seasonally from Mexico, harvest crops, and return. Mexican workers were supposed to be paid competitively to native wages, and 10 percent of their pay was for some reason sent to the government of Mexico, which was supposed to forward the payments to them. Needless to say, neither of those things happened very much, and these workers were horribly exploited from the start. During the war, around 40,000 to 60,000 braceros came every year. By the late 1950s, the number was more than 400,000 per year. The program was ended in 1964, but it had an impact well beyond its duration, as we'll see directly.

In 1952, Congress passed another restrictive law, the McCarran-Walter Act. This had several provisions, chiefly codifying the quota system from 1924. A couple of its provisions were somewhat liberal (it removed the ban on Asian immigration, although it kept the numbers exceedingly small). But mostly it was a Cold War law. Democratic senator Pat McCarran of Nevada was one of the Senate's leading anticommunists, so he, with Democratic congressman Francis Walter of Pennsylvania, pushed for language that would allow the United States to bar aliens whose presence it found to be "prejudicial to the public interest."[24] President Truman vetoed it as discriminatory, but there was more than enough cushion in both houses to override.

The Cold War sometimes had contradictory impacts on our politics. While on the one hand it produced anticommunist zealotry of the sort embodied in McCarran-Walter, on the other it made some elites realize that if the United States truly wanted to be the proverbial beacon of freedom to the people of the developing world, it probably should open its doors more widely to the people of said world. There was a collective guilt among elites about the Holocaust, and America's failure in the 1930s to take in more Jews. The Eisenhower administration imposed "Operation Wetback," which deported several hundred thousand (at least; the figures are disputed) Mexican farm workers in 1954 and 1955.[25] But Ike later urged liberalization of immigration laws, attempting to expand McCarran-Walter quota amounts in 1957, though Congress didn't take it up. Next, President Kennedy proposed comprehensive immigration reform in 1963. He did not live to pass it, but Johnson, with his customary zeal and mastery of the legislative process, took up the cause. And in 1965, the Immigration and Naturalization Act (INA) was passed by overwhelming—and again, bipartisan—margins: The Senate passed it 76–18, with Democrats voting aye by 52–14 and Republicans by 24–3; it sailed through the House 318–95, with roughly three-quarters of Democrats and four-fifths of Republicans in support.[26]

There was no controversy. There had been no great outcry for the bill. No marches, no demonstrations, no acts of civil disobedience. Either pro or con. "It is a very minor issue," said the lobbyist for the American Jewish Committee at the time.[27] Liberal groups supported it—the American Civil Liberties Union, Americans for Democratic Action, a major player at the time, and others—but there was no great hue and cry. Indeed, if anything the opposite: A Harris poll in May 1965 found the public opposed to easing immigration restrictions by a margin of 58 to 24 percent.[28] But they weren't so against it that they were moved to any big public act. Also, after the act's passage, Gallup found 70 percent saying they favored the new law.[29] Seesawing numbers like these indicate a classic case of the public not knowing much, not giving the matter much thought, seeing Congress do something, and thinking, especially in those days of far greater trust in government, "Oh well, okay, they must know what they're doing."

Few things as big as a major congressional overhaul of law can be put down to the efforts of one person, but if ever a case could be constructed along those lines, it can be made with respect to Congressman Emanuel Celler's efforts on immigration. Celler, a Jewish Brooklynite who grew up with his father's whiskey tank in his basement and who remains one of the longest-serving House members in history, was a freshman when Johnson-Reed passed, and it incensed him. He swore then that someday he'd have the power to undo it. He laid the paving stones in 1947, when he was the ranking Democrat on the Judiciary Committee—during a reorganization of the House, he got immigration moved from the jurisdiction of the Labor and Commerce Committee to his own. The move, writes Margaret Sands Orchowski in her study of the 1965 act, "made the focus of immigration law one of justice—family unification and antidiscrimination—instead of about work, jobs, and labor development of the country."[30] So finally, forty-one years later, Celler, with a big assist on the Senate side from Ted Kennedy, managed to run his steamroller over the old law.

Kennedy made a famous (or infamous, depending on one's point of view) assurance at the time that the law would not change the ethnic mix of the country. We'll leave to the side for present purposes the debate over whether he was being dishonest or naïve. But of course it did change the ethnic mix, chiefly through the family reunification provision, which allowed legal immigrants to petition to bring in not just spouses and children, but parents, adult siblings, some cousins. But again, as with 1924, the change was not dramatic and immediate. In the five years before the law's passage, the number of new legal permanent residents in the United States per year was about 222,000; in the five years after the law, it went up, but only to about 360,000 per year.

The civil-rights and feminist revolutions happened quickly and dramatically; but if they were volcanic explosions, the immigration revolution was the lava rolling slowly down the hill, unfolding over a much longer period of time. The 1970s brought the advent of many new arrivals from Southeast Asia, as the Vietnam War ended, and a slow but steady increase in immigration from Mexico and Central America.

These were legal immigrants and refugees. But around the same time, illegal immigration started to increase. The roots of illegal immigration are several, including first of all the vast wage disparity between the United States and the countries people were (and are) fleeing. Political strife—indeed, terror—in Central America and southern Mexico has been another factor. But according to Doris Meissner, who headed the Immigration and Naturalization Service for eight years under Bill Clinton, the deep roots were to be found in the networks created under the bracero program, and the always lax enforcement of U.S. laws governing employers' practices. She wrote in 2004:[31]

> ... the lasting effect of the *bracero* program has been that it spawned and institutionalized networks and labor market relationships between Mexico and the United States. These ties continued and became the foundation for today's illegal migration from Mexico. Thus, ending the agreement as a *legal* matter did not alter the migration behavior that had been established over the course of more than 20 years; the migrant flows simply adapted to new conditions.

In 1982, the Supreme Court decided, in *Plyler v. Doe,* by a narrow 5-4 margin that had conservative Lewis Powell joining the Court's four liberals, that children of what were then uncontroversially called illegal immigrants were entitled to the same education as native-born children (they were people "in any ordinary sense of the term," the majority held). In 1986, Congress passed a new immigration law to deal with these undocumented arrivals, in part by granting legal status ("amnesty," in other words) to all who'd arrived illegally before 1982 provided they pay a fine and back taxes and admit guilt. Yes, 1986—which means Ronald Reagan signed it. We weren't yet divided on immigration in those days that just barely, and not coincidentally, preceded the rise of right-wing talk radio. Three million undocumented aliens became legal in a matter of about three years. In exchange, sanctions were toughened (allegedly, anyway) on employers of undocumented workers. The roll-call votes, looked at from today's vantage of strict party-line votes, are interesting. It passed both houses comfortably—230-166 in the House, 69-30 in the Senate—but the ideological divisions were striking. Latinos and Ted Kennedy-style liberals were against it because of the sanctions, while most conservative members opposed the amnesty. Senate Republicans supported the bill 41–11, but House Republicans opposed it, 62–105 (although "Gingrich, Newton" voted yea!). Right there, in that 105 number, we see the seeds of what became by 2016 thousands of people chanting "Build the wall!"

It wasn't until the early 1990s—concurrent with the dawn of the broader culture war and the maturation of ethnic identity movements and a nascent but growing academic literature on multiculturalism—that immigration became a first-rank issue. Mind you, the broader public never supported liberal immigration flows. Gallup keeps data going back to 1965, asking respondents whether they supported immigration that was increased, decreased, or at current levels. In 1965, those numbers respectively were: 7 percent, 33 percent, and 39 percent. In 1972, "decreased" passed "current levels." By the mid-eighties, "decrease" held a solid lead. Then in the early 1990s the backlash kicked into gear: 65 percent supported a decrease, 27 percent said keep the status quo, and just 6 percent said increase.[32] And then we saw California's Proposition 187, which prohibited illegal entrants from accessing many of the state's social services (the voters passed it 59–41 percent), and other concrete manifestations of the backlash.

So again, a controversy that hadn't even existed in 1965 became, in this case not five but twenty and twenty-five years later, a stick of dynamite. And, as with race and abortion, it was inevitable that one political party would take one side of the argument, broadly speaking, and the other party would take the other side.

Coming Apart on Wages

As noted, 1968 was an *annus horribilis* if ever there was one. But by one measure—indeed the measure that is usually the bottom line in judging the success or failure of our politicians and political system, although not in those tumultuous times—1968 was a magnificent year. The economy was rarely stronger. Consider the phrase that recurs in that year's Economic Report of the President, issued that February: "the problem of prosperity."[33] The gross domestic product grew by nearly 5 percent.

The unemployment rate was a mere 3.6 percent. The median household income, adjusted for inflation, was $6,698, or just under $50,000 today in inflation-adjusted dollars.

That's actually less than the 2016 median household income in the United States of $56,516, but that is somewhat offset by the fact that in 1968, earnings were much more equitable. A CEO made about 20 times as much as his average employee, as opposed to the more than 300 times he makes now. And there was far less inequality all the way around. Economists have various means of measuring this, the main one being something called the Gini coefficient, developed in the early twentieth century by an Italian sociologist named Corrado Gini, whose early enthusiasm for Mussolini waned over the course of the 1930s enough that it hasn't harmed his historical reputation or lessened our reliance on his work. The Gini scale goes from 0 to 1.0, or is sometimes listed as 0 to 100, with 0 being a country where everyone owns everything equally and 1.0 (or 100) being a country where one person owns everything. As it happens, 1968 was the year of the United States' all-time lowest (and Gini scores are like golf, lowest is best) Gini number of around 35. It's climbed steadily ever since, especially after 1980, and by 2013 hit around 45.[34] For comparison's sake, the world's best Gini number is owned by Finland, in the low 20s, while South Africa claims the worst, around 62. The United States is rubbing shoulders with Peru, Singapore, Thailand, and Saudi Arabia.[35]

Things were still pretty good under Nixon for a while, but then the clouds gathered. Economists point to 1973 as the year that regular people's wages started stagnating. They use 1973 for a particular reason: That was the first year that wages and productivity started, as the economists sometimes put it, "decoupling." That is: Productivity is essentially the measure of how efficiently we make things. Productivity gains come from changes in technology, increases in investment, a whole host of factors. Productivity increased every year after the war in the United States, and usually dramatically. Wages increased right along with it. Then, in 1973, it snapped. If you Google "wage productivity gap," you'll see links to a lot of charts, and they all look the same: Two lines climbing almost exactly side by side from 1948 until 1973, and then, from 1973 onward, one line (productivity) continuing its steep ascent, and another line (wages) that's just about flat. Productivity has increased by 142 percent since then, and wages by just 15 percent.[36]

It was a hideous year, 1973. The OPEC oil embargo of the United States over the latter's military support for Israel stunned Americans. We're the United States! How can we be pushed around by these autocratic men in their funny outfits? But push around they could. The price of oil quadrupled in a matter of months. Americans had to change their habits in a hurry. I remember laughing to myself when my Aunt Tessie showed up at our door around then driving her brand-new Honda Civic. Honda, I thought; they make motorbikes, who'd want a Honda for a car? It sat in our driveway next to Dad's Chrysler Imperial, which looked like it could swallow Tessie's little Civic whole—and which got about twelve miles to the gallon.

The oil crisis exacerbated another ongoing crisis, the greatest economic cataclysm of the time: runaway inflation. Economists actually date what they call "The Great Inflation" to 1965. The reasons are many and complicated (and of course still debated by academics), but the rough consensus seems to be that it came down to government spending in the 1960s on the Great Society and the Vietnam War (and Lyndon Johnson's decision to run deficits rather than raise taxes), and to a Federal Reserve monetary policy that was implemented to adhere to the political priorities of the Kennedy and Johnson administrations that low unemployment was more important than low inflation and that led to excess growth in the money supply. Indeed, inflation did go up in that late-sixties period, from a 1960s average of just under 2 percent to 4 percent by 1968 and nearly 6 percent by 1970. But that was nothing compared to what was to come.[37]

It was a devastating combination: prices shooting up while wages were stagnating. At the same time: crime rates spiking; cities collapsing, becoming dysfunctional—"ungovernable," to use a word one heard a lot in those days. Normal rules of society seemed in some cases no longer to apply—it's unimaginable to us today, but in the 1970s, pornography was on open display in Times Square and in similar districts in other cities, with movie-theater marquees openly shouting the graphic titles of their current features. The Boston Strangler, the Zodiac Killer, Son of Sam, the Bronx burning during the 1977 World Series; these great citadels that had redefined the city and defined American greatness and innovation four decades before were now hellish moonscapes that no "decent American" wanted to set foot in.

And, of course, hovering over all this was the crisis of Watergate: the first time a president had been caught on tape lying and been chased from office in disgrace. And still Vietnam—it dragged on for two more years after Nixon had officially declared it over in 1973. These are commonly cited as the two events that made Americans lose trust in their government and leaders, and it's true—with them, a Rubicon was crossed. They forced upon the American people an introspection, not just about who their leaders were to have done these things, but who *they* were to have so long sanctioned their leaders doing them. Most people resist introspection; whole societies are no different. Liberals, however, tend to welcome introspection, and liberals and Democrats of that era, starting with the pious man in the Oval Office, did quite a lot of reflecting on what was happening to the national character. So surely one of the great secrets, perhaps *the* great secret, of the conservative movement's coming success, of Ronald Reagan's success in particular, was to free people of this responsibility of introspection, to release them from the guilt in which liberalism seemed to make them wallow.

A final bleak development began to catch observers' attention in the mid-to-late 1970s. The vast steel mills and other factories that had won the war and built the middle class started to shrink, or close, or move to nonunion states in the South and West (in many cases on their way, eventually, to Mexico and China). Union membership, which had peaked in the 1950s, began declining around this time: from 24 percent in 1973 to 20.1 percent in 1983 to 15.8 percent in 1993.[38] The phrase "Rust Belt" entered the national lexicon in 1982. The Homestead Steel Works, the great plant just south of Pittsburgh that had employed 15,000 men during the war, the one plant that symbolized that city's dominance of American and indeed global steel production, that epitomized the industry that gave the city's beloved football team its name, started downsizing in the early 1980s. In 1986, it closed. Wrote Jefferson Cowie and Joseph Heathcott of Homestead in 2003, "on that once world-famous bend in the Monongahela River are now a Loew's Cineplex; a McDonald's; a Target; a Bed, Bath, and Beyond; and other national chains displaying wares produced in an immense global network of production."[39] And, they might have added, stocked and sold by clerks making a fraction (in inflation-adjusted terms) of what the men at the Homestead Works had been paid.

Again, the consequences for our politics were obvious. During the era of general prosperity, there was labor strife, at times quite ferocious—major steel strikes in 1952 and 1959, the crippling New York City transit strike of 1966, and many others. And there were economic downturns, in 1958 and again in 1960, when unemployment peaked north of 7 percent. But for the most part from the end of the war until 1973—that is to say, for *almost thirty years*—wages were going up, factories were humming, people had job security, and inflation was under control. Under such circumstances, economic debates were mostly manageable. But after these stresses were introduced, the ideological polarities intensified. Liberals held fast to New Deal Keynesian principles, while conservatives over the course of the 1970s moved toward a radical critique of those principles. Both sides identified for their partisans the scapegoats for these new problems—the greedy owners for liberals, the bloated unions for conservatives.

Jimmy Carter made one effort to help unions, via a 1978 bill to make union shops possible in states where they had been outlawed. Labor leaders were desperate for the bill, but Carter didn't invest much political capital on it—he was obsessed at the time with passing the Panama Canal Treaty. The bill died in the Senate, where it was opposed by nearly as many Democrats as Republicans.[40] Those Democrats were from Southern and midwestern right-to-work states. Over time, there would be fewer and fewer such Democrats, who became more and more concentrated in the cities and on the coasts, while among Republicans, more and more conservatives replaced moderates, and that party's center of gravity moved South. The political chasm grew wider and wider.

The Right Gets in the Game

It's impossible to leave this discussion of the 1970s without considering one final factor that contributed to our widening divisions—the explosive growth of what's often called the conservative infrastructure, the network of nonprofit groups (think tanks, training academies, etc.) that pushed the Republican Party to the right. In some ways, this is *the* political story of modern times.

Most people don't realize the enormous role nonprofit associations play in politics—hundreds of millions if not billions of dollars spent every year by wealthy individuals and the foundations they establish for the express purpose of shaping political debate, getting a pet issue into the mainstream discourse, and so on. All such contributions are of course tax deductible, provided the organization follows a few loose rules about not being too capital-P Political. The first law providing tax exemption for these organizations goes all the way back to 1894, followed by two laws passed during World War I.[41] These laws paved the way for the existence of charitable organizations like the United Way and the Rotary Club— and also for nonprofit groups that did more policy-oriented work, such as the Ford Foundation, founded by scions of the motor company in 1936.

Ford was not and is not per se a political foundation—it doesn't get involved in electoral politics or track legislators' voting records. At the same time, many of the causes it has supported over the decades can fairly be called "liberal" ones, from public television (it was a Ford grant that initially brought you *Sesame Street*) to grants to law schools in the early 1970s to set up community clinics to provide legal services to poor people to voter-registration efforts to AIDS-prevention funding. Another major nonprofit, the Brookings Institution, was founded in 1916 expressly for the purpose of providing expert analysis of public-policy issues. (Robert Brookings had made his fortune in wholesale sales and was an innovator in warehousing and distribution—sort of the Jeff Bezos of the late nineteenth century.) Brookings was, and remains, nonpartisan in the sense that its mission is not to advance either party's agenda. And yet it's fair to say that insofar as Brookings exists to help government develop policy solutions to pressing problems, it leans to the left (especially on domestic policy; on foreign policy, Brookings was home to some prominent supporters of the Iraq War). As the twentieth century ended, Brookings ranked government's greatest accomplishments since World War II, and they were: (1) rebuilding Europe after the war; (2) expanding the right to vote; (3) promoting equal access to public accommodations; (4) reducing disease; (5) reducing workplace discrimination.[42] One can call these things "liberal" if one wishes, but they're also broad social goods that I hope few people would argue with, although conservatives today seem not to like number 2 very much.

There was one avowedly conservative counterpart to Brookings, established in 1938 to promote limited government. The American Enterprise Institute's founders included executives from General Mills, Chrysler, Johns Manville, Eli Lilly, Chemical Bank, and Paine Webber. Its endowment didn't match Brookings's, and, in an age when even Republican presidents accepted the basic premises of the New Deal, it didn't have nearly as much influence. Other think tanks existed, in Washington and elsewhere, but quite few compared to today. There was very little lobbying of Congress in those days, too. In fact, back then, according to Lee Drutman, a leading expert on these matters, businesses hardly bothered; and "to the extent that businesses did lobby in the 1950s and 1960s (typically through associations), they were clumsy and ineffective."[43]

So stood the Washington status quo through the late 1960s. But by this time, across America, young people were talking revolution; hit songs were celebrating it, and books like Yale professor Charles A. Reich's *The Greening of America*, a paean to the counterculture and a warning that revolution was indeed around the corner, were popping up on best-seller lists (and in Reich's case being excerpted in the venerable *New Yorker*). Corporate types and conservatives feared for the very future of the free enterprise system. Around this time, an official with the U.S. Chamber of Commerce named Eugene B. Sydnor Jr. was sharing some concerns along these lines with a neighbor of his. The neighbor happened to be Lewis Powell, a Richmond lawyer who was just a few months away from fate, in the form of Richard Nixon, tapping him on the shoulder and giving him a seat on the Supreme Court. Could you, Sydnor asked his friend, write something up for the Chamber describing how we might save capitalism itself?

Thus was born the famous "Powell Memo," dated August 23, 1971, in which the author, in the course of a few thousand words, lays out the dimensions of the crisis (name-checking Reich), laments the business community's "apathetic" response to these challenges, and lists a number of areas in which corporate leaders had to act posthaste. Fund conservative scholars. Create a campus speakers' bureau. Evaluate textbooks. Demand faculty slots. Monitor the media for unfair attacks. Publish books and pamphlets of their own. Get their hands much dirtier in politics ("as unwelcome as it may be to the Chamber, it should consider assuming a broader and more vigorous role in the political arena"). Fund some kind of judicial activism. The language of the memo is quaint today, as evidenced by that naïve "unwelcome" in the quote above, describing a time long-gone; reading it now is like reading a warning to pregnant mothers from the early sixties that they should give some thought to cutting back on the cigarettes and martinis.

The Powell Memo has been the subject of intense debate. It was barely noticed at first, although Jack Anderson, then a widely syndicated columnist, got a copy and published extracts around the time of Powell's Court nomination. The leak to Anderson, though, was not intended to showcase Powell's insight, but to raise questions about his temperament. Publicly, Powell was confirmed, and the memo quickly forgotten. Then, in the 1990s and early 2000s, liberals rescued it from history's dustbin. Some, realizing by then that liberalism had been outspent by conservatism by many hundreds of millions of dollars over the prior forty years, saw in it a veritable Rosetta Stone. It served a useful purpose for liberals, wrote the political analyst Mark Schmitt in 2005, "because it helps tell the story of the institutions that support the modern right in a tidy, accessible way, and one that shows how similar institutions of the left could be designed and built."[44] In the end, though, Schmitt is among those who think its influence has been overstated by liberals.

But whether the Powell Memo was or was not the engine that set it all in motion, the fact is that the conservative movement did indeed build its infrastructure in those next few years. The Heritage Foundation, the preeminent conservative think tank today, which guides much Republican policy thinking and recommended many of Donald Trump's appointments, opened its doors in 1973. A lot of the initial money came from Joseph Coors, of beer fame. The author Alyssa Katz, in her comprehensive history of the Chamber, *The Influence Machine*, directly credits the Powell Memo with having "inspired" Coors to act.[45] Richard Mellon Scaife, the Pittsburgh scion who became known for his role in trying to bring down Bill Clinton, was another early backer. Four years later, the Cato Institute, the libertarian think tank, was founded, with initial money from another billionaire whose name is also familiar—Charles Koch. Accuracy in Media, the first-ever right-wing media monitoring group of any importance, had been founded in 1969 but elevated its profile in the early 1970s with its

AIM Report, a biweekly newsletter devoted to cataloguing instances of liberal media bias. The Federalist Society, the conservative legal group, was founded in 1982 to fight liberal orthodoxy in law schools, and in part specifically, writes Steven M. Teles in his authoritative *Rise of the Conservative Legal Movement*, to check the influence at elite law schools of those Ford Foundation legal clinic grants.[46] Businesses aggressively stepped up antiunion activity. Law firms specializing in union-busting (though they denied the practice) proliferated in the 1970s and '80s. The AFL-CIO tried to make them controversial by circulating lists of these firms. They succeeded to a decent extent in raising awareness of their existence—but not in limiting their activity in any meaningful way.

It would be impossible to mention them all. If you're interested in the details, read Alan Crawford's 1980 *Thunder on the Right: The "New Right" and the Politics of Resentment* (and note well his subtitle; resentment against elites was the driver) and Sidney Blumenthal's 1986 *Rise of the Counter-Establishment: The Conservative Ascent to Political Power*. Crawford is a conservative, or was then, anyway, and Blumenthal a liberal, but the stories they tell are quite similar—of a movement that saw itself not as a normal American interest group, but as a vanguardist cadre taking on a mighty and malevolent establishment and funneling at first tens and then hundreds of millions of dollars into think tanks, advocacy organizations, training academies for young people, conservative newspapers on college campuses, all manner of enterprises. And here is a crucial point: Because they saw themselves as needing to persuade Americans of a whole new way of understanding political events, and indeed understanding society itself, they were avowedly ideological in a way that Ford and Brookings simply were not.

Eventually, it dawned on liberals that they were being dramatically outspent on idea dissemination and generation. Rob Stein, a progressive and Democratic operative, toted up the numbers in 2003 for a PowerPoint presentation he showed to Democratic insiders and wealthy donors. Conservative "idea groups," he found, were outspending their liberal counterparts about six to one, $180 million to $30 million.[47] Stein's PowerPoint gained such currency—you weren't a real insider if you hadn't seen it—that the *New York Times Magazine* wrote an article about it.[48] Today, he says, it's a little under two to one, as liberals have built large institutions like the Center for American Progress. But it means that for the better part of three decades, conservatives were pouring money into politics and creating disciplined organizations of a sort that simply hadn't existed before.

They changed the very way activists thought about issues and how to develop them. These funders took the long view, never demanding an immediate return on their investment. So the people at Cato and Heritage wanted, for example, to privatize Social Security. They'd produce white papers, an op-ed column here and there, maybe a book they'd disseminate to policy journalists. For the first ten years, everybody laughed. For the next ten, people still rolled their eyes, but they kept at it. Finally, George W. Bush was president, Republican majorities ruled Congress, and they had their moment. They didn't succeed, because a large majority of Americans thought it was a horrible idea. But they had their shot. On other matters, like the near-elimination of the estate tax, they've been far more successful, and their great patience has been rewarded.

So that's the political narrative of the unraveling. In 1964, we had one country; by 1974, we had a very different one, and by 1984 a different one still, as so many controversies exploded to the surface that hadn't even existed before. This is not a lament for the bygone days of 1964. Quite the contrary. African-American demands for equality, and women's, were necessary and just, as were the other movements that arose in their wake. I'm simply saying that America was deeply divided on these developments, and largely remains so, and for good reason: They're controversial, divisive matters that stir deeply held passions and prejudices, and there isn't all that much we can do about it.

Meanwhile, another change began brewing in the early 1980s, this one economic, that changed the character of the country in immeasurable ways. This change isn't normally part of the story of our political divisions, but I believe it to be crucial to the decline in civic spirit and the worsening of the class and cultural divisions that inevitably became part of our politics.

Steve Forbes, Malcolm Forbes, and Elizabeth Taylor at Malcolm's seventieth birthday party in Tangier, Morocco, August 1989.

FIVE

More Consumers Than Citizens

*How the Search for Credit and Yield Changed Us
as Human Beings • The Masters of the Universe Stake
Their Claim • The Compensation Boom—for a Few •
Amusing Ourselves to Death*

A S OUR CULTURE WAS FRACTURING ALONG LINES OF RACE AND gender, and as the old political consensus was in freefall, something else new and just as important was happening in the economic realm. American society was splintering here, too. Inequality was increasing— wages were stagnating in the middle, and zooming heavenward at the top. Wall Streeters, corporate CEOs, ballplayers, even university presidents, started making unheard-of salaries. A whole new media machinery was conjured into being to celebrate this wealth. Sharp entrepeneurs quickly figured out that these folks would spend $2 million on a Manhattan co-op (doesn't buy you a palace today but did then) or $3,000 on a handbag, and they set about to produce them.

These were the nouveau riche. They've existed in every society since the beginning of time, but they arise at certain moments—when a new set of economic conditions replaces an old set and creates new wealth out of what had been, to that point, nothing. The old rich, the people whose wealth derived from land, title, or a long-ago invention, whose names were in the Social Register and who could trace their family lineage back to the *Mayflower*, sneered at them, found them garish. And often they were garish. One of the prominent nouveau riche celebrities of the 1980s was the man who built that tower at Fifth Avenue and 56th Street in 1983, with the labor of "illegal Polish aliens working at rates one-half to one-third those of union scale," according to the late investigative journalist Wayne Barrett,[1] and lying through his teeth about promising to save two Art Deco friezes of Bonwit Teller, the legendary department store he tore down, friezes that the Metropolitan Museum of Art wanted preserved but that Donald Trump instead had destroyed ("they fell to the floor and shattered in a million pieces," wrote one Trump biographer).[2] Most New Yorkers weren't big fans of the tower, which some critics defended and others found vulgar (Paul Goldberger of the *New York Times* praised the rose-peach marble that struck many as garish); but millions of tourists flocked there every year to marvel at it, unsure whether they were supposed to be impressed or repulsed, but succumbing in the end to its self-promotional sense of spectacle and its proprietor's alleged golden touch.

But it wasn't just the nouveau riche. Regular middle-class people, or at least some of them, the ones in the right place and the right industry at the right time, were no longer so regular. They did better than their neighbors. They joined the investing class. Their houses got a little bigger. Sometimes gates and walls went up around their developments. Manufacturers and marketers quickly cottoned on to them, too. They could take slightly nicer vacations and drive ever-so-much-more-exclusive and gizmoed-up cars; before the 1980s were over, Toyota, Honda, and Nissan (née Datsun), known mostly theretofore for their reliably efficient models, were out with their respective luxury badges of Lexus, Acura, and Infiniti. They weren't rich, but they had just enough that they could sometimes act like it.

We go through life wearing many identities. Child, sibling, spouse, parent, grandparent; neighbor, friend; worker of some kind, most of us, although not of course everyone (by a long shot—around 150 million adult Americans work today, while 90 million do not, although they are not "unemployed" because they're not looking for work).[3] But in terms of our public rather than private identities, we have two main ones: citizen and consumer. Not every single person is a citizen of course, but the vast majority of us—93 percent—are.[4] And we're all consumers, whether we want to be or not.

Why do I highlight these two identities? Because in any democratic society, they are in tension. They make competing demands on us. As citizens, we're supposed to think of the other person's interest sometimes, or the common interest. At the very least, we're supposed to act in what is sometimes called "enlightened self-interest," which means we should understand that when we perform certain acts of seeming selflessness, it is also in our own self-interest to do so. An example here is that even people who don't have children in the local public schools still pay school taxes (hopefully willingly) on the understanding that having a well-educated population benefits the whole community and indeed them, since a well-educated community will function well economically and bring general prosperity from which all benefit (and if they can't get that through their heads, maybe they can at least be convinced that a good school system raises the value of their home). The simple doing of favors for friends constitutes enlightened self-interest, too: We're doing a nice thing because we like someone, yes, but also because we expect the favor will one day be returned (indeed, if enough favors go unreturned, we drop that person).

Citizens are engaged, too, in public matters. Whether we're on the left or the right or somewhere in between, our citizen-selves are regularly thinking and acting about politics and civic life. I'm not referring here to the lofty, theoretical concepts of citizenship that date back to Athens and that the founders hoped we would embody. I mean far more mundane things. Old high-school friends of mine come on my Facebook page to agree or disagree with something I've written. Those posts are acts of citizenship—every minute my old friends sit crafting those posts is a minute they're not thinking about buying, selling, consuming, bill-paying: about money.

In our other identity, our consumer identity, we don't think about the common interest or enlightened self-interest. We mainly just think about wants. The bigger TV, the newest phone, that latest version of that space-age device on the table that we can ask to play "Back to Black" or name us the capital of Ontario. The best balsamic vinegar, the array of carrots no longer merely orange, the exotic melons that go for $9 each even though they look like they have leprosy. Over these past thirty years, we have been trained by the market to want, want, want. And more than that:

We have been trained, relentlessly and really for the first time in history on such an all-encompassing scale, to want *in comparison* to what others want. This was always somewhat true; in the 1950s, Mr. Smith wanted a flashier car than Mr. Jones. But now this competition has seeped into every corner of our lives.

It is something that has happened in an astonishingly short period of time, in historical terms. Think back to what I wrote about the 1930s, how few people owned radios, telephones, stoves, other items. That was eighty years ago (and eighty years before *that*, in the 1850s, most people owned no consumer items at all). Today most people have all these things. Even families on the margins of poverty typically have a TV and two or three smartphones.

It has changed us, dramatically. In the 1930s, people barely had consumer identities. In the 1950s and '60s, they acquired such identities, a condition that was lamented by dozens of prominent sociologists and economists, perhaps most notably John Kenneth Galbraith in his famous book *The Affluent Society*. But even so, the consensus of the age provided for a kind of civic glue. Then came the period of collapse, from 1964 to 1980—the period of civil rights, Vietnam, the rise of movement conservatism, feminism and the backlash, immigration, wage stagnation and crushing stagflation. But even this was a period of intense public engagement, more intense, more head-spinning than any since the 1930s or arguably the Civil War. Our citizen-selves were called upon still, but now to argue rather than to agree.

So perhaps it makes a kind of historical sense that at a certain point, we as a people would grow exhausted of public engagement and retreat to more private concerns. And it happened just as two other things were happening: The country elected a president who signaled that this retreat was all right, and the country's economy began to emphasize status, acquisition, and difference.

And so, since that time, with some minor pivots back in the civic direction, our consumer selves have overwhelmed our citizen selves. That's not to say citizenship is dead. That's what books like this one sometimes tend to assert, in order to get attention, but that's overwrought. Citizenship isn't dead. But it sure isn't well. No country that could elect

Donald Trump is a country in which civic concerns are being properly nurtured. And it makes polarization worse and contributes to our current mess because once we've demoted the importance of civic culture in our brains, that's when the norms and traditions that kept the culture functioning become vulnerable to attack. It's when a republic's immune system is tested.

Countless great thinkers have written about the tension between our two selves. It was a constant theme of de Tocqueville's *Democracy in America*, now nearly two hundred years old. His view of the United States along these lines was pretty optimistic. The phrase he used was "self-interest properly understood," which meant basically the same thing as enlightened self-interest, and he marveled at how Americans "will obligingly demonstrate how love of themselves regularly leads them to help one another out and makes them ready and willing to sacrifice a portion of their time and wealth for the good of the state."[5] Another great Frenchman, Jean-Jacques Rousseau, was thinking not of the United States but of any modern commercial state when he wrote: "The cause of human misery is the contradiction . . . between man and citizen; make man one and you will make him as happy as he can manage to be. Give him wholly to the state or leave him wholly to himself, but if you divide his heart you tear it apart."[6]

In the United States since 1980, not only is de Tocqueville's assessment too sunny—so is Rousseau's! Our hearts are hardly even divided anymore. We have given ourselves to our private pursuits. How did it happen?

How the Search for Credit and Yield Changed Us as Human Beings

Lists of the tumultuous events that drove Americans apart in the 1960s and 1970s don't usually include inflation. But they should. The Great Inflation changed Americans' attitudes toward money and, Joe Nocera argues in his authoritative book *A Piece of the Action*, toward one another—toward the very idea of common purpose:[7]

Inflation splintered the status quo open every bit as much as the Vietnam War did. Among other things, it helped fuel the rise of special-interest politics, causing Americans to become selfish in a way they really hadn't been before. People had responded to the Depression by helping each other out as best they could, but inflation had the opposite effect on us. It created an ethos in which people felt justified in cutting special deals for themselves, even when the net effect of those deals was to ratchet up the inflation rate.

If you think that's overstated, you simply weren't around. Here are the yearly inflation numbers of the 1970s and early 1980s, and as you read them, bear in mind that the Federal Reserve Bank today considers the maximum acceptable inflation rate to be 2 percent:[8]

1970:	5.7 percent
1971:	4.4 percent
1972:	3.2 percent
1973:	6.2 percent
1974:	11 percent
1975:	9.1 percent
1976:	5.8 percent
1977:	6.5 percent
1978:	7.6 percent
1979:	11.4 percent
1980:	13.5 percent
1981:	10.3 percent

It was crushing. It helped bring down two presidents, Gerald Ford and Jimmy Carter. Neither responded adequately, because in truth there wasn't a lot either could do. Ford asked Americans to wear WIN buttons ("Whip Inflation Now"), and Carter implored them to lower their thermostats and put on sweaters around the house—a responsible request, and one many Americans took to heart, but hardly the kind of "we're America, we can overcome anything" rhetoric Americans were accustomed to hearing from their presidents.

It also tore apart the postwar economic order of fixed monetary exchange rates established at the famous Bretton Woods Conference in

1944. It produced four recessions, two severe energy shortages, and Richard Nixon's imposition of wage and price controls in 1971 (think about that—wages frozen by the government!) and his simultaneous decision to take the dollar off the gold standard. But even more than all that, inflation changed how people thought and lived. Up to that point for most living people, the American economy had just worked, and American products were the best. No longer. Cars—arguably the greatest source of American pride of the twentieth century, outside of winning the war—got smaller, and it soon emerged that the Japanese were a lot better at making fuel-efficient cars than Detroit was, which spurred the U.S. auto industry's decline. Japan started making better televisions, too. At the level of everyday consumption, for many people, every trip to the supermarket was a walk over hot coals. "From week to week, people couldn't know the cost of their groceries, utility bills, appliances, dry cleaning, toothpaste, and pizza," wrote the economics journalist Robert J. Samuelson in 2008. "People couldn't predict whether their wages and salaries would keep pace. People couldn't plan; their savings were at risk."[9] To an American who'd grown up during the great age of prosperity, the country was practically unrecognizable.

Inflation was finally tamed in 1982–1983, not by Ronald Reagan so much as by Fed chair Paul Volcker, who in 1979 began applying a tight monetary policy that eventually brought prices down. And once it did abate, naturally, what did people do? They started spending, like Americans had never spent before.

This had started, to some extent, during the decade of inflation, and for reasons having nothing to do with it. The expansion of credit across the broader middle class was one of the central defining characteristics of the 1970s. The credit card had barely existed in an earlier America. A man named Frank McNamara is generally recognized as having launched the first credit card, Diners Club, in 1950. But it wasn't really a credit card (the holder couldn't carry over balances), it wasn't even plastic (cards were cardboard until the 1960s), and only a comparatively small number of businessmen had them. Next came American Express and Carte Blanche—still mainly used by high-flying businessmen, at least at first. BankAmericard and Master Card began spreading credit somewhat more widely in the 1960s, but it wasn't until a man named Dee Ward Hock took over BankAmericard in 1970 that banks started making substantial profits from credit cards. Hock was a self-taught child of the Depression who could quote Voltaire and Yeats and was a passionate evangelical on the topic of credit. He compared himself and his executives to the founding fathers and "thought of himself as a revolutionary," one long-time employee told Nocera.[10] He cooled over the course of the 1970s to the name BankAmericard because he wanted something global. He wanted a word that had punch and that was "pronounced the same way in every language."[11] In 1976, he settled on Visa.

Even Hock's force of will, though, couldn't overcome state usury laws, under which credit-card issuers could charge customers an interest rate no higher than the one set by the state in which the customer lived. That changed in 1978. It may not live in history alongside *Brown v. Board* or *Roe v. Wade*, but in its way, *Marquette National Bank of Minneapolis v. First of Omaha Service Corp.* was just as revolutionary. It was a pulverizingly dull case—a dispute between two banks about which state's usury laws should apply when a Nebraska bank issued credit cards to Minnesota residents. Interpreting a national banking act that dated back to the Civil War, the Supreme Court held—unanimously; everyone from William Brennan to William Rehnquist!—that state usury laws could not be enforced on nationally chartered banks, which the Nebraska-based bank was. This allowed banks to charge interest rates in the state in which they (not their customers) were located. In effect, the least regulated state in the nation became the benchmark. In 1980, Citibank "moved" to South Dakota, which had no interest rate regulations. Citibank could now charge 20 percent, 22 percent, whatever it wished. The credit-card business exploded. Total credit-card balances were close to zero in 1970; in 1980, they were around $80 billion; in 1990, $240 billion; in 2000, $700 billion.[12]

Around the same time, another revolution was taking place in personal finance, this time on the investing side. In the 1960s, very few Americans invested their money. They kept it in the bank, and the bank paid them a small but reliable interest rate that helped their savings grow, and into the bargain gave them a free toaster or clock radio. For a long

time, this was fine. But as inflation rose, it was no longer so fine: If inflation was 7 percent and your savings account was earning you just 4 percent, you figured out pretty quickly that you were falling behind. But
banks couldn't pay higher interest rates because of a regulation dating
to the Depression called Regulation Q, which capped the rate of interest
a bank could pay to depositors. Back in the 1930s, banks were going out
of business competing with one another to offer attractive interest rates,
so the government imposed a limit. It fixed the problem then, but forty
years later, with inflation raging, the regulation was quite costly to normal people doing normal banking.

And so in the early 1970s, a few men simultaneously hit upon the idea
of letting people keep money in something that wasn't a bank account.
They'd scoured the federal laws and to their delighted surprise, there
seemed to be nothing to prevent it. Thus was born the money-market
account, into which Americans have subsequently placed trillions of dollars. They weren't covered by Regulation Q, so they could pay higher
interest. Now, personal investing started to achieve liftoff. Merrill Lynch
set the gold standard here, with offices and brokers in most decent-sized
American towns. E. F. Hutton was a big presence, too, and Charles F.
Schwab. They competed hard for clients. They even took the step—tacky,
to "real" Wall Street, the white-shoe investment houses who still did things
the way they'd always done them—of advertising on television (some of
you will recall the startling impression made by the "when E. F. Hutton
talks, people listen" TV ad campaign—the moment in those ads when a
man said, "Well, my broker is E. F. Hutton, and E. F. Hutton says . . ."
and everyone in the restaurant or bar stopped talking, leaned forward,
and cupped their ears).

But now the banks were peeved because they were losing deposits.
So Congress set about the business of fixing the problem. They could
have fixed it by imposing Regulation Q on money-market funds, but that
would have been politically impossible in an age of high inflation—it
would have constituted taking money out of depositors' hands. Instead,
Congress went in the direction of deregulating banks. Two major bills
were passed: In 1980, the Depository Institutions Deregulation and Monetary Control Act; and in 1982, the Depository Institutions Act, both of

which deregulated banks and savings and loan institutions in a variety of ways. These were big and complex pieces of legislation, but the main upshots were the demise of Regulation Q, allowing banks to compete with the new funds, and, oh yeah, one of the biggest financial scandals in the history of the United States—the S&L crisis. It resulted directly from the 1982 law, cosponsored by Republican senator Jake Garn of Utah and Rhode Island Democratic congressman Fernand St Germain (that's not a typo—there's no period in St Germain), which allowed savings and loans to stray from their historical purpose of financing the purchases of homes to speculating on all manner of enterprises. More than 1,000 S&L's would go belly-up. Around this same time, it was in 1980—under Carter, not Reagan—that the government allowed businesses other than banks to issue credit cards and offer other financial services. These "non-bank banks" came to include the Xerox Corporation, American Can, and the Baldwin Piano & Organ Company.[13]

In sum, in the late 1970s and early 1980s, Americans started to become a different people than they had been. Ever since *Poor Richard's Almanac*, Americans had for the most part lived cherishing thrift, discipline, doing without. This changed to some extent in the 1950s, the first real decade of consumerism in our history. Americans could laugh at it—watching, for example, *The Honeymooners*, contrasting the Kramdens' abstemious lifestyle, no telephone or television, with that of the upstairs best friends the Nortons, who were of the same social class but who bought a few modest luxuries "on time" (that is, the installment plan) and had a telephone, which Trixie Norton would dangle down the fire escape when Alice Kramden needed to call her mother.

But Ed and Trixie Norton would never have recognized the America that arose in the late 1970s and early 1980s, when the middle class started to become the investing class. Not everything about this was bad, by the way. Not by a long shot. Indeed, the goal of men like Schwab, and of Donald Regan, who ran Merrill Lynch in the seventies and went on to become Ronald Reagan's first secretary of the Treasury, was to give the small investor the same opportunity as the large investor. Bruce Bent and Henry Brown, the men who started the first money-market fund, were of course out to make money, and they made piles of it; but they undeniably offered people a better return than banks could.

So there was a lot about these changes that was positive. But the willingness to take on more debt—for millions of people, much more than they could plausibly sustain—and to search frantically for a better return changed society. One last time to Nocera, who is eloquent on the impact of the money-market fund:[14]

> . . . it instilled the idea that those who failed to chase yield would lose. Just as the aversion to risk would be ingrained in anyone who lived through the Depression, so would this new lesson embed itself in the subconscious of those who lived through the Age of Inflation. Long after inflation had been tamed, Americans would continue their sometimes frantic, sometimes giddy, sometimes sensible, sometimes insane, search for yield. Chasing yield would be the defining financial act of the middle class in the decade to come. It was how we had changed.

But the 1980s were defined only partially by the way middle-class people changed. The really important changes were happening at the top.

The Masters of the Universe Stake Their Claim

We sometimes call the 1980s the Decade of Greed or refer to the Go-Go Eighties—a time of self-interested pursuit, excess, getting, having, flaunting. It followed quite naturally, if you think about it, from the 1970s (the Me Decade), which in turn followed quite naturally from the 1960s. The sixties, by which we really mean the time from the Kennedy assassination and the arrival of the Beatles through all the political and cultural upheavals culminating in Nixon's resignation in 1974, were a decade that demanded of people a deep engagement in public concerns whether they wanted that engagement or not. It's no surprise then that the seventies saw a retreat to pursuit of individual well-being and enlightenment—the decade witnessed the explosion of the individual and small-group self-help movement. And in turn it's completely logical that the culture would move from self-help to even more intense manifestations of individualism: self-celebration, self-aggrandizement, self-reward, self-love.

But how, exactly, did the eighties become the Go-Go Decade? If you read journalism that looks back to that time, it will invariably reference the famous Gordon Gekko line from Oliver Stone's 1987 *Wall Street*: "Greed, for lack of a better word, is good. Greed is right. Greed works. Greed clarifies, cuts through, and captures the essence of the evolutionary spirit." The quote will often be cushioned in lots of rhetorical upholstery about how people somehow just became more materialistic, as if it all happened because of something in the water supply.

There is deep truth in the idea each age has its own ethos, and that a million little random events, imperceptible or seemingly isolated at the time, can eventually add up and boom, suddenly we're in a new era. But it's also the case that eras change because of specific actions taken by specific actors. I named some of them above. The *Marquette National Bank* Supreme Court decision and the two big banking deregulation acts of 1980 and 1982 were three such actions. These, I should emphasize, were bipartisan and even Democratic moves. The 1980 bill was really the handiwork of Wisconsin Democratic senator William Proxmire and was signed into law by Carter. He also oversaw the deregulation of the airline and trucking industries, with the support of no less liberal a figure than Ted Kennedy.

So the moves toward less regulation, more competition, and a less fettered private sector started under Democrats, anxious to tame inflation and try anything to jump-start the economy. But it's not pushing matters to say that Ronald Reagan's administration shoved all this into a much higher gear. First of all, he campaigned touting a theory of economic growth—supply-side to its evangelists, trickle-down to its foes—that argued for reducing the tax burden of those at the top. No one in modern American politics had ever said make the rich richer and everyone will benefit.

Next, he dramatically fired the striking (and unionized) air-traffic controllers in August 1981—more than 12,000 federal workers in high-tension jobs, safely guiding commercial aircraft to their destinations. They were public-sector workers, but the private sector got the message. It was okay now to hire replacement workers, and to start asking unions for concessions and givebacks instead of merely negotiating wage increases. Private-sector union membership has declined in this country since the mid-1950s, but from then until the 1980s, the decline was slow; go Google up a chart, and you'll see that from 1958 to 1980, the line slopes gently downward left-to-right, while from 1981 to the mid-1990s, it looks like an Olympic ski slope.

There was one more fateful deregulatory move to come. In 1982, one month after Reagan enthusiastically signed the Garn–St Germain bill, his Securities and Exchange Commission undid a key New Deal regulation and allowed corporations to buy back their stocks, which many experts say led to profit hoarding and disinvestment. They said it then, and they're still saying it, as profits today are hoarded at record levels, and they're right.[15] The new rule, called Rule 10b-18, combined over time with a shift toward more stock-based compensation, has resulted, in the words of Seattle-based venture capitalist turned writer and activist Nick Hanauer, in "a gigantic game of financial 'keep away,' with CEOs and shareholders tossing a $700-billion ball back and forth over the heads of American workers, whose wages as a share of GDP have fallen in almost exact proportion to profit's rise."[16]

Just as the great consensus of the 1930s and 1940s didn't merely happen but was forged through conscious thought and effort on the parts of various elites, the Go-Go Decade was also consciously made. It was made by politicians and their deregulating appointees. But no one did more to make it than a group of Wall Street men who discovered in the early 1980s that they could make a lot of money—crazy money, totally unprecedented money—through a miraculous process that required them to put up only a tiny amount of their own cash. The leveraged buyout—the hostile purchase of a company with mostly other people's money—had existed for decades. But it wasn't until the early 1980s that LBOs became all the rage. The first big one, weirdly enough, was of a greeting card firm, a company that owned the image of Garfield the cat. William Simon, who had been treasury secretary under Nixon and Ford, bought the company with a partner for $80 million, while putting up just $1 million of the purchase price. Simon personally anted up just $330,000. Within eighteen months, he'd made $70 million, on a silly greeting card company.[17] Quite naturally, on Wall Street, this development turned some heads.

Thus began the Gordon Gekko era. If you're old enough, you'll remember the names of these "masters of the universe," as Tom Wolfe dubbed them (or their fictional equivalents) in his 1987 novel *The Bonfire of the Vanities*: names like Michael Milken, Ivan Boesky, Saul Steinberg, Henry Kravis, and Carl Icahn, President Trump's friend. Icahn engineered one of the ugliest hostile takeovers of the decade, of Trans World Airlines—TWA, a once-glorious American company, along with Pan Am, one of the great flagship institutions of American commercial aviation. Historically, TWA was owned by Howard Hughes—a billionaire, but also a swashbuckling aviator who set a world record circumnavigating the globe in ninety-one hours in 1938. He acquired the young airline the next year. But over time, Hughes became a strange recluse, and he gave up TWA in the 1960s to a holding company, from which Icahn bought the airline in 1985. He paid for the purchase by selling off its assets, most notably its prized London routes, to American. The airline went bankrupt. Employees took pay cuts. Retirees lost significant portions of their pensions. Icahn became richer and richer, for example receiving $469 million when he took the airline private in 1988 (and saddled it with debt).[18]

By the end of the decade, some of these LBO titans ended up in jail, notably Milken, the so-called "junk bond king" from the firm Drexel Burnham Lambert (pronounced in the French way, Lam-BEAR), and his partner-in-crime, Boesky. Interestingly, Boesky, a very nonfictional character, actually said greed is good in real life, telling the graduating class of Cal-Berkeley (what a lesson for young graduates!) in 1986: "Greed is all right, by the way. I want you to know that. I think greed is healthy. You can be greedy and still feel good about yourself."[19] Just a few months after that speech, Boesky was convicted of insider trading, serving nearly two years in prison and paying $100 million in fines.

By that time, the culture had already changed. These men were lionized in the media, as magazine articles and books marveled over their prowess, their late-night negotiations held in luxurious Manhattan hotel suites, the lines of limousines double-parked on the street below, their toasts of $400 snifters of Armagnac to celebrate their deals, their ever-larger homes out in the Hamptons. The television show *Lifestyles of the Rich and Famous*, hosted by the Brit Robin Leach, purring over what he invariably called his subjects' glamorous "loifstoiles," debuted in 1984 to show us their kitchens and yachts and gold toilet fixtures.

Oh, they came in for plenty of criticism, both for their lives of excess and for the impact of their deal-making in the real world beyond Manhattan. When someone like (check this nickname, speaking of criticism) "Chainsaw Al" Dunlap came in to "restructure" a company, its assets would dwindle and hundreds or thousands of people would be laid off—6,000 people, in the case of the merger Dunlap forced between Scott Paper and Kimberly-Clark (he walked away with a $100 million golden parachute).[20] But these men not only defended what they did; they argued affirmatively that it was good for the economy. Practices that critics saw as heartless, they insisted were merely examples of market efficiency—the elimination of vast amounts of fat and redundancy that had been holding American growth back for decades. Not coincidentally, since they were almost all based in New York, it was a time too when New York—or at least, *their* New York—began to crawl out of the wreckage of the 1970s, as high-end real-estate prices took off like a space rocket. This created yet another class of men, the developers of these multimillion-dollar properties, to be celebrated in magazine profiles that gushed about their acumen, their enterprise, and of course their exquisite taste. They lost occasional battles, but mostly only when other really rich celebrities decided to oppose them: A demonstration against a double tower Mort Zuckerman wanted to build near Central Park, in which 800 protesters carried umbrellas through the lower park to dramatize the shadows Zuckerman's proposed skyscraper would cast over this urban oasis, was led by Jackie Kennedy Onassis.

Although on this one, in the end, Zuckerman didn't ultimately lose. The project was delayed more than a decade, and he was forced to chisel off a few stories (three from one tower, thirteen from another). But the resulting Time Warner Center does indeed exist, even if it is named for a corporation that no longer owns the flagship property from which it gets the first part of its name (*Time* magazine). With two fifty-five-story towers, it is a New Gilded Age pleasure palace if ever there was one: It's home to the Mandarin Oriental Hotel, where the most economical room tops $1,000 a night after taxes, and to the penthouse apartment that as of

July 2017 was Manhattan's most expensive, at $125,000 a month.[21] Down nearer the street you'll find a 70,000 square-foot Whole Foods, many of the usual high-end chain stores like Coach and Bose, and a range of absurdly pricey restaurants, including one, Per Se, where dinner for a party of four can easily set them back $2,500 or even more.

The Compensation Boom—for a Few

In the old days, young people on the go barely even thought about a career on Wall Street. It was powerful, of course. It was money. But it wasn't showy. It was the precise opposite of showy. It was built, as the historian Steve Fraser put it, on "'relationship banking,' that genteel world enclosed within mahogany walls hung with Old Masters where 'relationships' were premised as much on family and social ties as on mere moneymaking."[22]

In the 1980s and 1990s, all that started to change. As Milken and the rest became celebrities, and more and more young people looked to the Street for a career, compensation—especially the bonuses—went into the stratosphere. In 1985, the average Wall Street bonus was around $30,000 in 2012 dollars (that is, adjusted for inflation to 2012).[23] In 1995, the inflation-adjusted number was $62,000. In 2005, it was $176,000; in 2007, $197,000. After the great recession it fell back, to $121,000 in 2012. But even with that drop, bonuses increased from 1985 to 2012— remember, these numbers are adjusted for inflation—by 409 percent.[24]

Once the Wall Street compensation boom started, it didn't take long for others at the top to demand their share. The rise in CEO pay has been well and ably chronicled by many; to summarize, roughly speaking, the average CEO of a major U.S. corporation went from making 30 times the salary of the average employee in 1978 to 120 times that employee in 1995 to 384 times in 2000, according to the Economic Policy Institute, which tracks CEO compensation closely.[25] The ratio has dropped since that peak, but it is still around 300:1. Compensation for CEOs, says EPI, increased 937 percent from 1978 to 2013 (again, this is adjusted for inflation), while pay for average workers increased just 10.2 percent.

The defenders of these increases say that starting in the late 1980s, competition became fiercer for top companies to attract the best executives, so they had little choice but to offer more attractive compensation packages. There's little doubt that this is, to some extent, true, reflecting broader changes in society. Those changes went far beyond the matter of executive compensation. They were rooted in a change, perhaps even a revolution, in how elites thought of markets, and the story of that time is the story of the "rediscovery of the market,"[26] to borrow the phrase of Princeton historian Daniel T. Rodgers.

How did Americans come to accept this new embrace of the market? Again, this new consensus didn't just happen. It was manufactured. It came out of the academy, from a group of economists who disputed the Keynesian economics of the postwar period. The economic principles of British economist John Maynard Keynes—broadly speaking, that governments should create and manage demand through various forms of intervention in the private sector like public investment—had held sway in the United States since the 1930s. Every economist of note accepted it. Economics students all learned it; the seminal economics textbook of the twentieth century, *Economics* by Paul Samuelson and William Nordhaus, taught it. Nearly every politician of any consequence embraced it. Even Dwight Eisenhower and Richard Nixon declared themselves Keynesians. And as long as the economy worked, why shouldn't they be?

But in the late 1960s, when the inflation problem first arose, and especially into the 1970s, dissenters from Keynesianism began to find a wider audience, an audience they never would have found if the Great Inflation hadn't happened. "Because mainstream Keynesian economists lacked answers," wrote the historian Judith Stein, "they lost their monopoly on economic discourse and opened the door for outsiders."[27] These new gurus were centered in one place, the University of Chicago, and they were led by one man, Milton Friedman. They called their economic theory monetarism, because they argued that proper control of the money supply by policy-makers at the Federal Reserve Board would allow the economy to regulate itself, without government intervention. This is why we called it "supply-side," while Keynesian economics is "demand-side."

This was something a lot of people, especially very rich people, wanted to hear. It gave rise to supply-side economics, and to the idea that government intervention in the economy was doomed to fail and that the market should be left to its own devices. As with deregulation, Republicans embraced supply-side policies with far more enthusiasm, but Democrats sometimes drank the potion, too. The Carter administration at first opposed but then decided to back the Revenue Act of 1978, which cut capital gains taxes and according to Stein increased the tax burden of the middle class while granting great relief to the rich (and throwing a few beans to the poor).[28]

Carter was just bowing to political realities. But Reagan was a true believer, and once the monetarists had him in the White House, they were able to see their theories put into practice. Personal income tax rates were reduced aggressively in 1981 and again in 1986, such that a person making $100,000 then (close to $300,000 in today's dollars) went from paying a top marginal rate of 68 percent (on the last $18,200 earned) to one of 38.5 percent.[29] After the deep recession of the early 1980s, the economy strengthened and these policies seemed to work (the track record since then is quite bad, but Republicans all believe it, and conservative nonprofit institutions invest tens of millions a year in defending it). This changed the assumptions of much of the elite class—a staggering accomplishment, forcing a reassessment of assumptions people had held as sacred for forty years! Doesn't happen very often in history, something like that. Nearly half a century later, the Democrats are still struggling with coming up with an answer.[30] It changed the way the media presented economic questions to the public, which in turn changed public attitudes toward the relationship between the government and the free market. It changed the way economics was taught in the schools—by 1992, writes Rodgers, the Samuelson textbook, "its market share slipping and its once predominant command over the pedagogy of the subject eroded,"[31] reordered its chapters to emphasize the free market.

And this is really why Wall Street compensation and CEO pay shot up the way they did: Americans came to accept that if the market decided on something, it was probably right. And in the 1980s, and into the 1990s, the market was very busy indeed deciding that the people at the top deserved more.

Bankers, lawyers, doctors (particularly specialists), university presidents—they all started making a lot more. Also actors. Burt Reynolds was the top box-office draw of 1980, the year he appeared in *Smokey and the Bandit II*. He was paid a little more than $1 million. Fourteen years later, Tom Hanks earned (from points—he took no salary) about $40 million from *Forrest Gump*. The 1990s was the decade when actors' compensation first went completely bonkers: Hanks, Bruce Willis in the *Die Hard* films, Eddie Murphy, Tom Cruise, Mel Gibson (long before his downfall), Arnold Schwarzenegger, and Julia Roberts as the one woman Hollywood compensated on somewhat equal footing to these men.

And athletes—few examples illustrate the dramatic compensation increases of the top 1 percent as clearly as the pay of professional athletes, especially in Major League Baseball. Some of the astronomical rise in ballplayers' salaries can be explained by the unrestricted free agency that's been in place since the 1970s, and of course salaries in all sports have risen because of television contracts, which have been adding zeros every decade. Still, the increases reflected what the market would bear—that is, even with unrestricted free agency, salaries might merely have tripled or quadrupled. But they've done a lot more than that. The highest-paid player of 1977, Philadelphia's Mike Schmidt, made $560,000.[32] Adjusted for inflation to 2017, that would be just under $2.3 million. A very nice living, no doubt. But not particularly close to Los Angeles Dodgers pitcher Clayton Kershaw's $33 million. In fact, in 2017, Schmidt's $2.28 million would have ranked him 380th out of 819 players (some 300 or so rookies and part-timers who shuttle back and forth between the big leagues and the minors still make around $500,000).[33] By 1987, the salary scale had changed dramatically from Schmidt's time, and the highest-paid player, Boston Red Sox outfielder Jim Rice, was making $2.42 million. A nice number thirty years ago. But adjusted for inflation to a 2017 figure of $5.24 million, even Rice would have ranked only 249th, right behind Oakland A's third baseman Trevor Plouffe (during the first months of the 2017 season, he was hitting .214 for the A's, who traded him to Tampa Bay mid-season).

I tend not to begrudge athletes in particular these salaries, although one does wonder whether .214 is what the people signing Plouffe's paychecks had in mind. At least it has to be acknowledged that professional athletes are where they are because they're the best—they have the most talent, and they've all worked incredibly hard to make it to the pros, lived under a code of staggering self-discipline. You don't get to be a starting quarterback in the NFL because you have a nice smile. And of course, they're just making what the market says they should be making. Milton Friedman and other believers in the free market, presumably, wouldn't bat an eye at the fact that Kershaw made $13,090 per pitch in 2017, or $188,000 per inning pitched.[34]

But what this strict free-market view doesn't take into account is the consumers who are helping to pay these salaries. Economic theory would say that we have a choice—people can always stop going to movies and Dodgers games. But in real life, that's preposterous: People love movies and sports more than they love anything else in the world, practically, so they'll always go, wherever the price is set. And that brings me to the last way we changed starting in the 1980s—the percentage of our incomes we spend amusing ourselves.

Amusing Ourselves to Death

Robert Frank, the Cornell University economist, opens his 1999 book *Luxury Fever* describing the demise of his old propane grill. The ignition button went, which required him to throw a match into the grill's belly, a dicey proposition around propane; so reluctantly, he decided it was time to replace the grill, which had cost him $89.95.

What he found might have shocked some of his readers in 1999, but will come as no surprise to any of you today. He discovered that while he could indeed probably get a new grill for something around $89.95, he also saw that he could spend $400, $800, $2,000; or even, for a Viking Frontgate Professional Grill, which "comes with an infrared rotisserie that can slowly broil two 20-pound turkeys to perfection while you cook hamburgers for 40 guests on its 828-square-inch grilling surface," a full $5,000 (shipping and handling included).[35]

You've read descriptions like that in countless catalogues over the last twenty years. One day in late 2017, I pitched into the recycling bin the latest Orvis for Men catalogue; I seem to get about two of them a week once the holiday season begins, which of course these days means mid-October. If you fear that the $250 sweaters and $600 jackets just won't be quite enough to satisfy the man in your life, you can always throw down for the Handcrafted Cedar Kayak, a "sleek, nimble" craft that has "all the speed, tracking, and handling characteristics of the Aleutian baidarka-style kayaks after which it is patterned." That baidarka styling doesn't come cheap, bub. It lists for $18,000.

No regular person, indeed no person at all, needs to spit-roast two 20-pound turkeys while grilling 40 hamburgers. And of course almost no one reading that Orvis catalogue has probably ever even heard the word "baidarka," let alone being able to attach any meaning to it (Microsoft Word doesn't even recognize the word, which turns out simply—and quite unglamorously—to be a Russian word for "sea kayak"). And yet, these images and words seduce us powerfully, and these things sell. The person buying the $5,000 grill or the $18,000 kayak or the $350 copper sauté pan from Williams Sonoma knows that she doesn't "need" said grill, kayak, or pan. She also knows very well that a piece of $22-per-pound branzino will taste just as crappy if overcooked in a $350 pan as in a T-fal pan that you can buy on Amazon for $20.

That said, there is probably a way in which a $100 sauté pan is superior to a $20 one. It may distribute heat more evenly, be more resistant to scratch, be a little easier to clean, last longer. But this style of consumption isn't really about product quality. It's about status and self-reward: that little frisson of self-satisfaction the high-end consumer feels when he retrieves the $350 pan from the cupboard and fires up the burner and salts the fish.

High-end frypans are an example of what the economist Fred Hirsch called "positional goods."[36] That is to say, their value is derived not necessarily from their inherent qualities, but from how they compare—how they are positioned—to competitor goods, and how that comparison makes us feel about ourselves. Positional goods have existed since consumerism has existed. In the early department stores of the late nineteenth century, whether Bergdorf Goodman in New York or Galeries Lafayette in Paris or Marshall Field's in Chicago, there were of course high-end items and more affordable ones. Come the 1950s and 1960s, there were better televisions and worse ones, luxury cars and no-frills cars, dishwashers that were a little more expensive—the Maytags, which came to dominate the market with that clever ad campaign about the Maytag repair man who sat around all day with nothing to do because Maytags never broke down—and the others that were less expensive, like the Kenmores, the Sears house brand.

Now, though, it seems—and this started, again, in the 1980s—that this concept of positionality has spread into nearly every crevice of consumerism you can name. Take, indeed, dishwashers. If you've been in the market for one in the last decade or so, as most of you probably have, you know what I mean. The parade of brands and styles is endless. They run from about $400 up to $2,000. As near as I can tell, the $2,000 ones have one concrete thing going for them: They're a lot quieter. You could run one near the circulation desk of the town library. That's a genuine technological advance. And I guess they have a lot of whiz-bang features (which most people surely never use). But they're no faster than the $400 ones, which would seem to me a logical and key point of technological advancement; in fact, some of them take *longer* than your mother's dishwasher, and they don't even dry your dishes. When I bought a new dishwasher five years ago, I was told by the fellow at the Home Depot that while they're mostly all made in China, the American-"badged" ones (Maytag, Kenmore, GE) come with heating coils, while the foreign-badged ones (Samsung, LG, Bosch, etc.) do not. At first it astounded me that anyone would want a dishwasher that costs $1,500, takes longer to run a cycle, *and* leaves water spots on your glassware. But then I stopped and realized, this is precisely the logic of positionality! The goods that attain and confer status aren't necessarily the best or most efficient ones; they're the ones that offer the richest psychic reward to high-end consumers. The reward here is that they're getting something more newfangled and cutting-edge than the boring old brand names their mothers trusted.

We live now in a world of relentless positionality. It's driven in the first place by the massive increases in compensation for the top 1 percent, who have a lot more money and want to spend it—on bigger mansions, longer yachts, kitchens with $12,000 refrigerators, luxury sky-box Giants tickets, what have you. Then the people the next rung down read about what the rich have been up to and decide they want more themselves: kitchens with $3,000 refrigerators, lower-level seats at the Giants games. Then the people the next rung down read about that and want more, and the next rung follows, and so on down the line.

The dramatic rise in inequality over this period excludes some percentage of people from participating in this relentless dance of acquisition, probably the bottom third or quarter of the people, who are the reason Kenmore keeps cranking out $400 dishwashers and who couldn't dream of going to a Giants game. But for the top two-thirds or three-quarters, a new market has arisen in the last thirty years that never existed before. It's a more enticing market, full of fancy coffee machines and olive oils and you name it, but mainly it's a more expensive market. We're spending so much more on amusing and entertaining ourselves than we did forty years ago, without most of us quite realizing how dramatic the change has been.

For starters, we spend billions we'd never spent in the past before we even walk out of the house. When I was a kid, watching television was, in essence, free (except for the cost of the electricity required to run the box): You bought a TV, plugged it in, fiddled with the rabbit ears, and watched. Of course, there were only ten or so channels. But still—free. Then came cable, which first appeared, surprisingly, in the late 1940s, to serve rural areas in Arkansas, Oregon, and Pennsylvania, but which wasn't in widespread use until a landmark cable deregulation act in 1984.[37] Today, about 92 million households spend an average of $103 a month just to watch television.[38] That's down from a few years ago, because young people especially are "cord-cutting" by the millions, though even they are paying for Netflix and Hulu and Amazon Prime. In any case spending on cable TV still amounts to nearly $9.5 billion a year. Add to that the video gaming industry, which barely existed when I was young and did $19 billion worth of business in 2018.[39]

Once we walk out the door to take in live entertainments, we're spending mountains more than our parents and grandparents did. Let's look, again, at baseball. A CNBC.com article in October 2013, on the occasion of that year's World Series, compared ticket prices for that year's contest, between the Boston Red Sox and the St. Louis Cardinals, and for the 1963 series fifty years before, featuring the Los Angeles Dodgers and the New York Yankees.[40] A field-level box seat at Dodger Stadium for the '63 series went for $12. Adjusted for inflation to 2013, that ticket would cost $91. So what did actual tickets to the 2013 series fetch? $100, $200, $400 . . . $600? Try $1,291. That's a little more than fourteen times as much, even factoring in inflation. And that's an *average*, not a field-level box seat to see Sandy Koufax duel with Mickey Mantle up close. Dugout seats—especially in Boston, where the prices were considerably higher than in St. Louis—were going for several thousand dollars.

On eBay, I found someone selling a ticket to the 1980 World Series, between the Philadelphia Phillies and the Kansas City Royals. The face value was $20. Adjusted for inflation to 2017, that ticket would cost $58.18. But for the 2017 Series, between the Houston Astros and the Los Angeles Dodgers, you probably could hardly take a taxi to the ballpark for $60. The Dodgers organization set face-value prices at $166 to $531.[41] And of course, most normal people who aren't season ticket holders or who can't make time to camp out at the stadium the night before the few unallotted tickets go on sale no longer have access to face-value prices. They buy on the secondary market, where tickets generally ran from $1,100 to $1,800—and again, several thousand for the ace seats near the dugouts and the plate.

This is hardly limited to baseball. Let's look at the NFL, which in the years we're discussing here went from being less popular than baseball (still the "national pastime" in the mid-1970s) to vying with it to conquering it and every other sport in terms of spectator popularity. In 1985, the average price for a ticket to a Dallas Cowboys game was $18.30. In 2000, it was $47.90. And in 2016, it was $110.20.[42] Making our usual inflation adjustments, $18.30 in 1985 would have equaled $40.70 in 2016, and $47.90 would have been $66.42. So today's prices are roughly double or triple the old prices, with inflation factored in. Then of course there's the cost of going to a game: parking (which can run $60 alone in some venues), food and drink, a little souvenir for the kids. An outing to a Cowboys game for a family of four can easily run north of $500.

And, of course, all this isn't limited to sports. You prefer Broadway shows? The change has been just as dramatic there. You could go see Zero Mostel in *Fiddler on the Roof* in 1965 for around $9, and *A Chorus Line* in 1975 for $15. Adjusted for inflation, those figures translate into $70 and $68, respectively. Great, groundbreaking shows (I had the good fortune to see both, although Mom always said I slept through most of *Fid-*

dler, as I was only four). And huge hits. Quite comparable to *Hamilton* today. The lowest-price ticket for *Hamilton* I could find when I checked while writing this was $285. Of course, every show isn't that expensive. You can actually get into most shows for around $100, but they won't be good seats. For actual good seats on broadway.com, you need to spring for something they call "Premium" seating, which for most shows starts at around $250, but for *Hamilton* at $750. (You may be wondering here about movies; interestingly, the price of a movie ticket has roughly kept pace with inflation, a little more, but the difference isn't glaring.)

Rock concerts are probably the craziest of all. I found on Google Images a picture of a field-level box seat to see the Beatles at Shea Stadium in 1965. The face price? $5.65. That's $44.13 today, to see the most famous concert by what is still the rock era's most storied band (granted, they played for just half an hour, but that was standard then). In 2016, the highest-priced concert ticket was to go see Adele, for which a fan paid on average $469.[43] Bruce Springsteen fetched $249. (And these are two artists with great working-class appeal.) Paul McCartney, still plucking at that same Höfner violin-shaped bass guitar that he strapped across his back at Shea Stadium, averaged $195. Even Twenty One Pilots, of whom I confess I'd never heard, averaged $108. Meanwhile, for $44, you can buy a Beyoncé baseball cap (and hey, have $4 left over!).

Why this hyperinflation? You're helping to pay the salaries and compensation expectations of the stars, certainly. You're helping to pay (in sports) for these fancy new stadiums. Some would say unions are a reason. But the real reason is obviously that plenty of people—and corporations, which buy most stadium sky boxes—have the money and are willing to pay these prices to see these things. The market for high-priced entertainment exists in a way it simply didn't thirty or fifty years ago. And this market isn't merely willing to pay high prices. A good portion of this market *demands* it; wants to pay higher prices to have a special parking spot near the gate, to sit behind home plate with the option of going to the restaurant at the top of the first deck, to meet the actors backstage, to use a special entrance or private restroom, or otherwise separate from the riffraff who paid a mere $100. I don't mean to criticize these things in traditional leftish class terms. If I were a rich man, I readily admit I would probably take a bite out of some of these tempting apples. I've been to a few Washington Nationals games sitting right behind home plate, the guest of a journalist friend who scored the corporate tickets, and availed myself of the free buffet and open bar at the top of the section. Trust me when I tell you it's a better way to see a game than sitting in the bleachers. I'm simply pointing out how different it all is from just a few decades ago, how *necessary* it is today, whether you're selling concert tickets or sauté pans or olive oil, to offer premium versions of your product—what Fred Hirsch would call positional goods—so that people of means can have the experience of knowing that they purchased something that regular people can't.

These days there's a premium or positional version of just about everything, in categories where it would have been unimaginable not long ago. The most visible manifestation of this may be in amusement parks, where for a price, often a hefty one, you can skip the lines. "To avoid offending ordinary customers," writes the political philosopher Michael Sandel in his book *What Money Can't Buy*, "some parks usher their premium guests through back doors and separate gates; others provide an escort to ease the way of VIP guests as they cut in line."[44] Sandel's great book is a catalogue of such offers: Washington lobbyists paying people to stand in line outside committee hearing rooms; concierge medical services offering people "absolute, unlimited, and exclusive" access to their family physicians; Inuits of Canada letting hunters kill walruses for $6,000; services that write apology notes for people who've offended friends, and much more. All of these services are new, having popped up in the 1990s or 2000s, to cater to the "needs" of a new moneyed class for whom consumption has become a competition.

★

So: a period of inflation like the modern United States had never seen; a massive expansion of credit to the middle class, but extended at rates of 15 and 20 percent; banking deregulation that increased Americans' savings but also led to the S&L crisis; explosions in compensation for the top 1 percent, in every walk of American life; and finally, an age of unprecedented consumption. Meanwhile, two things I didn't mention yet: The value of the minimum wage started decreasing, and middle-income wages were increasing, but at lower rates than they previously had. In 1979, Congress raised the minimum wage to $2.90, which is $9.44 in 2015 dollars. It immediately began to drop precipitously and plummeted throughout the 1980s, hitting a modern low of $6.38 in 2015 inflation-adjusted dollars in 1989. It's never been close to $9.44 since.[45] As for wages in the middle—again, they peaked in 1979, in terms of percentage increase over the previous year.[46] Since that year, wages in the middle have grown by anywhere from 6 to perhaps 20 percent, depending on who's crunching the numbers and how, while wages for the top 1 percent have grown 138 percent.[47]

All interesting, you might say; but what's it have to do with political polarization? Plenty. These new class divisions didn't merely creep into our politics. They barged into them. It's not a coincidence that money started to dominate politics in this same decade, as this "New Class" of Americans—these Sub-Zero Americans, we might call them, after the leading high-end refrigerator brand—came to have inordinate influence in political affairs. Both parties catered to them. In very different ways of course—the Republicans genuflected before oil and chemical and old economy money, while the Democrats tended to kneel to Silicon Valley and new economy wealth. But both parties grew more responsive to the top 10 or 15 percent (in the Democrats' case), or the top 1 or 2 percent (in the Republicans'). The seeds that sprouted into Trumpism were planted with these transformations of the economy that began in the 1970s because of the Great Inflation and that changed who we were.

And this economic maelstrom forced an even deeper change. Let's now think back to those de Tocqueville and Rousseau quotes I invoked toward the beginning of this chapter, and the whole subject of the competition within each of us between citizen and consumer. Let's say for argument's sake that in the 1930s and 1940s, most Americans were more citizen than consumer; then in the postwar economic boom, people were about evenly split, or maybe consumerism nudged into the lead at some point.

Well, how is that race looking now? Our consumer selves have lapped our citizen selves a few times over. I often wonder what might happen in this country in the event of a major war, a really major war, along the lines of World War II, when people accepted rationing and planted victory gardens. How would we respond if we found ourselves in such a circumstance today? I think many Americans might still plant gardens, provided they weren't convinced by their favorite talk-radio hosts and Russian Facebook trolls that the war in question was really a secret project of George Soros. But I think there's zero chance this country would ever accept rationing again. A black market would arise instantly; someone would invent an app (actually, many someones would invent many apps) that would allow users, for the right price, to get as much sugar or bacon or gasoline as their hearts desired. No doubt a sophisticated system of credit-swapping would soon emerge, along with secondary-market websites selling gasoline the way StubHub sells event tickets. And this would all be offered, of course, on guilt-free terms ("don't worry, your purchases through this app will not affect the amount of bacon received by our soldiers!") and defended by some on the grounds that all this consumption was good for the economy.

My civic self has rarely been more depressed than it was after September 11, 2001, when President Bush, New York Mayor Rudy Giuliani, and others said that if citizens want to help their country, they should go shop. The greatest tragedy in recent American history, I might have thought, just might have been an occasion to ask of people some sacrifice—see if that old spirit could in any way be summoned by the leaders of our government. Bush does deserve credit for his "Islam is peace" speech at the Islamic Center of Washington shortly after the attacks, but he and other leaders could have done much more. They might have implored us to go visit a mosque, get to know a Muslim family; do something for our soldiers, for we will likely soon be asking a good deal more of them; have your children write notes to the children whose parents were killed; make efforts to get to know people in your communities you usually ignore in the push of daily life. They could have said a dozen things that would have helped strengthen civic bonds in a bereft nation. Instead, they said: change nothing, be normal, and go shop.

But what made me even more depressed was the realization that on some level, they were right. By 2001, the world was less interested in gestures of civic humanity than in how quickly the market would bounce back. In this sense, shopping—propping up the economy—*was* a civic act. The truth of it couldn't be denied. But it still symbolized for me what a different country we'd become than the country that pulled together to win the war; a place, now, where consumerism had so subsumed citizenship that it in fact *became* it.

Bob Dole, Bill Clinton, and Newt Gingrich negotiate under the watchful eye of Thomas Jefferson, 1993.

SIX

From Gingrich to Trump—
the System Explodes

★

*How Money and Technology Changed Politics • For Better
or Worse, the Most Influential Republican of Our Time •
The Rise of the Right-Wing Media Machine • The Pledge:
The Best-Kept Secret of the Age of Polarization • How the Two
Parties Became Different Creatures • And Finally,
Obama and Trump*

I**T'S 1990. THE ECONOMIC TRANSFORMATION OF AMERICA HAS TAKEN**
firm root. The political flashpoints of the 1970s and '80s have now
fully planted themselves in the culture as well. It's a more divided country, and a more unequal country.

Consider how this might have looked to a twenty-year-old woman
in 1990. She was born in 1970. She may have the vaguest memories of
hearing Mom and Dad discuss Nixon's resignation, if she was raised in
a political household. She'll remember them cursing high prices. She'll
have been old enough to have understood, on some level, the Iranian
hostage crisis—her great nation brought to heel by this country her parents never had to give a moment's thought to. Maybe she went to school
in a district where there was a huge and divisive busing controversy. If
she was raised in a Republican household, her parents were telling her
during her teens that Mr. Reagan was doing great, but there were too
many Americans who wanted something for nothing. If she was raised
in a Democratic household, her folks spent her teenage years in a state of

alarmed disbelief that the American people could elect and reelect that man, and that so many of their own friends could have voted for him.

If she was white and middle-class, she could probably watch all this tension mount as an indifferent spectator. If she was African-American or Latina, or if she came to realize that she was gay, she could likely not afford the luxury of indifference. History was acting on her; her very identity was contested. So she perhaps grew to feel that she had to act, too.

If she was going to college in 1990, really any college but particularly an elite school, and taking certain kinds of courses in the women's and black studies departments that universities agreed under student pressure to create in the 1970s, she was reading critiques of American culture and society that were nothing like the ones her parents might have read. If her parents had read such critiques, they were largely made along the lines of economic class, or of the national-security state. But these new attacks were based on race and gender, and they were framed around two core ideas: first, that "the personal is political," a phrase first used in a women's liberation newspaper in 1970, which meant to show women that their seemingly isolated experiences were taking place within larger social and political contexts and were happening to millions of women, and were thus a legitimate basis for political action; second, that biological identity is destiny—that human society had for centuries or even millennia privileged the work of white men chiefly because they were white men, and had done the opposite to everyone else.

Thus were born the "culture wars," a phrase that crept into general usage in the early 1990s. The famous precipitating incident of the culture wars, the Fort Sumter so to speak, was a demonstration by students at Stanford in 1988, who chanted, "Hey-hey, ho-ho, Western Civ has got to go!" referring to the university's survey Western Civilization course that as far as the students were concerned leaned too heavily on the works of dead white males. The students were correct that many valuable works by women and writers of color had been overlooked. But in other respects the critique went too far. *The Adventures of Huckleberry Finn* was much ostracized in those days, but no matter how many times it used the n-word, it was obviously a work of staggering literary merit (and was a strongly antislavery tract to boot).

Conservatives like William Bennett railed against this activism, this seeming defenestration of America's history and traditions and moral lodestars. The more interesting tension, not generally caught by the media at the time because it was too subtle for most of them, was the animosity that arose over all this between liberals and radicals. Liberals took the position that welcoming Zora Neale Hurston and Albert Murray, two African-American writers who were finally getting their deserved academic due, into the room didn't have to mean throwing Mark Twain and F. Scott Fitzgerald out of it. Radicals did not trust this liberal tendency to find the inoffensive middle ground. And as we saw in the 2016 Democratic presidential primary, they still don't.

All this didn't directly impact the kingdom of politics, not just yet. Politics is usually a lagging indicator of social change, not a leading one. In 1991, George H. W. Bush was president. He wasn't above using a little racial fear to get elected in 1988 (the ads featuring the mug shot of the black convicted rapist Willie Horton, whom Michael Dukakis had pardoned), but he was no culture warrior. He lived through the Depression (although he was raised in wealth), enlisted in the Navy on his eighteenth birthday, fought bravely in the war (he was a hero fighter pilot), and had developed a sense of responsibility about tending the garden of the republic. In the 1990 Americans with Disabilities Act, he signed a historic piece of civil-rights legislation that vastly expanded the federal government's reach into the private sector. He supported environmental regulation—his EPA commissioner was the first to talk about climate change. He compromised with Democrats, even agreeing in 1990 to a tax increase. He didn't think of Democrats as his enemy. And he was among the last of his breed.

How Money and Technology Changed Politics

The Republican leader of the House of Representatives during Bush Sr.'s presidency was a man named Robert Michel. He was about as decently Middle American as a person could possibly be. For starters, he was from the city that had been since the late nineteenth century *the* archetypal Middle American town: Peoria, Illinois. You may have heard the phrase

"Will it play in Peoria?" which is a stand-in for whether the people of Middle America will accept a particular idea or thing. It comes from an 1890 novel by Horatio Alger, who is himself an American archetype: A "Horatio Alger story" is a tale of a person who went from rags to riches. Appearing as his novels did in the (first) Gilded Age, they helped convince a generation of young readers that the idea was not to resent the swells in Manhattan and Newport but to become one of them. He invoked Peoria as a place where a traveling theater troupe was putting on its next performance. Ever since, Peoria has stood for good, sturdy, small-town America (even though it's really a small-to-sizable city, with a metro area population of more than 350,000).

Born in 1923, Michel was of prime fighting age during World War II. He joined the army and served as an infantryman; he participated in the Normandy invasion and ultimately won a chestful of medals, including a Purple Heart. He came back from the war, went to college in Peoria, and got involved in Republican politics. He made it to the House of Representatives in 1956 and spent nearly forty years there. In 1981, when then-sitting House minority leader John Rhodes retired, his GOP colleagues chose Michel to succeed him. Michel was conservative, there was no doubt of that. But he did not breathe fire. He played golf and poker with Democrats. In 1981, his first year as GOP leader, he had to persuade at least twenty-six Democrats to vote for the Reagan economic package. In those days there were still plenty of Democrats who were not only moderate but even conservative, the so-called "Boll Weevil Democrats," who went extinct by roughly 2000. So they made for a willing audience. But still, someone had to talk to them, cajole them, twist their arms. Michel did it. The headline on his 2017 *New York Times* obituary said: "House G.O.P. Leader Prized Conciliation."[1]

But as the 1980s dragged on, the House of Representatives began to change. One thing that changed it: money. Money changed the rest of the culture in the 1980s, so there's no way it wasn't going to change politics, too. The Supreme Court played a role here, just as it had in the credit boom. Its 1976 decision *Buckley v. Valeo* ruled on various aspects of some sweeping 1974 campaign-finance-law amendments that Congress had passed. The decision upheld limits on campaign contributions by individual donors; but, more important, it said that campaigns and candidates themselves, as well as independent groups, could spend as much as they wanted to spend, because money, the Court held, was the same as speech. The impact was clear. *Buckley* "perpetuated an arms race that has consistently driven up the cost of campaigns faster than inflation."[2] The decision also made it easier for candidates to self-finance, leading to both parties recruiting more wealthy individuals to run. Result? From 1986 to 2016, the cost of winning a House seat roughly doubled, from $787,418 in 1986 (that's in 2016 dollars) to $1,516,021 in 2016.[3] This increase also had the effect of kick-starting the mad money chase on Capitol Hill that is so familiar to us today. This changed the culture of the place, forcing representatives and especially senators to spend far more time raising money—and from big donors, not their constituents—than they ever had before. It's not something your average citizens knows, but senators—who are not allowed to raise money from their official offices—going back to the 1990s, rented small offices in the older townhouses that surround the Senate office buildings; during down moments, they'd sneak off to these "political" offices to call donors and plead for money. More recently, the parties have set up call centers on Capitol Hill; if you happen to be on the Hill at the right time of day, you might see a phalanx of legislators walking to these centers. Senators and House members in tough reelection races may spend a few hours a day in those cubicles.[4]

The other half of the money chase took off around the same time: corporate lobbying. The long-standing corporate view of politics had been that it was a messy business best avoided. But this started to change in the 1970s. It changed in part because of the Powell Memo and the way it urged corporate America to get involved in politics. But the scope of the change went far beyond what was outlined in that memo, because starting in the 1980s virtually every business you could name started hiring lobbyists. Many of them had little or no concern about the grand ideological direction of the country. They just wanted more favorable legislative treatment: the avocado growers, the drywall manufacturers, the flatware council, what have you. Once this explosion occurred, corporate America began to see that it could get something out of having an active presence in Washington—companies could win favors, steer federal policy. By 1982, a Harris Poll of corporate leaders found 90 percent saying "they were better able to get their message out than five years ago" and "75 percent saying that they felt business has more clout than it did in the recent past."[5]

Another big change in Congress in the 1980s, which walked hand-in-hand with money, was the professionalization of political consulting. Going back in time, most politicians used advisers who were often just their old buddies. Some had professional consultants going back to the 1940s. By the 1960s, journalism started to get curious about these men behind the curtain, and a few of them became famous: New York's David Garth, who engineered Mayor John Lindsay's upset reelection victory in 1969, and Roger Ailes, who ran Richard Nixon's 1968 campaign, three decades before he launched Fox News and five decades before he was revealed to be a serial sexual predator. Garth and Ailes both came out of television—Garth directed the telecasts of New York–area high-school football games, and Ailes had worked for Mike Douglas, a popular daytime talk-show host of the 1960s and 1970s. In the seventies, the number of consultancies and polling firms grew. By the eighties, they were ubiquitous. Also coming into vogue that decade: the focus group. Focus groups had been used in the retail sphere since the 1950s; their inventor was a man named Ernest Dichter, a native of Austria who had been an acolyte of Sigmund Freud and had fled the Nazis in 1938. A successful ad man in New York by the 1950s, he used focus groups to help Jell-O, Plymouth, and others learn from consumers how best to market their products. By the 1980s, a few political consultants, mostly on the Republican side, brought the focus group into politics.

All this dramatically and permanently altered the practice of politics. Now, for the first time, candidates could know exactly how many percentage points taking a certain position would gain or lose them. They could see what specific language fired voters' brains and what words left them cold. And they learned, quickly, that even though voters might say they didn't like nasty attacks—they worked. The other great change that occurred then was in the culture of Capitol Hill, which many have written about. Those days when Mike Mansfield made senators car-pool on a bipartisan basis were now long gone. They were replaced by a schedule that allowed little time for such interparty socializing. Today, and actually since the 1980s or '90s, House members drive or fly back to their districts every weekend ("weekend" often defined as Thursday evening to Monday evening), and what time they do spend in Washington is more and more taken up by visiting those fund-raising call centers.

These changes were taking place, remember, while the country was splitting into two camps over race, gender, and sexuality. These were inert gases, sitting in the lab. All that was needed was for someone to come along with the smarts to combine them; merge them into something combustible. Someone who could unite money, technology, and the culture wars; who could marry corporate cash and all these fancy new campaign techniques to the project of awakening the fears and anxieties of the broader white middle class that didn't want all this change. That person could revolutionize politics.

For Better or Worse, the Most Influential Republican of Our Time

Newt Gingrich ran for Congress twice in suburban Atlanta as a kind of standard-issue, moderate-to-conservative Republican in a state that still strongly favored Democrats, albeit pretty conservative ones. He came close to the Democratic incumbent both times but lost. Then, in 1978, that incumbent, seeing that his district was changing and that his likely Republican opponent was relentless, retired, and Gingrich won easily, running this time as more of an exponent of the new "movement conservatism" that arose from the antisixties backlash and the politicization of the religious right. Forty years later, I think it's clear that in terms of the influence he's had on conservatism and on both the discourse and practice of politics, he has been, for better or worse, the most influential Republican of his age.

He was the anti-Michel. There was to be no golf or poker with Democrats in Gingrich's spare hours. While campaigning in 1978, he seemed to be attacking Michel and his style directly: "One of the great problems we have in the Republican Party is that we don't encourage you to be nasty. We encourage you to be neat, obedient, and loyal. . . .This party does not need another generation of cautious, prudent, careful, bland, irrelevant quasi-leaders."[6]

The difference in outlook was partly a matter of personality, but there can be no doubt that it was substantially driven by the different eras that produced them. Michel was another of the men who were raised during the Depression, who fought in the war, who were shot at and shot down, who saw the all-but-dead surviving Jewish prisoners of Dachau and Buchenwald. When they got to Washington, they arrived with humility and the awareness that they bore the responsibility of upholding certain traditions and practices. Gingrich, born in 1943, grew up in the greatest era of prosperity ever known (he was not rich, but lived comfortably as the adopted son of a career army officer), and he never fought in a war. He received student and parental deferments during Vietnam (he had two young daughters). Surely the fact that he'd never known actual battle permitted him to believe and say things like the eye-popping remark he once made to the journalist Jane Mayer in 1985. She was asking him about his deferments. "Given everything I believe in, a large part of me thinks I should have gone over," he acknowledged. But then he added: "There was a bigger battle in Congress than Vietnam."[7]

His early antics in the House are well known and don't need retelling in detail. The defining episode came in May 1984, when he took to the House floor to question the patriotism of certain House members by name. The speech was captured on C-SPAN, the then-new station that covered House floor action gavel to gavel. He delivered it to a nearly empty chamber, but of course his intended audiences—viewers back home, movement conservatives and donors across the country—would have no way of knowing that. But to an empty chamber or a full one, this sort of thing was not done back then, and Speaker Tip O'Neill was enraged. He ordered that thenceforth, the C-SPAN cameras would pan across the empty chamber so that viewers would know such speeches were pointless theatrics. But Gingrich had succeeded in doing two things he would do extraordinarily well for the next twenty-five or so years: bringing attention to himself, and defining down the standards and norms of whatever institution he was associated with.

In a phrase, this is what Gingrich did: He brought the culture war to

Congress. He didn't really start swinging for the fences on such matters until he was more senior and Bill and Hillary Clinton were in the White House. Just before the 1994 election that would make him speaker, after a South Carolina mother named Susan Smith drove her car into a lake and drowned her two sons, Gingrich said the crime "vividly reminds every American how sick the society is getting and how much we have to have change. I think people want to change and the only way you get change is to vote Republican."[8] In other words, things like this happen because of what the Democrats have done to the country. When it emerged that Smith had in fact been raised by a stepfather who was a local Republican Party poohbah and Christian Coalition leader—and who had sexually molested her[9]—Gingrich didn't think it necessary to correct the record. In the days after that election, he vowed to destroy the "Great Society, counterculture, McGovernick" legacy the Democrats had imposed on a supine nation.[10]

In the early and mid-eighties, the country was sending more and more people to Congress who would have agreed with Gingrich's assessment of the Smith horror completely. They didn't all have Gingrich's flair for self-drama or the flesh-piercing sound bite, but they were nearly all movement conservatives who weren't very interested in socializing across party lines and who shared Gingrich's view that politics was war and liberals were the enemy.

I return us now to my atlas of congressional districts, that twelve-pound tome that reveals so much history. In the 95th Congress, which sat from 1977 to 1979, the last Congress before Gingrich became a member, the Democratic hold on the South was still almost total. All of Georgia was Democratic, most of both Carolinas, and twenty-two out of twenty-four districts in Texas. Elsewhere, rural Minnesota, Wisconsin, and Missouri were chiefly Democratic, as were about half the Big Sky State districts. West Virginia was solid blue. It was still, electorally speaking, Roosevelt's America. These things change slowly because of the high rate at which House incumbents are reelected, but over the course of the eighties, change they did. For his first three terms, Gingrich was the only Republican from Georgia (out of ten representatives). By the time he became speaker in 1995, eight out of eleven were Republicans, and all of them movement conservatives to one degree or another. This happened all over the country.

Was the same thing happening across the aisle, you may be wondering? Sort of, but not in the same way. Democrats did not think of themselves as part of a new movement that had to take on and shake up the establishment in anything like the way Gingrich Republicans did. The Democrats had held power in Congress for so long that they *were* the establishment, at least politically speaking. So they had nothing to "insurge," if you'll permit me that verb, against. They had institutions and traditions and habits to protect. Totally different mindset.

Nevertheless, the Democratic contingents in the House and Senate did start to get more liberal on the whole in the 1980s and 1990s, for two reasons. The first has to do with the rising influence of single-issue interest groups, which became more powerful during this period. As certain social issues became more bitterly contested, the interest groups that worked on those issues started raising more money and gaining in prominence. This gave them more clout (this whole business of dozens of groups rating and scoring legislators' voting records also started around the same time). It made for less tolerance for departures from the party platform. In the 1970s and '80s, there were plenty of prolife Democrats in Congress. In 1985, there were 76 prolife Democrats. Even Ted Kennedy was prolife in the early 1970s; former *Boston Globe* editor Matt Storin recalls hearing him thunder at a 1970 campaign rally, "Don't tell me there isn't enough love in the world to care for all the unwanted babies!"[11] By the mid-1990s, that 76 had shrunk to 54; by 2005, to 32; and by 2015, to 3.[12] Similarly, as African-American and Latino voter participation increased, those groups acquired more political muscle, and more and more (white) Democrats adopted positions favored by their interest groups. The most notable example of this is that organized labor had initially opposed a path to citizenship for immigrants who'd arrived illegally on the grounds that they undercut wages. But labor changed this position in 2000, after a critical mass of its membership had become Latino. The dwindling but still significant number of Democratic legislators who took their cues from labor did the same.

Second, it stands to reason that as all those rural and exurban districts switched from Democratic to Republican representation, the Democrats lost a number of their more conservative members. This happened in rural areas all across the country, but the change was most striking in the South. Remember: Except for those two oddball districts in eastern Tennessee, the South had barely sent a Republican to the House of Representatives since the late 1870s. But after the Gingrich Revolution election of 1994, as the journalist E. J. Dionne Jr. noted, "Republicans outnumbered Democrats in the South for the first time since Reconstruction: 73 Southern House members were Republican, only 64 were Democrats." Also: In 1990, 50 percent of white Southerners voted for Democratic candidates, and by 1994, only 36 percent did.[13] This meant curtains for Southern Democrats, who had wielded enormous power since the New Deal as chairmen of the most powerful committees. "The once-mighty 'conservative coalition' of congressional Republicans and Southern Democrats found itself relegated to the sidelines," reported the 1995 *CQ Almanac*[14]—which if anything was a severe understatement.

Was it all Gingrich and the Republicans? Wasn't Bill Clinton, too, a polarizer and a culture warrior? Not like Gingrich was. He didn't seek to inflame partisan ideological passions in the same way Gingrich did. Hillary Clinton did a bit of that, though less by intent than by tone deafness— the way she seemed to demean mothers who stayed at home and baked cookies, for example. But the Clintons were mostly culture warriors by dint of their biography: the first liberal Baby Boomers to make it to the White House. He, the first Southern governor to become president who had cut his political teeth fighting the old-line racists in his state, like Orval Faubus and "Justice" Jim Johnson; she, the first feminist First Lady, so unimpressed with tradition that she could barely be bothered to buy a dress for her wedding and did not (at first) take her husband's name. They worked for McGovern in 1972. Old photos popped up of them in law school, particularly that one of Hillary with no makeup, large glasses, and plain straight hair she seemed barely to have combed, and another of Bill sporting a shock of hair and beard that made him look as if he might have been the designated roller for the Allman Brothers. They made conservatives crazy just standing there.

So it came to pass during that 1992 campaign that this newly muscular movement conservatism set about the business of trying to turn the Clintons into some kind of anti-American double agents. The story—true, and politically quite damaging—that Bill had reneged on a promise to a University of Arkansas ROTC officer to join the officers' corps and later wrote him a letter thanking him for "saving me from the draft"[15] threw several gallons of gasoline on that fire. By the fall, an innocent trip Clinton had made to the Soviet Union during his time as a Rhodes Scholar at Oxford was converted by certain critics into a secret mission to collude with the Kremlin to help America lose the Vietnam War. No actual proof was ever adduced that he did anything other than visit the place to see what life was like there, but those Americans who were inclined to believe the criticism no longer demanded things like proof.

In an earlier time, these allegations wouldn't have made it beyond Clarence Manion's mimeograph machine. But by the 1990s, the right had its own megaphone. That's another important piece of our story.

The Rise of the Right-Wing Media Machine

The radio was invented around the dawn of the twentieth century—the beginning of the electronic media revolution that is still shaking up the world. It is wireless. Signals are transmitted via a process called amplitude modulation—that is, AM—over a certain band of frequencies. This was a new technology, and it was different from previous ones in one key respect: Whereas the supply of potential newspapers was theoretically infinite in that anybody with the resources could start one, anybody with the resources couldn't broadcast a radio show on the AM dial. The frequencies were finite.

So the government said: Not just anyone can own a broadcasting license. We will award them. Possessing one will be privilege, and it will carry with it a civic responsibility. First the Radio Act of 1927, and then the Communications Act of 1934, which created the Federal Communications Commission, sought to regulate these new broadcasts. The 1934 law placed a responsibility on licensees to devote a reasonable portion of their broadcast hours to news and public affairs and the airing of different viewpoints. This provision was amended and challenged here and there; and then, in the late 1940s, a new medium arose, television, where there were only a few networks that had enormous power over the way public issues were discussed. The folks at the FCC thought about the implications of all this, and in 1949 they produced a report called "In the Matter of Editorializing by Broadcast Licensees," which made the obligation more explicit. The report left it to licensees to decide exactly how to cover public affairs, but then said:[16]

> This choice, however, must be exercised in a manner consistent with the basic policy of Congress that radio be maintained as a medium of free speech for the general public as a whole rather than as an outlet for the purely personal or private interests of the licensee. This requires that licensees devote a reasonable percentage of their broadcasting time to the discussion of public issues of interest in the community served by their stations and that such programs be designed so that the public has a reasonable opportunity to hear different opposing positions on the public issues of interest and importance in the community.

This was the Fairness Doctrine. It was enforced throughout the period of consensus. The Supreme Court smiled on it in a 1969 case, holding unanimously in *Red Lion Broadcasting v. FCC* that requiring equal time did not infringe on a licensee's First Amendment rights and agreeing that possessing a broadcast license conferred special responsibilities on those who had one. Congress agreed. It was the settled law of the land.

But starting in the 1970s, the doctrine came under attack, on two fronts. First, critics began to assert, and accurately so, that what had been true in 1949 was no longer true with respect to the limited number of frequency positions and electronic news outlets (the "scarcity" problem, in the argot). There were more radio stations by then than there had been in 1949, and many more television stations. The presumption was that a market as robust as that would by definition adequately represent all points of view. This fed right into the second argument, which was that with such a proliferation of outlets, the doctrine actually impinged on broadcasters' First Amendment rights. If there was now a fellow across town presenting the liberal point of view, the conservative licensee asked, why must I also devote air time to that point of view? (Of course, the liberal across town had to devote time to the conservative argument, but that point was often glossed over.)

These debates continued throughout the 1970s, but it wasn't until the country had a conservative, antiregulation president that the doctrine's critics donned their battle gear. Ronald Reagan supported repeal, and Oregon Republican senator Bob Packwood, who chaired the relevant Senate committee and held hearings in the early eighties giving a platform to repeal advocates, took to calling the Fairness Doctrine the "fearness doctrine."[17]

In 1984, Mark Fowler, Reagan's FCC chair and a repeal advocate, put out word that the commission was considering repeal. It's kind of amusing today to look at who was lined up for and against. Most repeal advocates were indeed conservatives, on ideological, deregulatory grounds. But a number of conservative leaders and interests opposed repeal, worried that the "liberal media" would never broadcast a conservative point of view. Pat Buchanan, Reagan budget director Richard Darman, Senator Trent Lott, and Newt Gingrich were among them.[18] Corporations like Exxon and General Motors liked the doctrine because they were able to invoke it to get equal time to answer attacks they considered unfair. Both Ralph Nader and Phyllis Schlafly testified for the doctrine, out of fear that their side in the political debate might be marginalized.

As the FCC took public comment, a few voices warned that repeal might lead to one point of view dominating the market, especially on radio. But Packwood dismissed the thought. Commissioner Mimi Dawson, a Reagan appointee who had once worked for Packwood, allowed that yes, the commissioners had seen it argued that repeal would be "a boon to conservatives,"[19] but it did not seem to her a prevalent or persuasive viewpoint.

Congress disagreed with the administration and passed a law to protect the doctrine in June 1986, and it did so with bipartisan support: Fully 79 Republicans joined 223 Democrats to back the measure in the House.[20] In the Senate, 18 Republicans joined 41 Democrats in voting aye.[21] But President Reagan vetoed it. Three months later, a three-judge panel of the Court of Appeals for the District of Columbia ruled by 2–1 that implementation of the doctrine should be discretionary (those two judges? Antonin Scalia and Robert Bork).[22] The doctrine was repealed in August 1987. That year, 7 percent of AM stations followed the talk/ public affairs format. By 1995, 28 percent did.[23] They were virtually all conservative. Conservatives saw the opportunity and flooded the zone. And they got ratings and sold ads. Rush Limbaugh was the first and most famous. In 1987, not too long after he'd wrapped up his stint as director of promotions for the Kansas City Royals, he was still a local talk-radio personality in Sacramento. The year after the repeal, he moved to New York and went national. Dozens followed. Soon enough Limbaugh and his imitators owned the AM dial, and in time the best-seller lists, too. Today, conservative screeds against Godless liberals occupy three or so spots on the *New York Times* bestseller list most weeks; yet another phenomenon that started in the late eighties and early nineties.

AM radio was the vanguard of this new media brigade. But it wasn't just radio. Wealthy conservatives were now pouring millions into media, without a care about how much money they lost, because they covered the losses from their other profitable ventures and because they knew every dollar they burned was buying them at least a dollar in political influence. The leader here was Rupert Murdoch. He bought the *New York Post* in 1976. The *Post*, up to that point, was a liberal newspaper under owner Dorothy Schiff—its readership was largely Jewish (while the *Daily News* catered more to Catholics), and it was pro–New Deal and pro-Zionist back when Zionism was a liberal thing. Murdoch turned the paper hard to starboard in a hurry, making it his mission to defeat Mario Cuomo in the New York City mayoral race of 1977 and to elect Alfonse D'Amato to the Senate in 1980. He lost many millions of dollars a year with the *Post*; still does today. At one point, owing to an FCC rule that forbade ownership of a television station and a newspaper in the same city, Murdoch had to sell the *Post*. A few years later, in 1993, when the paper was on one of its serial death beds and 700 jobs were at stake, he was able to buy it back—with the help of liberals no less, including Ted Kennedy, who (it was thought at the time) feared that if he didn't facilitate the repurchase, Murdoch would flagellate him in his home state with the *Boston Herald*, which Murdoch also owned (in another city where Murdoch also owned a television station). Kennedy was facing reelection the next year, 1994, and in 1993 he was at something of a low ebb (the 1994 race—against Mitt Romney no less—was the closest reelection battle of his career). Mario Cuomo, the New York governor at the time, helped out too, at the prodding of his old friend, the legendary liberal *Post* columnist Jack Newfield. The dual-ownership prohibition was thus ended in the 1990s, by liberals, for Rupert Murdoch.

That year of 1993, when Murdoch bought back the *Post*, was of course the first year of Bill Clinton's presidency. By this time, there were hundreds of talk-radio stations around the country, virtually all of them conservative. There was Murdoch's *Post*. There was the Unification Church's *Washington Times*, which cult leader Sun Myung Moon launched in 1982 and which President Reagan made a point of citing from time to time. In the 1980s, the exotically named editor Arnaud de Borchgrave sponsored fund-raising drives for the Nicaraguan contras. By 1992, the paper was edited by Wesley Pruden, who even today unironically peppers his copy with phrases like "the Cruel War of Northern Aggression."[24] There was the editorial page of the *Wall Street Journal*, that most sober of newspapers, owned then by the Bancroft family, which sold it to Murdoch in 2007. The *Journal* didn't even have photographs in those days, and its news pages were as trusted as any in journalism. But its editorial and opinion pages began to mix the time-honored defenses of conservative monetary policy with aggressive and sometimes groundless demonization of all things liberal and of aides in the Clinton White House it decided to slander. And there were magazines, most notably the *American Spectator*, a far-right opinion journal that had existed since the late 1960s without making much of an impact. But in 1992, a young journalist named David Brock published a major attack on Anita Hill, the woman who had come forward to accuse Supreme Court justice Clarence Thomas of making repeated sexually lewd comments and advances toward her. Washington finally noticed the *American Spectator*, and would do so again. (Brock became a liberal in the late 1990s and has been ever since.)

This was something that hadn't existed in the old consensus America: A conservative, a *very* conservative, media solar system all of its own, with real power and reach. It had important validators, like Reagan and some of the more articulate politicians he swept into office, such as Texas senator Phil Gramm. It had some intellectuals, like William F. Buckley Jr. and Norman Podhoretz, who had been a leftist as a young man and moved right during the 1970s (and had written more than one memoir detailing the reasons for his change of heart). It had television personalities, notably John McLaughlin, the former Jesuit priest who worked in the Nixon White House and whose pugilistic *McLaughlin Group* debuted in 1982 and paved the way for the decibel increase in political talk that hasn't stopped since (and whose momentum was not slowed a whit by the host's settlement in 1989 of a $4 million sexual harassment claim).[25]

They played by different rules: Win at all costs. "Whitewater is about health care," Limbaugh instructed his 20 million listeners in 1994—in other words, the point of the Whitewater investigation was not to find out whether in fact either Clinton had done anything improper on that land deal; it was to drive up the Clintons' disapproval numbers and make it harder for them to pass the health-care bill. Facts became "facts." Some months after White House aide Vince Foster committed suicide, Limbaugh told his listeners that Foster, far from shooting himself in suburban Fort Marcy Park, as the police had ruled, had been "murdered in an apartment owned by Hillary Clinton."[26] This "fact" was somehow traced back to New York Democratic senator Daniel Patrick Moynihan's office, which declared it "breathtakingly untrue." The *Wall Street Journal*'s editorial page—which had helped drive Foster to suicide with its fusillade of innuendo about his supposed role in covering up various Clinton crimes—carried on hinting that the cover-up about the "real" cause of Foster's death was a scandal of scarcely imaginable proportions. Foster's death was investigated five times. Each one found that a deeply distraught man had in fact committed suicide.

They discovered, these new avatars, that it was easier than they'd ever have dreamed to get the liberal mainstream media interested in their narratives and allegations. Yes, most reporters are liberal; but (a) not *all* reporters are liberal; (b) reporters who do lean left privately sometimes give conservatives the benefit of the doubt to show they're not biased; and (c) even the ones who are liberal are usually more interested in breaking a scandal and getting their stories on the front page than anything else. On top of that, the Clintons, Hillary especially, had hardly endeared themselves to the press. Most mainstream reporters felt no great love for them. So the new right-wing media mandarins came to have enormous power in driving the national agenda.

This time frame, the early to mid-1990s, marked the beginning of the age we know so well today—of two different sets of facts, two different realities, which drove the country apart even more. Murdoch's Fox News Channel debuted in October 1996, with the slogan "We report—you decide." In other words, we, unlike those liberal outfits, won't guide you by the nose toward a desired conclusion. But of course Fox did exactly that. That was the whole point of it.

The change in the media culture, over a short ten-year period, was hard to comprehend—and indeed, most people didn't comprehend in real time how different things were. Walter Cronkite had retired in 1981, but metaphorically, we were still living in Cronkite's media world in the mid-1980s—three networks, three anchors, two big papers (the *New York Times* and the *Washington Post*), CNN still kind of an afterthought, and no one to question the big outlets' authority. By the mid-1990s, this had changed dramatically. And once the Internet exploded in the second half of the nineties, the number of voices increased five-, ten-, twentyfold. It was as if a solar system that had consisted of five or six large planets exploded into pieces. The cores of the larger planets were still there, and still dominant, but hundreds of smaller rocks were now constantly jostling them, challenging their orbital paths.

And the Fairness Doctrine? A faint memory. Democrats have tried to revive it from time to time. Republicans, obviously aware of the endless dividends that its repeal has paid to their side, have blocked it. Groups still exist trying to get it reinstated, but the doctrine comes from a different America. They might as well try to reinstate gas rationing. The idea that the government can referee ideological balance is ghastly to conservatives, and even to many liberals, it's quaint. Technically, the doctrine remained on the books after 1987, because that year's repeal meant only that the FCC stopped enforcing it. In May 2011, Republican legislators asked President Obama's FCC chairman, Julius Genachowski, to wipe it from the code officially. Deciding that the doctrine was not a hill he was going to die on, he obliged them. "Striking this from our books ensures there can be no mistake that what has long been a dead letter remains dead," Genachowski said.[27]

The Pledge: The Best-Kept Secret of the Age of Polarization

The year 1990, the year the culture wars arguably started, turns out to have been a rather important year in the story of our coming apart. It was in 1990 that President George H. W. Bush did something he had promised during his 1988 campaign he would never do. He raised taxes. "Read. My. Lips," he'd famously said at his party's New Orleans convention. "No. New. Taxes." What grew from that broken promise is one of the biggest—and least-known—drivers of today's polarization.

What changed to make Bush renege on his promise? Reality, in a word. Bush was hit with the savings and loan crisis shortly after taking office, which required huge government outlays. The deficit, which had been going down in the later Reagan years, shot back up. Fed chairman Alan Greenspan refused to ease the money supply until he saw evidence of deficit reduction. So Bush needed to do that. Democrats controlled both houses of Congress. If he wanted a budget deal that would convince Greenspan to change course, he'd have to play ball with the Democrats, who were insisting that the deficit reduction could not come entirely from budget cuts. So, in late June 1990, Bush announced that he was open to tax increases being part of a final deal. That deal, with $159 billion in revenues, was struck in late September at Andrews Air Force Base, better known to us as the home of Air Force One (and called Joint Base Andrews today). Conservatives were enraged. Republicans voted against the deal—against *their president*—by 163–10 in the House, while Senate Republicans were about evenly split. There was a recession, which had started before the deal was signed, but whose duration allowed conservatives to blame it on the tax hikes. Most economists, in fact, didn't blame the deal for the bad economy, and many budget experts came to agree that the compromise, in the words of former conservative Bruce Bartlett, "deserves much of the credit for the subsequent improvement in the deficit."[28]

That was not how Grover Norquist saw it. Norquist, just shy of thirty-four when that budget agreement was negotiated, was already Washington's leading antitax advocate (which he remains today). He seemed to spring so formed from the womb. He grew up in Massachusetts, went to Harvard, joined the *Crimson*, alongside such now-prominent liberal writers as Jonathan Alter and Nicholas Lemann; but he was fixated on conservative-libertarian politics from his youth to the exclusion of most of the diversions typical of a young American male of the early 1960s. When a *Crimson* editor assigned him to cover a baseball game, according to the journalist Nina Easton, he "had never even read a sports page."[29]

In 1985, he was chosen to run a new group called Americans for Tax Reform, which was to do grassroots lobbying in behalf of Reagan's 1986 tax bill. That accomplished, Norquist hit upon the idea of drawing up an antitax pledge that he would ask all Republican candidates to sign—a promise to their prospective constituents that they would never vote to increase a tax. In 1988, Bush Sr. signed it.

The fact that he signed it and broke it and went on to lose the election shot Norquist's stock on the right up to the heavens. He looked like he had the power to make and break presidents. After Andrews Air Force Base, or "Andrews" as conservatives call it in a shorthand synonym for capitulation that is not so far removed in spirit from "Munich," nearly every Republican running for House or Senate (as well as hundreds of candidates for lower offices) has signed the "Taxpayer Protection Pledge," which reads: "I, _____, pledge to the taxpayers of the (____ district of the) state of _____ and to the American people that I will: ONE, oppose any and all efforts to increase the marginal income tax rate for individuals and business; and TWO, oppose any net reduction or elimination of deductions and credits, unless matched dollar for dollar by further reducing tax rates." In the 115th Congress, seated from 2015 to 2017, 46 of 52 Republican senators and 210 of 239 GOP House members were signatories. President Trump, interestingly, did not sign. He never publicly stated his reasons.

The result is pretty straightforward: Since 1990, not a single Republican House member or senator has voted for a tax increase. Oh, there are a few asterisks in there. From time to time, Norquist has defined some small thing as a "fee" rather than a tax increase. A couple of times, Republicans in Congress have agreed to mild tax increases that were offset by spending cuts or deductions or other moves, which Norquist's group scores as a wash. An increase in the top marginal rate on dollars earned above $400,000, agreed to under Barack Obama's term, was judged to be all right because the agreement made the Bush Jr. tax cuts permanent (they had been about to expire), so overall it was a cut.

But fundamentally, the Republicans in Congress have never supported a broad tax increase for a public purpose since 1990. The real-world policy impact has been beyond profound. During the late-Clinton boom times, tax revenues came to around 20 percent of the Gross Domestic Product. They got down to 15 percent during the worst of the Great Recession, and in 2017 they were around 17.5 percent[30] (that's before the December 2017 passage of the GOP tax bill, which will presumably reduce them). So the government has had less to spend, on scientific and medical research, on infrastructure, on public investments of all kinds.

The political impact has been equally dramatic; maybe even more so. The pledge has been one of the great drivers of polarization, and an often unacknowledged driver. I've written about it, as have a number of observers. But the general public hasn't the slightest idea of the role the pledge has played. They ought to know.

Here's what I mean: In the prepledge days, Democrats would push for a tax increase to meet some newly arisen need. Republicans in the Bob Michel mold would typically say well, okay, if we must, but not that much; this much. And so, there would be compromise, as there was in 1990. As there was throughout the modern history of the country—going back to the New Deal, say—up through 1990. During World War II, taxes were increased substantially, and on a bipartisan basis, in 1942. Another (much smaller) Revenue Act passed in 1943. Of course, those were for the war effort. Most people didn't mind. Irving Berlin even wrote a song called "I Paid My Income Tax Today," which the popular song-and-dance man Danny Kaye made into a hit. But it wasn't just at wartime. Fuel taxes chiefly built the interstate highway system. Payroll taxes finance Social Security and Medicare.

People complained about their taxes in consensus America, as people have in every society since taxation began. But there was no antitax movement until 1978, when a right-wing California businessman named Howard Jarvis led an effort to get an initiative on that year's ballot to slash property taxes. Property taxes increased with a home's assessed value, and what with the raging inflation and the California population explosion, assessed valuations were rising astronomically. Proposition 13, which capped assessments, was opposed by nearly every major politician and newspaper but passed two to one; instantly, property taxes were slashed by 58 percent and counties and municipalities were staring at large shortfalls.[31] They cut services. They resorted to local sales and utility taxes, which are regressive. Californians often comment on the crazy quilt of valuations, in which two identical homes next to each other can have wildly different tax bills, but the main economic impact was described well by the *Los Angeles Times*'s Michael Hiltzik:[32]

> Proposition 13 didn't necessarily relieve Californians of paying for the services they demand from local government; but it did produce a change in who pays the price. In many respects, the burden has been shifted down the income scale, so that poorer taxpayers are shouldering more of these costs.

Prop 13 kicked off a dramatic transformation in the way people thought about their tax bills, and politicians (mostly Republican) started feeding the antitax beast. But even into the 1980s, constructive compromise still happened from time to time. Social Security provides us with the classic example of the old-style tax negotiating that the taxpayer pledge has now rendered impossible. Social Security was in trouble in the early 1980s, and Ronald Reagan's first instincts toward addressing the problem were all about cuts, notably a steep reduction in benefits for people who took early retirement. But all of Reagan's ideas along these lines were unpopular, so he appointed a commission, chaired by Alan Greenspan, which told Congress that either taxes would have to go up or expenses down. In 1983, a small group of expert negotiators appointed by Congress, including Democrat Robert Ball, one of the key figures in the history of Social

Security, and Republican Richard Darman, who would later run the Office of Management and Budget for Bush Sr., did a bit of both. They struck a deal that they then sold to the commission, the president, and Congress that raised the retirement age for people born in 1960 to sixty-six and later to sixty-seven (that's a benefit cut, since it means two fewer years of benefits) and bumped up the payroll tax contribution from both employers and employees by .8 percent in stages over the course of the next seven years. At one point, negotiators were stuck: Democrats argued there still wasn't enough revenue, and Republicans wouldn't move on the payroll tax. So they hit on the idea, which originated with the liberal Ball, of taxing some benefits for high-income recipients, according to the author Paul Light, who wrote an authoritative book on the deal.[33] It was a tax. But the Republicans agreed, and Reagan went along with it. He hadn't signed any pledges. The Social Security trust fund drew away from the precipice.

The text of the pledge refers specifically only to personal income taxes, but it has been understood to be far more universal. Take the gasoline tax, which is the main source of revenue for the Highway Trust Fund, which provides the money for roads, bridges, tunnels, and some public transportation. The tax hasn't been increased since 1993, when a 4.4 cent hike was folded into a larger budget bill that passed with no Republican votes in either chamber (they opposed it mainly because it had a personal income tax increase, but they railed against the gas tax increase as well). That bill raised the tax to 18.4 cents (24.4 cents on diesel fuel), where it's been ever since. If the tax had been indexed to inflation, at least it would be around 31 cents today, but it was not.

Republicans have held the line on the gas tax ever since. As the GOP's presidential nominee in 1996, Bob Dole even proposed repealing the modest '93 increase. That didn't happen, since he lost, but it remains the case that in a quarter-century, Congress hasn't increased the tax. In the meantime, the Highway Trust Fund has been in the red since 2008; Congress has to kick in money from elsewhere to cover the shortfall. Also, states have been raising their own gas taxes to beat the band. More than half the states—most of them red; Alaska, Oklahoma, Mississippi, and Louisiana are among the biggest increasers—raised their gas taxes between 2013 and 2017.[34] A broad coalition of interests, including the U.S. Chamber of Commerce, supports increasing the tax. President Trump, to his credit, has said he's open to an increase. And disappointingly, to his noncredit, Senate Democratic leader Chuck Schumer told the *Daily Beast*'s Sam Stein in 2017 that he was against an increase.[35]

You read all the time about our collapsing infrastructure. Talking heads on cable television bemoan it and ask why Congress won't do something about it. They usually leave the impression that it's everyone's fault equally, that they just can't get together and reason anymore. But it's not that at all. Schumer's recently taken position notwithstanding, historically, the problem is the pledge. No tax—even one whose justification is ample and obvious, one that is supported by the Chamber of Commerce and that majorities of Americans regularly tell pollsters they support[36]—can be considered. It's just out of the question. (Although today's Republicans did sneak in a "tax increase" in their 2017 bill by capping the state and local deduction; that was just to stick it to filers in high-tax, Democratic states.)

The first task of a legislative body in a representative democracy is to assess the society's public needs and figure out how to address them fairly and adequately. That will include finding ways to pay for them. Simply put, the pledge makes carrying out that first task impossible. If one of the two major parties simply will not discuss revenue, compromise on this first task is by definition impossible, since compromise involves giving a little in exchange for getting a little, precisely as Reagan and O'Neill did in 1983. If compromise is impossible, then governance is impossible.

In some sense, everything else I've written about in this book pales in comparison to this intentional logjam. If Congress can't discuss revenue, then by definition it can't do its job. In addition, the fact that the parties can't negotiate on this most basic of legislative questions—the proper balance between spending and revenue—has over the decades created a mindset by which they can't compromise on anything else, either; whereas if they'd been in the habit of compromising on budget deals, maybe they'd have been able to carry that habit into other realms. They "compromise" on budget deals now—but only on the size of cuts. Never on revenue, because revenue is undiscussable. That's not real compromise. It's stalemate. And stalemate is where the pledge has left us.

How the Two Parties Became Different Creatures

That's the historical context for the polarization that we've been living with for the past quarter-century. The middle disappeared. It disappeared in part because of particular decisions made by particular men, like Gingrich. But it happened mostly because of all the historical and institutional factors I've previously described; factors that were well beyond any specific person's control, factors to which even Gingrich was responding. It's very hard to see how things could have gone differently, given the history that unfolded.

I won't go into great detail on these last twenty-five years, as hundreds of books have. Arguably it goes back further. Supreme Court fights were the first highly polarizing events in our modern history. Conservatives would say, and not wholly indefensibly, that the trouble started with Robert Bork's Supreme Court nomination in the fall of 1987, and it is true that Democratic opposition to Bork, who on paper was qualified to sit on the Court, was without precedent. Democrats would counter that Bork was unusually extreme in his views, and that Reagan had nominated Bork to replace the much more moderate Lewis Powell, who held a swing seat on the Court, and so Reagan was trying to radically alter the character of the Court (and indeed when Reagan advanced the less conservative Anthony Kennedy after Bork was defeated, the Senate confirmed him unanimously). Then came the vicious Clarence Thomas fight of 1991. It stands to reason, in retrospect, that the first partisan mud-wrestling matches were over the Court. It had been controlled by a liberal majority since the 1950s. Conservative legal activists had their sights set on flipping that the moment Reagan was elected, as their liberal counterparts well knew. Both sides knew that the stakes were enormous, as indeed they have proven to be.

Conservatives who think it unconscionable what Democrats did to Bork in 1987 do not, I notice, express much outrage about what Republicans did to Merrick Garland in 2016. In any case, the toxin spread from the realm of judicial nominees to everything else in fairly short order. Indeed, the only politically memorable moments of the past quarter-century were ones over which the country was bitterly divided. The momentary exception to that judgment is 9/11, but that little flicker of national unity was very short-lived. Other than that, they've made for a bleak political landscape, these last two-plus decades.

There were two seminally divisive battles that set the template for the era of modern polarization. The Clinton impeachment in 1998 was the first big national freak-out of the 24/7 cable news era. All three of the major cable news networks existed by then, although MSNBC was still at least a decade away from fashioning itself the "liberal" channel; in fact, the MSNBC of 1998 featured a show in which Laura Ingraham and Ann Coulter starred, and another hosted by Alan Keyes. The country was not evenly split over Clinton's fate, not by a long shot—polls consistently showed that 60 to 65 percent of Americans opposed Republican efforts to remove Clinton from office over lying about a consensual affair, and the voters penalized Republicans at the polls that November. The party lost seats and Gingrich resigned the speakership (partly over the losses, partly over other long-standing grievances within the House Republican caucus). Clinton left office with a 66 percent approval rating,[37] but the modern electronic battle lines were drawn.

They hardened over the 2000 election, which became the second seminal event. It went nearly five long and bitter weeks from election night until the still-controversial *Bush v. Gore* decision was handed down by a 5–4 Supreme Court majority on December 12. As in 2016, the loser (in the Electoral College and the Supreme Court) was the winner (of the popular vote). The infamous "butterfly ballot" that had some Jews in Palm Beach County voting for borderline-if-not-outright anti-Semite Pat Buchanan, the paper-thin 539-vote margin in Florida, the "Brooks Brothers riot" by Republicans at the Miami-Dade election headquarters that stopped a recount in a county Al Gore won, the dueling marches outside the Supreme Court Building the night the decision was handed down, with supporters of Gore and George W. Bush screaming in each others' faces, all relayed to the millions at home on cable news; you could palpably feel the gulf widen in this country over those five weeks, could tell we'd crossed a bridge from which there was no going back.

On September 11, for a short moment, virtually all of us reacted to a public event in the same way, with something like the same mixture of shock, horror, anger, and sadness. For a few weeks, it was as if we were back in World War II—we were drawn together in shared grief, as we watched the television specials profiling the fathers and mothers and Little League coaches who'd lost their lives at ground zero and the Pentagon, and the impossibly brave passengers who brought that plane down in central Pennsylvania. Some guardians of the culture announced the end of irony. But soon enough, irony returned, and so did our political and cultural divisions. Within two months, the country was at war, though this was a war (Afghanistan) that the vast majority of Americans supported at first, never imagining that it would still be going on all these years later. Within a couple more months, President Bush identified Iraq as part of the "axis of evil" in his 2002 State of the Union address. By that fall, it was clear that Bush and his team were pressing for another war, this one much more divisive.

The 2000s were the first decade when we began to associate political leanings with certain lifestyle and consumer preferences, and with where one chose to live. It was in 2000 that David Brooks published *Bobos in Paradise*, his sharply original analysis of the new class of "bourgeois bohemians" whose lifestyle combined an embrace of resplendent capitalism with an adherence to certain countercultural values. Before too long, the kind of car one drove, music one listened to, and salad greens one preferred were taken as indicators of political identification. It nearly goes without saying that when churned through the crude sausage grinder of political journalism, these choices were never equal in terms of the moral weight they purported to carry. The simpler, more straightforward choices (Branson, iceberg lettuce) were the preferences of "real" Americans, while the fussier alternatives (Sonoma County, arugula) marked their adherents as elitists.

In Congress, the period from 2000 to 2010 saw striking changes. For one thing, the decade nearly wiped out the very idea of the Southern Democratic senator. When the decade began, there were eight Democratic senators from the eleven former Confederate states. By the time of the 112th Congress, which was elected in 2010, that eight was cut in half down to four. By 2015, it was down to three, and two of those were from Virginia, which over the course of the decade became a much bluer (and less culturally Southern) state because of the explosive growth of the Washington suburbs of northern Virginia. As of late 2017, there was one more, Doug Jones of Alabama. He narrowly beat an accused pedo-phile, which shows just how bad things have to get for Southerners to decide to send a Democrat to the Senate. Likewise, the New England Republican has virtually disappeared. In 1989, ten out of twenty-four House members from the six New England states were Republicans. By 2017, there was one.

By 2010, the *National Journal*, the respected Congress-watching publication, found that the then-seated 111th Congress was more polar-ized than any before it. For many years, the *Journal* had rated every sena-tor on an ideological continuum. In the old days, there was much overlap between the parties—several Democrats more conservative than the most liberal Republican, and several Republicans more liberal than the most conservative Democrat. As years went along, the overlap decreased. By 2010, the most conservative Democratic senator, Ben Nelson of Nebraska, had a voting record that still put him to the left of the Senate's most liberal Republicans—Olympia Snowe and Susan Collins of Maine, and Ohio's George Voinovich. No more Senate overlap. Also that year, the ideological overlap almost disappeared in the 435-member House, consisting of just five Republicans and four Democrats who formed an overlapping subset in the middle. Back in 1999, even after the Gingrich era, more than half of all House members compiled a voting record that had placed them in between the most conservative Democrat and the most liberal Republican. Half. By 2010, that overlap was all but gone.[38] Congresses have just been getting more partisan ever since.

All this happened, as the foregoing paragraphs suggest, because of changes in the media landscape and other broader changes in the cul-ture. But it also happened for another very specific reason: the hundreds of millions of new dollars spent on electoral politics by just a handful of extremely rich and extremely conservative players, most notably the Koch brothers. The Kochs began putting money into politics in the 1970s. But that was on idea creation and dissemination, and to some extent grassroots activity, through Americans for Prosperity (AFP) and other groups. They did not put money into *electoral* politics—supporting Republican candidates through independent committees—until fairly recently. Theda Skocpol of Harvard, who has tracked Koch spend-ing closely, states that the Kochs spent essentially nothing on electoral politics up through 2006, then spent just under $100 million in 2008, an amount that went up steadily to about $750 million in 2016.[39] This spending made them first-tier players. For years, they'd held wonkish policy retreats that drew donors and policy thinkers. By 2009, writes Jane Mayer in her meticulous *Dark Money*, the retreats were attracting the likes of Antonin Scalia, Clarence Thomas, senators, House members, and media stars.[40]

The impact of all this spending on the Republican Party has been both profound and clear. The Kochs and their associates are interested in a handful of issues: low taxation, less regulation (especially on polluters), reduced entitlement spending, lower social-welfare spending, and anything that will help cripple unions. Republicans already supported all these things, of course; but they have learned in these last few years that the more they hold the line on these issues, and the more aggressively and creatively they pursue them, the more access to Koch money—which, thanks to *Citizens United*, is unlimited—they will have. The Kochs have even taken a page from Grover Norquist's book and cooked up a "No Climate Tax" pledge, which they have compelled more than half of the GOP legislators in Congress to sign. Their power within the GOP is such, write Skocpol and Alexander Hertel-Fernandez, that they constitute a veritable third political party. "Yet AFP is not a separate political party," they write. "It is, instead, organized to parallel and leverage the Republican Party" and to pull GOP officeholders "to the far right on political-economic issues."[41]

So the parties have grown more polarized, which is usually the whole story when it's told by most political journalists. But it's only half the story. The other half of the story, and indeed the more important half, is the *way* the parties have become polarized. Because they are not simply mirror images of each other. This is a crucial point that even many fairly close observers of politics either don't understand or dismiss.

The two parties are totally different creatures. As I noted earlier, Gingrich was the leader of an insurgency toppling an establishment. That has been the mindset of movement conservatism since the late 1970s. It is, after all, a *movement*. And it has taken over the Republican Party almost completely. Therefore, the Republican Party is a movement party. That makes it a unique thing in American history, at least for major parties. As we saw previously, our parties have been amalgams of interests; have even contained different movements within themselves. But today's GOP basically *is* the conservative movement.

The Democratic Party, meanwhile, is a different kind of vehicle. It's a patchwork of the various interest groups that have come into being over the last forty or fifty years. They're all liberal to one degree or another, but they're too disparate to add up to a movement. The distinction is well and thoroughly explained by Matt Grossman and David A. Hopkins in their book *Asymmetric Politics*. Their thesis states: "While the Democratic Party is fundamentally a group coalition, the Republican Party can be most accurately characterized as the vehicle of an ideological movement."[42]

This difference affects nearly everything both parties, and their candidates, do. To take an obvious and very public example: You've noticed, I'm sure, that Democratic candidates are great laundry-listers. Their speeches name cause after cause, issue after issue. When they name one group of Americans, they have to name six. These tics are no coincidence or accident; they reflect what the party is. Democratic speechwriters down in the boiler room know that the boss's speech will need to check exactly twenty-three (or whatever) boxes. So they check them. Republican politicians' speeches are not like this. Republicans have far fewer interest groups. Think about it. There's no conservative environmental group, or conservative antipoverty group, or conservative transgender rights group, or a dozen other things. The conservative policy agenda is far narrower than the liberal policy agenda. To be a liberal in good standing these days, you have to be affirmatively for a large number of different things. To be a conservative, you have to believe in only two things: less government, and a strong defense (in the age of Donald Trump, I've tossed—or rather, the Republicans themselves have tossed—"traditional values"). So Republicans don't have to give speeches that pat a dozen different interest groups on the head.

The Republicans are an ideological party. This is true not only at the leadership level, but at the rank-and-file level. Indeed, it's true at the leadership level precisely *because* it's true at the rank-and-file level. Political leaders (quite badly misnamed in this sense) follow the will of their voters, as we have seen so excessively during the Trump era. And the

Republican base wants ideological purity far more than the Democratic base does. Grossman and Hopkins adduce reams of evidence to support the point. They gathered Pew data from 2008 to 2014 on the question of whether members of both parties prefer ideological purity to moderation. Republicans top Democrats on this by 58 to 41 percent. On preferring principles over compromise, Republicans top Democrats 54 to 36 percent. On liking politicians who make compromises to get the job done, 88 percent of Democrats said they did, while only 70 percent of Republicans said the same.[43] Similarly, they find (using 2012 data) that about 50 percent of rank-and-file Republicans call themselves "conservative" or "extremely conservative," while just 25 percent of rank-and-file Democrats say they're "liberal" or "extremely liberal"; also, 31 percent of Democrats, but only 19 percent of Republicans, call themselves "moderate."[44]

The authors also note when asked to define politics, "Strong Democratic identifiers consistently describe politics as a competition among social groups for favorable concrete policies and benefits, whereas strong Republicans explain the salient differences between the parties as concerning a more abstract conflict over the proper role of government."[45] Not surprisingly, legislators in both parties have responded to their bases' demands. I return here to the research of congressional voting by Keith Poole, Nolan McCarty, and Howard Rosenthal. They score congressional votes on a scale on which 0 represents perfect moderation; they then plot roll-call votes to see how far both parties diverge from 0 in their voting patterns (the Republicans above the mean, and the Democrats below it). They find that over about the last thirty years, the Democrats have gone from -.3 to -.4; farther away from the middle. The Republicans, however, have zoomed away from the middle, from +.3 to +.75.[46] In other words, Democrats became 33 percent more left, while Republicans became 150 percent more right.

They're just different beasts. This shouldn't be so shocking. But it has been hard for people to accept because it defies most of American political science for the last five or six decades, which has generally (with some notable exceptions) discussed political parties as if they are all the same and respond to stimuli in the same way. They did. But they don't any longer. It's certainly been hard for many political journalists to accept because, aware of their own personal liberal biases, they want to be fair to conservatives; or failing that, they at least fear being attacked by conservatives if they show signs of bias. So journalists are hesitant to say that Republicans are more ideological. It sounds like an aspersion. But it's not. It's simply a descriptive statement, supported by data.

And Finally, Obama and Trump

The most fundamental and consequential difference between Democrats and Republicans, liberals and conservatives, is not about ideology or issues or taxes. It's psychological. Conservatives, despite the fact that they control every branch of government as this book is written, still think of themselves as an insurgency, a brave minority resisting the social changes forced on them by the elite establishment; standing athwart history yelling stop, to use Bill Buckley's oft-quoted phrase from 1955 that is just getting more apt each year. Liberals don't see things that way at all. Liberals want more change still, but they want it to be managed in a prudent way (I mean here mainstream liberals, as distinct from Bernie Sanders–style leftists). Liberals want to fix the house up. Conservatives want to burn it down and build a new one.

This brings us to our current era, and the Obama and Trump presidencies. It's interesting to observe how well each man reflects the condition and nature of the party that nominated him.

Conservatives tried very hard to turn Barack Obama into a crazy radical, and a lot of shameless people made a lot of money doing it. But the narrative never took outside hard-shell conservative circles, and it never took because that's not what your average person saw when he or she looked at Obama. He's a liberal, certainly; he is practically a walking embodiment of coalitional liberal politics, and the coalition he put together to get to the White House of young people, urbanites, people of color, and well-educated white professionals was quite liberal. But even so he was no ideological warrior. Recall the beginning days of his presidency, which were more exasperating to the far left than to the far right: He refused to prosecute any Bush administration officials over the war; his Justice Department pursued no high-profile cases against the bank CEOs who caused the meltdown; he didn't nationalize the banks; he invited the conservative minister Rick Warren to deliver the convocation at his inaugural.

In the beginning, he actually thought he could unite the country. He gave interviews in 2008 saying that he thought that maybe because he wasn't a member of the Woodstock/Vietnam generation, Republicans might not be quite so irate at him as they were at the Clintons. I half believed this myself, I remember. Obviously, it was a very naïve view. We're going to keep fighting over the sixties for as long as the country keeps changing. Besides, Obama was—how to put it?—black. A big chunk of the GOP base never got over this, and elected Republicans never pushed back adequately or responsibly against "birtherism" and all the rest of it.

Obama was genuinely shocked to see the Republican opposition be as implacable as it was. It took him aback, and it seemed to take him years to figure out that they really meant it and weren't going to change. He made his mistakes, too, of course. It can fairly be said of a man who lived his life in Honolulu, Los Angeles, New York City, and Chicago that he didn't have much of a feel for the America that the media keep telling us is the "real" one. Hence that hideous verb "cling," in the infamous quote from his first campaign about how rural people who fear cultural change "cling to guns or religion or antipathy to people who aren't like them." He was quite wrong to say the Cambridge, Massachusetts, police "acted stupidly" in arresting Harvard professor Henry Louis Gates Jr. at his home. The policeman arguably did act stupidly, or in a biased fashion, as reports seemed to indicate his disbelief that a black man could own a nice house off Harvard Square. But a president shouldn't have been the one to say so, especially with race involved.

Police officers weren't part of the Obama coalition, and this provides a representative expression of the broader shortcoming of that coalition, and of twenty-first-century American liberalism more generally. Liberalism became so identified with those Obama parts of America that it shrank to such a point that it had no footing in vast swaths of the country that weren't part of Obamaland. This surely has something to do with the fact that Democrats and mainstream liberals like Hillary Clinton were shocked to discover in 2016 the depths of the white working-class anger that was out there—although in fairness to Obama it has to be noted that he pressed hard, for example, for the kind of infrastructure spending that might have helped that America. And he even proposed it without a tax increase. But the Republicans wouldn't cooperate with him on it because their strategy was to give him no victories.

Whomever one blames, the fact is that the Democratic Party's map shrunk severely by 2016. In 2009, the Democratic Party was dominant in the House of Representatives and competitive at the state level in a number of states we tend to think of as red (there were Democratic governors that year in Tennessee, Oklahoma, Arkansas, Kansas, and Wyoming). By the time Obama left office, the Democrats were the congressional minority, and at the level of state politics, Republicans were in their strongest position since the 1920s.[47] This culminated in Hillary Clinton winning just 487 out of the country's 3,141 counties (a mere 16 percent) in the 2016 election.[48] Obama made history, and he left office with a 59 percent approval rating[49]—no mean feat in this divided age. And in the sense that he helped steer the economy back from the brink of disaster and saw through to reality some important progressive goals like the passage of universal health-care legislation and the legalization of same-sex marriage, he did fix up the house. But as far as his party's fortunes were concerned, he lopped a floor off of it.

As for Trump, there are conservatives who like to say he's an aberration, but in fact he's the embodiment of what the Republican Party let itself become over the course of these last thirty years: a movement in which rage against liberal elites, against political correctness—a phrase that means many different things but generally refers to codes of speech and thought liberals are said, sometimes accurately and sometimes inaccurately, to be forcing on society—is by far the dominant gene. Not much else matters. Tax cuts matter, some. But little else. As long as Trump seems to be offending liberal opinion, and taking the occasional poke at black people and immigrants—pokes that, psychically, are really still aimed at outraging white liberals—his constituents will adore him. This is why he is permitted his various departures from conservative orthodoxy. It's why even his promises aren't taken too seriously by his backers. The wall is a perfect example. Would they like to see it built? Sure. But if it's not, Trump's hard-shell supporters will make two rationalizations in their minds, perhaps not explicitly but instinctually: first, that the wall is more important as metaphor than as actual brick-and-mortar thing—it represents Trump's commitment to the worldview that people like them are under attack; and second, to the extent that Trump fails in building it, that will be effortlessly chalked up to the undermining liberal elites and media who want this country to fail.

Trump doesn't merely sow division. He depends on it, wouldn't exist without it. As I write these sentences, it's impossible to know where the Trump presidency and the country are headed. It seems more likely than not that this will not end especially well for either entity. But it must always be remembered that the mess Trump makes couldn't have happened without the mess that preceded him—a mess that has deep historical roots, and that seems, most days, completely and utterly unfixable.

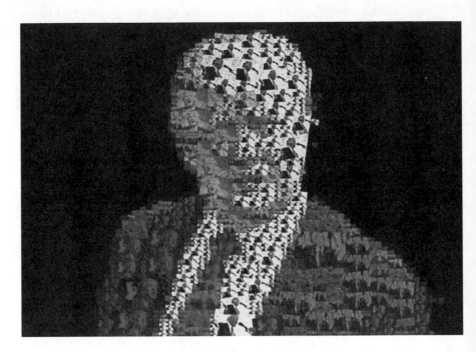

Everywhere, all the time.

OLI GOLDSMITH.

SEVEN

If We Can Keep It

A Fourteen-Point Agenda
to Reduce Polarization

★

The Four Ages of the United States • Fixes to the
Political System • The Most Important Project in
American Politics • Trump • If We Can Keep It

The Four Ages of the United States

THE STORY I'VE TRIED TO TELL IN THE FIRST SIX CHAPTERS OF this book is a story about our country that's real. It's darker than the story that we learned in school and that most Americans carry around in their heads. But it's also the story of an ambitious and audacious nation that was the first on the planet to lay out for itself some noble ideals and that has succeeded at key moments in living up to them.

If We Can Keep It has shown that we've been beset by divisions, very deep and difficult divisions, from the start. The battles between today's blue staters and red staters are surprisingly close in spirit to the feuding between Hamiltonians and Jeffersonians in our country's first days. Certain other disputes even predate our first days—questions about how to set up our representative government, most notably. Certain customs we've stuck to weren't the product of a grand design, but instead were matters to which little thought was given at first, such as the creation of single-member legislative districts, which were just kind of inherited from England and are a global outlier, used to elect national legislatures in only a few advanced countries. Certain of our methods of self-governance weren't acts of brilliance consummated by men of great genius and foresight, as we were taught in grade school; they were hard-won compromises that sometimes pleased no one but were the best they could do under the circumstances.

Notable here is the Connecticut Compromise, struck during the 1787 Constitutional Convention, which created the Senate and the House of Representatives. It's emblematic of the way we've been taught to think about these things that the Connecticut Compromise is also widely known as the *Great* Compromise. But no one thought it was so great at the time. It passed by a one-vote margin of 5–4–1. What if it had failed? What if the representatives of the large states (who mostly opposed it) had been unyielding and said no, as they considered doing the next day? It's hard to know, but in any case, the point is that it was an outcome that no one was thrilled about. The United States of America is different in this regard from other countries, the European nations we feel closest to. Those countries are centuries old, and the framework of their laws and procedures took shape over the course of those centuries. The framework of our laws and procedures was written by fifty-five men over the course of four months in an intensely political and very high-pressure process. So the United States has always been a compromise, and often a distasteful one, especially on the topic of slavery, which was countenanced by many men, men who were indeed great in other ways but who knew better.

I think of our history as consisting of four ages. First came the Age of Creation, which lasted from the Constitutional Convention through the Civil War. This is when the republic was under formation. We had this new nation and constitution. We had all this land, these endless vistas of land to the West, which settlers struck out for and turned into territories (usually at high cost to the indigenous populations) and eventually states. We had a fast-growing and transforming economy. But most of all, we had one great and terrible matter to settle: the evil of slavery, which the founders had put off in the interest of forming the republic. For decades, antislavery politicians, like Martin Van Buren, continued to brush the matter to the side and let the South have its way, as Van Buren did in the 1820s when he put together the coalition that became the Democratic

Party. Three decades later, the antislavery men (and women, like Harriet Beecher Stowe, arguably the most influential novelist in American history, at least in terms of impact on the political discourse) had had enough; they could no longer brush it aside. With Van Buren now firmly among their number, they knew that a country that permitted slavery anywhere could not rightly call itself a republic.

One exchange summarizes the moral stakes well. In late 1858, Stephen Douglas, planning an 1860 presidential run and trying to pander to Southern voters and unite the then-divided Democratic Party, went on a speaking tour down South. In Memphis that December, he criticized the notion of a firm latitudinal line deciding the slavery question, the line that had been designated in the Missouri Compromise of thirty-eight years prior. He said, in essence, that the nation could exist half-slave and half-free. "The Almighty had drawn a line on the continent," he said, on one side of which the soil would be tilled by slave labor, and on the other side by "white labor." That line didn't run "inflexibly" along the 36°30' parallel but "meandered through the border states and territories" according to the self-interest of the white inhabitants. Four months later, in a speech in Chicago, Abraham Lincoln issued his response:[1]

> Suppose it is true that the Almighty has drawn a line across this continent, on the south side of which part of the people will hold the rest as slaves; that the Almighty ordered this; that it is right, unchangeably right, that men ought there to be held as slaves, and that their fellow men will always have the right to hold them as slaves. I ask you, this once admitted, how can you believe that it is not right for us, or for them coming here, to hold slaves on this other side of the line?

That little excerpt could be read as the speaker endorsing slavery everywhere, but the speaker was Abraham Lincoln, and his meaning was the opposite. In other words, said Lincoln—this was nine months after his famous "house divided" speech—if part of the republic is slave, then all of it is slave. And that is unacceptable. Six years and 620,000 deaths later, the country was cleansed of its original sin and finally deserved the name republic. (And it's always worth remembering how full of accidents and strokes of luck history is—Lincoln won in 1860 in part because Douglas failed to unite the Democratic Party, and Southern Democrats ran their own man, John Breckinridge, while the mid-South states backed a fourth candidate; if Douglas had united all these forces and won, slavery would have continued, and the war put off.)

The second age we might call the Age of Power, in two senses. First, it was the age when great power was first amassed in this country. It was the time of the Industrial Revolution, when modern social classes first took shape. It was the Gilded Age, the era of the first great fortunes in America, held by men whose power over what we now call the 99 percent was abetted by Congress (especially the Senate, which was dominated by a few wealthy men), a string of pro–Wall Street Republican presidents, and the Supreme Court, whose 1905 decision *Lochner v. New York* upheld by a 5–4 vote employers' rights to "freedom of contract" and thereby struck down (along with other similar decisions) federal and state laws that sought to regulate working conditions. Thus was political and economic power in the fast-growing country concentrated in few hands. The great battles of the era—between labor unions and owners, between Teddy Roosevelt (the one president of the era who challenged wealth) and the trusts—were all about this concentration of power. Power almost always won.

In the second sense, it was the age when the United States first became a world power, after its entry into World War I and the guiding role—and catastrophic one, as it would turn out—that Woodrow Wilson played in forging the peace at Versailles. Often in human history, war is what historians and economists call a "great leveler"—that is, its consequences for a society are so terrible and overpowering that it reshapes the society in profound and permanent ways. This certainly happened in several of the nations of Europe, where history was dramatically rewritten to punish those who'd been responsible for all those utterly pointless deaths. In the war's wake, the German kaiser was replaced by a republic (all too feeble, alas), the Tsar in Russia was toppled by a communist dictatorship, the Austrian Hapsburgs were stripped of the crown and their empire broken up into several independent nations. But nothing like this happened in the United States after 1918. The losses sustained weren't great enough for World War I to have that effect here. Our human losses (116,000, more from disease than actual combat) were small compared to those of the European powers; our soil was not ravaged as France's was; and hey, we won.

So after the war, the United States returned to business as usual, the ruling class picking up right where it had left off. Power and wealth became more and more concentrated, almost completely unchecked by any countervailing force. Into the bargain, New York replaced London as the world financial capital, so there were even greater fortunes to be made. Yes, there was enough wealth and enough technological innovation that some of the bounty was spread around, but not very much of it. It all went great until, on October 29, 1929, it didn't. The country, and the world, sank into depression.

The Depression helped bring on the third age, the Age of Consensus, characterized by the growth of the concepts the "American Dream" and the "American way of life," even in the midst of economic depression, and the way that corporate, labor, civic, and religious leaders, along with entertainment moguls and stars, worked to get Americans to believe in these notions. They didn't all have the same vision of this way of life. Far from it. The New Deal was heavily contested and bitterly fought. But the key point is this: Even the forces that opposed the New Deal knew that unchecked capitalism had failed. A 1928 newspaper ad for GOP presidential candidate Herbert Hoover bragged: "Republican prosperity has *reduced* hours and *increased* earning capacity, silenced *discontent*, put the proverbial 'chicken in every pot.' And a car in every backyard, to boot."[2] But after the following October, Republicans couldn't talk like that for a long time to come; they and the business interests they represented had to offer a new story to people, a story to compete with Franklin Roosevelt's, about how broad prosperity was to be achieved.

It's a striking paradox that this faith in the American way became unshakable during precisely the decade when the country was grappling with the gravest economic crisis in its history. But then again, maybe that makes sense. Crisis fixes the mind. For the same kinds of psychological reasons that a good football team might play poorly against a mediocre rival, a people might not necessarily rouse themselves to meet a modest challenge, but will surely resolve to answer a great one. It was precisely when things were at their worst that people needed to believe in the American way the most.

Then came the seminal event of the twentieth century—World War II. The first war had been no leveler, but this one surely was. Everyone was affected, and everyone pitched in—scrimping housewives, victory gardeners, 4-F men leading town rubber drives, and even the rich, who now paid strikingly more in income tax to support the war effort. And once Hitler and Tojo were vanquished and Stalin became the new enemy, the perceived need for consensus still held fast among both the elites and most of the people. In some ways, it intensified in the 1950s. It intensified in part because by now, the broad parameters of the New Deal were more widely accepted, especially after Eisenhower embraced them. And it intensified as the men who'd fought the war found their way to Washington. This new phenomenon, this awareness of the need to nurture American civic life, wasn't limited to politicians reporting to work in Washington. Around 16 million men, along with 350,000 women, served in the armed forces during the war. That was 12 percent of the total population, and nearly 20 percent of the adult population between ages 18 and 65[3] (it's never been as high as 1 percent of the total population in recent years, even as we fought two wars). As those millions of young men returned to civilian life and assumed their places in society and then began to take leadership positions at their jobs and raise their families, they made for a generation that believed in the consensus without reservation.

This third age was defined by reduced polarization, at least after the 1930s. That made it different from the first two ages. But even with that important difference, the third age had one big thing in common with the first two ages: that our two major parties were divided within themselves as much as they were divided against each other. The Democrats were split chiefly between liberals and segregationists, while the Republican division was between the dominant moderate-liberal wing and the upstart conservatives who began building their movement in the 1950s.

Then the 1960s arrived, and with them, the central political development in this country of the last fifty years—the great ideological sorting out of the parties over issues of race, war, feminism, immigration, the law, and an economy that no longer delivered for workers the way it had since the 1940s. Those who'd been left out of the consensus wanted in, but it turned out that they met with a lot of resistance, especially once the economy started faltering. And so we entered, at first slowly and fitfully, and by the early 1990s with accelerating speed, the fourth age, for which I'll borrow the name of the extraordinary recent book by the Princeton historian Daniel T. Rodgers, from which I quoted earlier: the Age of Fracture. The fracturing has been not just political, but economic, as we became a far more consumption-driven culture and as the United States changed from a society in which prosperity was broadly shared to one that the economists Robert Frank and Philip Cook named the "winner-take-all society": one in which "a handful of top performers walk away with the lion's share of total rewards," and not just in fields like entertainment, but in "law, journalism, consulting, investment banking, corporate management, design, fashion, even the hallowed halls of academe."[4]

And so here we've sat, for a quarter-century now, in this ever-worsening Age of Fracture. Politicians keep insisting to us that they hope to work together in a bipartisan fashion. Presidential candidates keep promising to try to heal our divisions, or least George W. Bush and Barack Obama both did; I give Donald Trump a perverse kind of credit for so bluntly acknowledging that he has no such intention.

Division is the American condition. About a decade ago, I used to think that a new depression and world war would return us to a state of some harmony. Not that I was cheering for them to happen, but I thought at least they'd yield that silver lining. I no longer believe this. We're not the same people we were in the 1930s and '40s. We're too stratified and too materialistic. As I noted earlier, today's better-off Americans would never sit still for something like rationing. And unless the morality of the war were absolutely crystal clear, we'd be at loggerheads about it from the start. This would be, let's face it, especially true if it were a Democratic president who got us involved in the hostilities—the conservative media, which knows only attack mode, would be full of reasons about how it was all preventable or brought on by the weakness and implicit anti-American posture of the incumbent. A colleague once joked to me that maybe an alien invasion could unify the country, but the more we thought about it, the more even that scenario fell apart. If we were invaded by the green people of Planet Zanthon, in time, we'd discover something about life on Zanthon—say, that the green majority was oppressing a restive purple minority. From there, it wouldn't be long before Fox News was agitating for a white-green interplanetary alliance to beat back the black-brown-purple hordes. No—for now, we're stuck here.

What, if anything, can be done about it? There are some ways out of this mess. But before we get to those, two points must be made. First, it's useless to hope that politicians can just go back to getting along the way they once did. They didn't get along better in the old days because they were nicer people, or because they once had the will to do so. They got along better because a particular set of historical forces and circumstances produced a degree of social cohesion that called on them to cooperate more. Today, a totally different set of historical forces and circumstances exist, and they produce social atomization rather than social cohesion. Our politicians can't overcome that. I'm sure the 2018 party leaders in the House of Representatives, Nancy Pelosi and Paul Ryan, are at least as nice as Sam Rayburn and Joe Martin were (the respective Democratic and Republican House leaders back in the consensus era), and I'm sure they'd prefer to cooperate more. But social and institutional forces don't permit it. So being romantic about how "they" were "better" in the "good old days" is both inaccurate and a waste of time.

I should also pause here to give fair consideration to a question some people ask during such discussions, to wit: Is this really so bad? Maybe all this division is fine. Maybe it's good, as Franklin Roosevelt suggested to Wendell Willkie, that the people have two clear choices placed before them. So maybe there's nothing to "fix" here at all.

This is not an unserious position. It was a strange, or at least unusual, thing to have parties that blurred ideological distinctions. No other country did, historically. In an odd sort of way, the Europeans moved a bit in our direction as we moved in theirs. That is, their parties nudged away from their old fixed identities to some extent. In France, for example, François Mitterrand's mid-1980s "U-Turn" away from the left started a process that over time reduced the differences between the main left and right parties (and, by the way, helped give rise to the far-right, anti-immigrant National Front). In Italy, the Five Star Movement arose as an explicit left-right mishmash. Here in America, we've done the opposite. And I think most of us would agree that the rancor has gotten rather out of hand. And because poisonous atmospheres tend to reward dispensers of poison, it's just going to get worse until some awful breaking point is reached.

So I do think there is something to fix here. My position, though, is that we don't want an *end* to polarization. We want some polarization, but we want manageable polarization. We want clear differences between the parties, but not differences so vast that the members of Team A think it's an existential crisis if Team B wins. I don't even know if that sweet spot exists, let alone whether we can find it and agree to live in it. But it's where a well-functioning democracy has to live.

There are no easy and quick fixes. It took us a quarter of a century to dig this hole, and we'll need another quarter-century—at least—to dig out.

Reform Agenda to Reduce Polarization

Fixes to the Political System

So now we get to the "answers" part of *If We Can Keep It*. This section is itself divided into four sections, and it will include some political fixes as well as some suggestions that go well beyond the political realm. As the previous chapter revealed, politics is a lagging indicator of change. Politicians don't usually lead the way to change. They drink from that trough only when forced to. When social forces and conditions no longer tolerate this kind of polarization, then politicians will react, and they will change. That has to be driven by others, as I'll argue later in this chapter.

Nevertheless, there are some changes to our political system that we could contemplate that might help ease the situation. Most of these aren't especially realistic, to be honest, at least in the near future; but we have a dire situation, and we have to think outside the box and be open to making root-and-branch changes to the political system. Far from disliking this, the founders, I think, would have approved; isn't that exactly what they did?

★

1. END PARTISAN GERRYMANDERING

If you asked 1,000 close political observers to name one concrete fix that could alleviate polarization, I'd guess that less partisan gerrymandering would top the poll. Districts are drawn now with such detailed knowledge about where the Democrats live and where the Republicans live that state legislators, who draw the districts in most states after every census, can stack the deck enormously in their party's favor. And while both parties do this, Republicans do it more by virtue of the simple fact that they control more state legislatures. Consider this little fact. In the wake of Doug Jones's historic win in the Alabama Senate race in 2017, it was reported that if that same turnout had elected Alabama's delegation to the House of Representatives, it would have changed . . . nothing. Alabama is represented by six Republicans and one Democrat. So think of it: The turnout that elected a Democrat to the Senate from Alabama for the first time since 1992, a heavily African-American electorate, would not have gained the Democrats a single House seat (assuming people voted the same way).⁵ That's how precisely these districts are drawn.

Or consider the well-known case of Pennsylvania. At the time of the last redistricting (2011–2012), Democratic presidential candidates had carried Pennsylvania five straight times. Enrolled Democrats outnumbered Republicans in the state by 1.2 million. In 2008–09, the state's delegation to the House of Representatives reflected those advantages, if perhaps a bit inequitably: twelve Democrats, seven Republicans. But the Republicans won the statehouse in 2010 as part of the Tea Party wave, and with it the right to draw the map. The result after the 2012 elections was thirteen Republicans to five Democrats (the state lost one seat). The Republicans scored their resounding legislative win, by the way, in the very same election in which Barack Obama beat Mitt Romney by 310,000 votes in the state, and in which Democratic House candidates collectively won 2.7 million votes to Republicans' 2.6 million.⁶ The Pennsylvania State Supreme Court invalidated the lines in 2018, and the U.S. Supreme Court refused to overrule the state court. The same thing happened in North Carolina, Michigan, Wisconsin, Iowa, and other states, where districts have been drawn to ensure Republican dominance and high incumbent reelection rates.

The solution some seek is to take the redistricting power out of the hands of state legislatures and give it to independent commissions. Yes, the commissioners would be appointed by politicians and would themselves be party members, but the thought is that at least they would be slightly insulated from the mud wrestling that often goes on in state legislatures. Several states have set up such commissions: California, Arizona, New Jersey, Washington, a few others. Whether these commissions will change anything won't really be known until after the next redistricting, in time for the 2022 elections. It's worth noting that this is one area of law in which the normally conservative Supreme Court has been handing down liberal decisions. The Court upheld the existence of Arizona's independent commission in a 2015 decision in which Anthony Kennedy joined the Court's four liberals in rebuffing a Republican challenge, and it has taken what can fairly be called the liberal side of the argument in three other recent decisions, whose majority opinions were written by Elena Kagan, Ruth Bader Ginsburg, and Stephen Breyer.

A less politicized redistricting process can help around the margins by producing districts (and representatives) that are less hyperpartisan. In some parts of the country, independent commissions could draw genuinely competitive districts that would be more likely to produce more moderate winners, from whichever party, because the winner would have to have received some votes from independents and voters of the other party. But partisan districting also reflects in part the way we've grouped ourselves, with liberals living among liberals and conservatives among conservatives. And if we are to preserve "majority-minority" districts to ensure the election of minority-group representatives (as we should), that will mean that the surrounding districts will be heavily white, and that will maintain the status quo in and around most cities. So there are limits on how much reform this change can produce.

★

2. BRING BACK AT-LARGE CONGRESSIONAL ELECTIONS

Meanwhile, here's a much more interesting idea: Why don't we revisit the whole concept of single-member districts? They are inherently and definitionally unfair, leaving a significant chunk of a given district's citizens with their views completely unrepresented. They are not mandated by the Constitution, and some states used to use "general-ticket" voting, which we now call "at-large" voting. What if we were to return— and I'm well aware that this is politically unfeasible for now, but just go with me on the thought experiment—to some at-large voting? Say, for example, that states with more than a minimum number of districts— six, perhaps—had to elect their congressional delegations half by district, and half at large, either from the entire state or, if a large state, from commonsensical, nongerrymandered regions? This notion of regions is at the core of what is called multimember voting, under which legislators are elected from larger districts—three per district, say—and which is actually used in some state legislatures. (And I should note that the choice of how exactly to do it would be left up to the states.)

Let's think about New York in this hypothetical. Right now, New York has twenty-seven congressional districts, with eighteen Democrats and nine Republicans. Now let's say I waved my wand and only fourteen of New York's representatives were chosen from individual districts, and the other thirteen were elected from three different geographic entities: five from Long Island, Queens, and Staten Island; four from Manhattan, Brooklyn, the Bronx, and two or three suburban counties up through the lower Hudson Valley; and four from the rest of the state (one would have to study the population distribution, but this seems roughly fair to me). What would such a system produce? Probably a few more Republicans! Certainly, the first region would tilt somewhat Republican. And at least one of the four at-large representatives from the Manhattan-Hudson region would likely be a Republican, meaning that Manhattan would see Republican representation in Congress for the first time since the tenure of a man named Bill Green, a supermarket-fortune heir and dyed-in-the-wool moderate Republican whose later campaigns in the 1990s I covered as a young reporter. And that's the point. This person would probably be from the Hudson Valley, but he or she would have to be more moderate than your average House Republican to have garnered enough votes to win the seat. And the upstate New York region would certainly lean Republican, but upstate New York has enough urban areas that this district would typically elect one at-large Democrat, who would again be more moderate than your standard Democrat.

Replicate this all over the country and what happens? You have a chance at having maybe fifteen or more Republicans who would not sign Grover Norquist's pledge and would play some legislative ball with Democrats at budget time. It's also reasonable to assume that a lot of these new Republicans would take middle-ground positions on guns and would not live in fear of the National Rifle Association. Fifteen may not sound like much, but when we're talking congressional votes, fifteen is a lot—maybe enough to swing an outcome. Concomitantly, you'd have that many fewer very conservative Republicans and very liberal Democrats from ultrasafe districts, many of which would be eliminated.

I'm well aware of the resistance a scheme like this would face, which is to say, right now, it's basically unimaginable. But things change. If some group of bipartisan rich people liked this idea and put serious money behind it and kept at it patiently but doggedly, persuading the public of its benefits, and if a future president endorsed such a change, it's not inconceivable that Congress might be forced to consider it in time for the 2030 census. And remember, it's just a matter of changing a law—undoing the 1967 law that mandated single-member districts—not passing a constitutional amendment.

3. INTRODUCE RANKED-CHOICE VOTING

There is, in fact, a bill in Congress that would do something very like what I sketch out above, sponsored by Don Beyer, a Democrat of northern Virginia, long known in the capital district for his eponymous car dealerships. It would allow states to create multimember districts, and it would allow voters to rank candidates in order of preference.[7] "Ranked-choice" voting is a good idea, too, and in fact a necessary component of any changes like the one I'm discussing. In this system, voters don't vote just for one candidate; they rank them all from first choice to last. The idea behind it is this: Candidates will work harder to ensure that voters who aren't in their corner will hopefully rank them second or third, which means they have to make themselves more acceptable to an ideologically wider swath of voters. Its proponents argue that ranked-choice voting also reduces negative campaigning, because if you want voters who aren't for you to rank you second or third, you're probably less likely to run a negative campaign—to be seen as the race's mud-slinger. Of course, most mud these days is slung by noncandidate operations fueled by dark money, so I'm not wholly persuaded of this claim. But certainly candidates running under a system in which every voter in the district or region or state got to rank them first choice to last would have some incentive to campaign in such a way as to ensure that the voters who don't support them also don't despise them. And once elected, they'd have some incentive to legislate and vote in such a way as to ensure that as few voters as possible hated them, which would mean they'd be casting fewer polarizing votes.

Beyer introduced his bill in 2017, so it hasn't gone anywhere and probably won't for some time, but it deserves the attention and support of concerned citizens. It's very hard to convince people that something like the way we elect Congress should be different. It's like convincing people that lightbulbs should be different. But we've done that! It took a decade, and inevitably enough, some conservatives saw in the new lightbulbs a socialist plot (not a joke; a conservative political action committee fundraising appeal, invoking President Obama, warned in 2011 that "a silly little light bulb is merely a small piece of the larger puzzle of global socialism that he feels is his agenda to enslave the American people").[8] But most people use them now un-grumpily. So it would go with this change.

4. EXPAND—YES!—THE HOUSE OF REPRESENTATIVES (UNDER ONE CONDITION)

While I'm tossing pies in the sky, here's another thought. The House of Representatives has been at 435 members since after the 1910 census. The population in 1910 was 92 million. Today it's 320 million. A congressman in 1910 represented about 260,000 people. Today, one represents more than 700,000. The founders intended the lower house to be close to the people. It's awfully hard for a representative to be close to 730,000 people. I'm well aware that "Hey, let's make Congress bigger!" is a line that . . . well, there aren't enough rotten tomatoes in all of America to arm all the people who'd want to pelt me with them. But there needs to be a balance between the size of a legislature and the size of legislators' constituencies. Compare our House to the U.K.'s House of Commons, one of the few other legislatures in the developed world whose members are chosen from single-member districts. It holds 650 members, each representing around 100,000 constituents. The 577 members of the French Assembly each represent around 115,000 people. The 150 members of Australia's House of Representatives each represent on average around 160,000 people. At those sizes, a legislator can know his or her district very intimately, which is just what our founders intended.

We can't go that small—going down to 100,000 constituents per district would give us a lower house with 3,200 members! And mind you, I would never favor increasing the size of Congress if the new members were elected on the same single-member basis. Any increase in size would absolutely have to be tied to and predicated upon de-mandating single-member districts. If new members could be elected according to a scheme like the one I laid out above, or under Don Beyer's proposed law, I think expansion should merit the most serious consideration. If we could add, say, 65 seats, up to a nice round 500, and if we could ensure that the bulk of those 65, or indeed all of them, would not be elected from ultrasafe conservative or liberal districts but from ideologically heterogeneous districts or regions or whole states, the very nature of the House of Representatives would change for the better. You'd have a critical mass of compromisers.

Maybe much of the above could all be combined someday into a big, new Apportionment Act akin in scope to the 1842 one (except of course that it reduced the size of Congress). Combining my points two, three, and four, it's conceivable that if all those changes were to happen, perhaps a fifth or so of the House of Representatives would consist of legislators who had reason to fear they might lose reelection if they got too extreme—who would have incentives to cooperate. That's the opposite incentive than exists for most of them now.

There have been serious problems in the past with multimember and at-large districts. Often, minority representation was diluted. Some cities (New York among them) used to elect some City Council members on an at-large basis in the past specifically because black candidates were less likely in those days to be able to win at-large seats. They ran afoul of the Voting Rights Act, and cities had to stop using them. That's a concern, but there is some evidence now that times may have changed for the better on this front. Some cities use multimember districts and/or ranked-choice voting in local elections, and they have elected minorities: Hmong, Somali, and Latina council members in Minneapolis, and more people of color in San Francisco than were elected previously from single-member districts. Of course, everyplace isn't Minneapolis and San Francisco, but one can plausibly argue these days that most cities are diverse enough, and minority voting rates have increased enough, that minority groups would have a fair shot at electing one or more of their own in a multimember district. Obviously, such districts should be drawn with an eye toward ensuring fair representation. But remember, both the Beyer proposal and mine do not eliminate single-member districts, so majority-minority single-member districts would still exist.

5. ELIMINATE THE SENATE FILIBUSTER

Enough about the House. What about the Senate? Most observers, certainly most liberals, point to the Senate as the far bigger problem, given the outsized influence it hands to the small states, which tend to be more conservative. The numbers have gotten completely out of hand, as I showed in Chapter One discussing the California-Wyoming disparity. It's totally indefensible. Remember from the first chapter, when Earl Warren said the principle of "one person, one vote" was by far the most contentious and important one that his Supreme Court laid down? The United States Senate violates it every day.

It has real-world consequences. Here's just one noteworthy example. Clarence Thomas was seated on the Supreme Court in 1991 by a vote of 52–48. The scholars William Eskridge and Suzanna Sherry sat down and figured out what would have happened if senators were allocated in proportion to each state's population and each senator within a state's senatorial delegation voted the same way. Thomas would have lost 52–48.[9] I'm not arguing that this would have necessarily been the more "democratic" outcome; polls at the time consistently showed that pluralities—not majorities, but consistent pluralities—favored Thomas's confirmation (most people have no opinion on any Supreme Court nominee). At the same time, though, opinion was nearly universal that Thomas was clearly not the most qualified available jurist. So it arguably would have been a more democratic outcome if George H. W. Bush had been forced by the Senate to choose someone else—equally conservative, according to his wishes, but more qualified (and someone who might have asked a question once in a while over the last twenty-eight years).

As for how this can be changed. . . . It probably can't be. Could you imagine someone seriously proposing, for example, that states have between one and four senators based on population? Any such change would require a constitutional amendment, since the Constitution explicitly says that each state shall have two senators. That requires a two-thirds vote of both houses of Congress, or the vote of two-thirds of state legislatures. (The changes I discuss about the House above, in contrast, would require only that Congress pass a major new apportionment law and then leave it to the states to figure out the specifics.) Seemingly impossible. We're stuck with the Senate. Maybe some liberal billionaire can pay liberals to move to Wyoming and these other states by the tens of thousands, which would change Wyoming. You can sooner change Wyoming than change the Senate.

Here's something that might happen, however, if some conservatives have their way. We could be returned to the days when state legislatures elected senators. The people have been electing senators directly since 1913. But conservatives, led by the American Legislative Exchange Council (ALEC), which receives funding from corporations like ExxonMobil and grants from right-wing foundations including the Charles G. Koch Charitable Foundation,[10] argue that the 17th Amendment "disenfranchised states."[11] That's the public argument, anyway. But why do conservatives really want this? Simple: Republicans control more state legislatures than Democrats do, so they think this would result in more

Republican senators. And they're right: During the 115th Congress, seated from 2017 to 2019, twelve Democratic senators represented states where the GOP ran the statehouses. There was just one GOP senator from a state under Democratic control. I expect you can do the math on that as well as the people from ALEC can.

The only Senate reform that seems remotely realistic that would reduce gridlock would be elimination of the filibuster. It's absurd that it takes sixty votes to clear a "cloture" vote to pass something meaningful. We're told we live in a country where the majority rules. But we don't. In the Senate, forty-one people can block a bill, meaning that those forty-one can effectively be the majority, since what they say goes. In Federalist No. 22, Alexander Hamilton wrote: "To give a minority a negative upon the majority (which is always the case where more than a majority is requisite to a decision) is . . . to subject the sense of the greater number to that of the lesser number." He added that such a provision ran the risk of handing power to "an insignificant, turbulent or corrupt junto."[12]

The filibuster isn't in the Constitution or any law. It's just a rule of the Senate, and it could be changed. The Senate has already done it with respect to judges and could end it for everything else with sixty-seven votes, or, under cover of some parliamentary trickiness, a simple majority at the beginning of a new session. The idea of ending the filibuster is horrifying to Senate traditionalists. And it's scary to partisans on both sides. If there had been no filibuster in the first two years of President Trump's term, for example, he and the Senate GOP majority of fifty-two could have passed all manner of antiregulatory and other conservative laws. Yes, they could. But then a Democratic president and Senate could turn around and unpass them and pass other laws of their own. It would be a mess. It would be hectic. It would also be democracy.

★

6. GET RID OF THE ELECTORAL COLLEGE (OR MAKE IT OBEY THE POPULAR VOTE)

Another reform some people speak of frequently is eliminating the Electoral College and electing our presidents by national popular vote.

Republicans are resistant to this for the obvious reason that Al Gore and Hillary Clinton would have been president, and let's be honest—if the situation were reversed, Democrats would be resistant, too. But there's a nonpartisan case for it all the same.

The founders put it in the Constitution because they didn't really trust the people to make the right choice (and this was when "the people" meant only propertied white men). We should simply be over that. In addition, there's also the distasteful fact that in the beginning, the Electoral College rigged things for the slave states. The college, combined with the three-fifths rule that counted 60 percent of slaves for census purposes, heavily advantaged the states with the most slaves. For example, in 1800, Pennsylvania had about 60,000 more free citizens than Virginia did. But Virginia had nearly 350,000 slaves, who obviously could not vote, but of whom around 225,000 counted toward Virginia's Electoral College total. And so, in the 1800 election, that mess that the House of Representatives needed thirty-six ballots to settle, Virginia had 21 electoral votes, Pennsylvania 15.[13] Ever wonder why eight of the first nine presidential elections were won by slaveholding Virginians?

Getting rid of it would have big consequences, and not all would be positive, truthfully. On the plus side, candidates would have to campaign where the voters are, and not just in the same handful of swing states. In 2016, 94 percent of about 400 campaign rallies by the major candidates were held in twelve states, and two-thirds in just six states.[14] That would mean that Republicans would have to campaign in California, because under a popular-vote scheme, it would matter whether the Republican lost California by 10 points or 20 (it does not now, of course). Ditto New York. And the Democrat would have to campaign in Texas. This could have a somewhat moderating effect on the kinds of campaigns they ran, especially in terms of hot-button cultural "wedge" issues. California is particularly important here. If a Republican has to try to come close there instead of just ceding the state, then he or she will probably have to downplay some hard-core cultural politics positions that would play poorly in the state. Something similar would be true of a Democrat trying to keep things close in Texas or Georgia. Of course, depending on the circumstances, the opposite could happen: It could just mean the Republican would do everything he could to get right-wing California voters to crawl out of the woodwork to the polls, and the Democrat would do the same to jack up the Texas minority vote. Some political professionals say that candidates would also do less campaigning and would spend more on TV ads, most of which of course would be negative.[15]

Abolition of the Electoral College might also hasten the breakdown of the two-party system, in the following way. Right now, it's basically impossible for an independent or third-party candidate to win a presidential election, because such a candidate can't plausibly get to 270 electoral votes. But under a popular-vote system, it's possible that an insurgent could win. He or she would almost certainly have to be rich, and able to spend billions on a campaign. Presumably, some candidates would run for House and Senate under this insurgent's standard, and some number of them would win, so we'd have in effect three parties. We'd also have a president who in all likelihood won with less than 50 percent of the vote (in a three-way contest), which would raise issues of what kind of mandate this new president had. It's hard to know whether these would be good things.

The plan that has gotten the most traction is something called the National Popular Vote movement, which would not wholly eliminate the Electoral College. Under it, states would agree to give their electoral votes to the winner of the national popular vote, so we'd never again have the Gore-Bush, Clinton-Trump, Tilden-Hayes problem. As of early 2018, it had been enacted into law in eleven states, which have 165 electoral votes. Once it has been passed by states totaling 270 electoral votes, it will kick in, and those states will (theoretically) agree to give their votes to the winner. Of course, given recent history, it's widely seen as being a Democratic vehicle, and the eleven states that have passed it are all blue states. Some Republicans suspect that states might not actually honor their commitment. Say for example a conservative Republican wins the popular vote but lost California by 15 points; would California really give its electoral votes to that Republican? The law is built in such a way to command it, but laws can always be superseded by other laws. In any case, the hill to 270 is a steep one here.

So the campaign-related impacts of getting rid of the Electoral College would be mixed. Where I think it might have a clearer moderating effect, though, is on how presidents governed. They'd have to be thinking more about maximizing their popular vote in the next election than they do now. Presidents would think twice before pushing divisive issues that might alienate the middle of the electorate.

All of these changes are right now pretty far from being politically feasible, and none of them would "solve" the polarization problem. To believe that, you have to believe that polarization is wholly a function of our electoral system. It's plainly not. We're polarized over real, substantive matters—immigration, race, religion, and more. Collectively, we're polarized over what kind of society we want to be—whether multicultural or monocultural, whether a society that wants to make broad public investments and maintain social insurance programs or one that does not want to do those things. Germany has a much better electoral system, but Germans are polarized too, and basically over the same things. Changing the ways we elect people can help, but it won't get to the core reasons for our divisions.

★

The Most Important Project in American Politics

The above reforms, if they were ever to happen, would have an impact on both parties. But let's be real. The Republicans are the bigger problem. The Poole, McCarty, and Rosenthal numbers tell us so, and our own eyes and ears tell us so on a weekly basis. The Republican Party has become the vehicle of a single movement, the conservative movement, which has no competition or counterweight in the party to battle it and thus just keeps moving further and further to the right. This wasn't what our parties ever were or were supposed to be.

And it's not what the Democratic Party is or has been, although the Democrats, too, are moving in that direction and might become a version of the Republican Party if Bernie Sanders and his followers have anything to say about it. Sanders is a movement guy through and through, and even though he refuses to actually become a Democrat, he unquestionably emerged from 2016 as one of the party's most prominent leaders, maybe *the* most prominent. He wants a party much more eager to take on the corporate elites, the banks and Wall Street in particular; his critique of the Democratic Party as having been captured by elite corporate interests was exaggerated here and there—he tended to paint with far too broad a brush, accusing all Democrats of corporate perfidy. But the gist of it rang true for millions of voters because the gist of it *was* true. He also demonstrated in the 2016 election that it's possible for a major candidate to raise many millions of dollars in small contributions ($134 million, to be precise), which freed him from having to worry about taking positions that would offend big donors.

The extent to which *Bernie-ismo* has captured the Democratic Party isn't clear as I write these words in the summer of 2018. More leftish insurgents have challenged incumbent Democrats this primary season, with the support of new groups like the Justice Democrats, and a handful won primaries, most famously Alexandria Ocasio-Cortez in New York City. Most of the others who won Democratic primaries did so in districts that are heavily Republican. We will see more of these challenges, particularly if Sanders wins the presidential nomination in 2020 (everyone assumes he's running, even though if elected, he would turn eighty during his first year in the White House). But the number of congressional districts where a left-wing candidate can win a general election is probably not very large.

Another reality the Democrats face is this. While Republicans can win a majority of 218 seats in the House of Representatives by electing only conservatives, the Democrats cannot get to 218 by electing only liberals. Because liberals are concentrated in more densely packed areas, and because there are simply fewer liberals than conservatives in the United States, there aren't 218 liberal congressional districts in the United States. The Democrats need moderates to get a House majority. When the Democrats had their majority from 2007 to 2011, they picked up a lot of seats in swing districts far away from either coast: in upstate New York and northeastern Pennsylvania and Ohio and Indiana (three seats!) and Kansas and Arizona and North Carolina and rural Wisconsin and rural Minnesota. Winning those districts is the only way the Democrats can get a majority, so they can be either a pure liberal party or a majority party in the House, but they can't be both.

The Democratic Party as a whole is certainly moving left. They have a long way to go to become like the Republicans—their march to the far right took two generations. But if that happens, then it won't be long before our two-party system ends. We've had an enduring two-party system because our parties have been broad coalitions. One has already stopped being that. If the other does, then in time, and I think it won't take long, the parties will splinter. And I suspect we're likely to have not three but four: a left-populist party, a left-moderate party, a right-moderate party that distinguishes itself from the left-moderate on abortion rights and a few economic matters, and a far-right party. And if we have four parties, that will probably force a change at some point to a more European-style parliamentary system, which could mean a pretty major rewriting of the Constitution. But I'm getting ahead of myself.

So. Back to the Republicans. This matter of intraparty primaries is of the highest importance. You cannot understand American politics today unless you understand the way Republican incumbents in the House and Senate live in fear of "being primaried" from the right. Authoritarian regimes enforce party discipline by threat of demotion, arrest, or death. In democratic societies, parties enforce discipline by the threat of a well-financed primary challenge. And after the experience of Indiana senator Dick Lugar in 2012, all Republican legislators are keenly aware of this. If a highly respected and plenty conservative legislator who spent nearly four decades in the Senate could be defeated by a journeyman right-wing challenger (who went on to lose the general election to a Democrat), then any of them could.

Barney Frank put the matter pithily in an interview with Jason Zengerle of *New York* magazine when he was retiring from Congress, making reference to the Minnesota congresswoman who was at the time a kind of poster child of Republican extremism:[16]

So do you look across the aisle and still see people who share your faith in governance?
A few. But they are mostly so intimidated by the fear of losing a primary that they can't do much. There are a couple of Republicans on the committee that I can work with because they're sort of independent and tough-minded.

People ask me, "Why don't you guys get together?" And I say, "Exactly how much would you expect me to cooperate with Michele Bachmann?" And they say, "Are you saying they're all Michele Bachmann?" And my answer is no, they're not all Michele Bachmann. Half of them are Michele Bachmann. The other half are afraid of losing a primary to Michele Bachmann. So, no, there are maybe three Republicans I can work with, on a couple of issues, out of the thirtysomething on the committee.

This dynamic paralyzes Congress. Nothing will change until it is ended. So, how can that happen? The answer is obvious. Republicans need to fear primary challenges from the center. If they do, they'll start acting and voting more like centrists.

★

7. REVIVE MODERATE REPUBLICANISM

There is no project in American politics more important, none that could do more to reduce polarization, than reviving moderate Republicanism. I say that as a liberal and an enrolled Democrat. That's the precise inflection point at which the system is really broken. If some person or group of people will put money—and serious money: billions, not millions—into this project, that person or persons can help rescue the republic. A Club for Growth of the center can save this country.

Why? Imagine a typical conservative Republican House member. Not a radical, just a typical conservative. When he got to Congress—say, back in the early days of the Bush administration—he was a right-wing freak. Now things have shifted enough that he's just a run-of-the-mill conservative. And the only pressure he ever gets back home is from his right. The district is cut in such a way that he doesn't really have to pursue Democratic or independent votes. The voters he does care about take instruction from Rush Limbaugh and Sean Hannity and the local Christian broadcaster. The local newspaper is right-wing. His money comes from right-wing sources. There are four or five ambitious people eyeing his seat—a few state legislators, a rich businessman or two. Each of them is more right-wing than the last. It's unrelenting, and it's why these people vote the way they do.

Now imagine that some of that machinery existed in moderate form. Some of it could not be re-created—the media, for example. But some could. Suppose this organization identified more moderate voters, organized them, turned them into a bloc. And suppose this organization also recruited candidates and supported them financially. Given time, this organization would make a difference.

This would be a massive and perhaps impossible undertaking. But surely there are some rich moderate Republicans out there who could fund such a pressure group. It would take a long time to have an impact. Some people I've discussed this idea with say they don't think there even *are* many moderate Republicans anymore. They may be right. But atrophied muscles can be brought back to strength. I suspect that millions of Republicans might choose moderation over extremism if someone just placed it on the menu for them. The problem is that for decades, no one has.

When ideas like this are proposed—ideas that try in some measure to conjure back to life a lost past—the wise cynics always say two things. First, that the past can't be re-created; second, that even if it does work, its success will be quite limited. On the first point, I agree that the past can't be re-created. It will never be like it was in the 1950s through the 1970s. There aren't going to be any more Jacob Javitses or Charles Mathiases or Lowell Weickers, to name three former Republican senators who were genuine liberals. But here's my response: The country doesn't need liberal Republicans. It needs Republicans who are basically conservative but who harbor a few moderate instincts and who—this is the key thing— actually *want to come to Congress to compromise and get a few things done.* Surely those Republicans exist. And on the second point: Again, critics are correct—this project wouldn't work in a lot of districts, which are too right-wing to bother with. But it doesn't need to work in a lot of districts. It needs to work only in a handful. A half-dozen such wins in House races begins to alter the nature of the Republican caucus. A dozen constitutes a real voting bloc.

A revival of moderate Republicanism along these lines, especially coupled with the electoral reforms outlined above, would end the insidious "Hastert Rule," which the Republicans decreed in the early 2000s and under which they will not let a bill come up for a vote unless it has the backing of a majority of Republicans. The Hastert Rule has meant that for Republicans, bipartisanship—a bill passing the House with, say, 140 Republicans and 100 Democrats—is something they no longer even pretend to strive for. It was the Hastert Rule that prevented then-Speaker John Boehner from bringing the immigration reform bill of 2013 to the House floor. It would almost certainly have passed, and on a bipartisan basis—but with a minority of Republicans. The Republican Party is not going to just wake up one day and decide to change the rule. But a critical mass of a different breed of Republican can force such a change.

All of these ideas I'm mentioning in this chapter are long-term projects, the work of ten or twenty years, or more. But imagine a Congress a generation from now in which are seated twelve to fifteen moderate Republicans in the House, and three or four in the Senate. They would vote with Democrats for a tax increase, as part of a budget deal or to shore up Medicare or to fund a no-bullshit response to the opioid crisis, which would really mean hundreds of free treatment clinics across the country. Next would come the crucial step: They'd have to survive reelection after so voting, because the right will come after them with everything. But if they did survive, it would send a loud and clear signal to other Republicans. It would break the back of the antitax pledge, and Congress could start governing again.

If lots of money could be directed toward efforts that would force the Republican Party toward the center, then maybe we'd see some positive change. Politicians and the political system will resist this change, and all the changes discussed so far. Politicians don't just wake up one day and decide, "Gee, I'm going to do the right thing today, even though I'd be unleashing an unknowable chain of events that might cost me my job." They respond to pressure. That pressure has to come from the broader society; from sources that have credibility with the broad public and can change public opinion. And that is the point on which this book will conclude. But before I get to that, we have to grapple with a more immediate threat.

Trump

Everything that's been written so far could have been written without changing a word if Hillary Clinton were president, or Ted Cruz, or Jeb Bush. If Clinton were in the White House—the reality I anticipated when I started thinking about this book—the Republicans would have been on the warpath. There would be hearings on the emails, and still another investigation (which would have been the eighth) into the Benghazi deaths of four Americans in 2012. And if one of the other Republicans had made it, Congress would be just as dysfunctional, and the parties just as divided, as they are now.

But they're not president. Donald Trump is, and things are different. Trump has done two things that mark him as a graver threat to the republic than any president since at least Richard Nixon (I think quite graver; Nixon at least knew and cared about policy) and that place the nation's future in a precarious position. First, he has weaponized the white ethnonationalist resentment of a percentage of the Republican base, a resentment that other more mainstream Republicans have fueled in less blatant ways for five decades. I have no wish to argue percentages, and it's pointless: Even if the percentage of Republicans who can fairly be described this way is low, that's still millions of people. And we know, because we've seen plenty of manifestations of it, that Trump has brought joy to the hearts of open white supremacists. David Duke said at the white-supremacist rally in Charlottesville that the event "represents a turning point for our country" and then specifically added that "we are going to fulfill the promises of Donald Trump."[17] That should mortify any decent person, to know that this man who has been the country's most prominent public racist for four decades was speaking so tenderly of the sitting president of the United States. And that Trump himself said there were "very fine people" on both sides at Charlottesville—that is, that some white supremacists are very fine people!—should have been grounds for a serious discussion about his fitness to serve the whole of the American people as president, but this is a discussion Republicans have been unwilling to have.

I used to wonder, at moments of racial strife like a controversial police shooting or jury verdict, what it would take for racial violence to erupt in this country. One could see scenarios then, but they were all pretty abstract. They're not so abstract now. It's not hard to imagine that another Charlottesville could end in many more deaths than one. It's not hard to imagine, now, any number of incidents that might bring a white person or persons into conflict with a black or brown person or persons that could ignite rioting and violence, with the president of the United States himself gleefully throwing gasoline on the fire. And it's not hard to imagine Trump's loyalists sparking violence, since some have promised to do exactly that. Alex Jones, the radio host who said the Sandy Hook elementary school shootings were a hoax, and Roger Stone, the longtime GOP dirty trickster, have promised "civil war" if Trump is removed from office. They went to a shooting range in late 2017 to prepare to "defend" themselves. "If there is a coup d'état, if there is an illegitimate unconstitutional effort to remove Donald Trump on trumped-up charges by a biased and partisan prosecutor or an illegitimate takedown by the 25th Amendment, there will be a civil war in this country," Stone vowed.[18] With his choice of words, of course, especially the word "illegitimate," Stone signals to followers that by definition there can be no such thing as a *legitimate* constitutional effort to remove Trump, so civil war is inevitable if Trump is removed, and he and Jones and other Trumpists will say that any resort to violence was forced on them. This "civil war" would not be racial per se, although as a practical matter the Trump side would be 98 percent white and the vast majority of non-white America would be on the anti-Trump side, so it wouldn't take long for it to become racial.

The second thing Trump has done that is virtually without precedent in our history is to demonstrate that he has no respect for, nor the slightest concern about, our civic institutions and practices and customs. Does anyone think he's ever read the Constitution? A book about it? An *article* about it? His statement in May 2017 to NBC's Lester Holt that he fired FBI Director James Comey because Comey was investigating possible ties between his campaign and Russia was a direct admission of obstruction of justice, on national television no less. A president firing a prosecutor who was investigating him—in a less partisan time, with a Republican Party less cowed by the president and his rabid supporters, the House would have opened impeachment proceedings instantly.

Again, scenarios that were once hard to imagine happening in the

United States are now all too easy to foresee. As dark as it got during Watergate, there was always the sense that the Constitution and our institutions would survive Nixon. Republicans were different then; when the House Judiciary Committee charged Nixon with obstruction in late July 1974, six of the committee's seventeen Republicans joined all twenty-one Democrats in voting to refer the charge to the full House.[19] Those six, while a small number, were crucial; they were proof that the president's party wasn't wholly in his pocket, that if a moment of crisis arrived, Congress, with the assent of about a third of the president's party, would step up and fulfill its obligations. Also, Republicans were not going to extraordinary and shocking lengths in an attempt to discredit Nixon's attackers, as House Republicans are doing for Trump. Nixon also didn't have a cable news channel whose leading stars defended his every action and egged him on; indeed, John Dean has said that Nixon "might have survived if there'd been a Fox News."[20] And of course, Nixon saw that enough Senate Republicans would vote to convict him, and so he went peacefully when the time came. We can't be at all sure that Trump would do that, if the moment arrived.

Trump's need to stoke racial tension and his absence of respect for the Constitution and the law really could lead to ruptures that would push the country to a point from which there's no going back, that could make the country in certain ways unrecognizable. One obvious example is this. Remember when Nixon said "if the president does it, that means it is not illegal"? Almost no one agreed with him on that in his time. Today, Trump obviously believes it, and from the looks of things a majority of Republicans either agree with him or if they disagree are too afraid to say so. And what about the current Supreme Court? Would its five conservative members agree, too, if the question arrived to them on just the right platter? So in other words, it's not at all outlandish to worry that it could *become law* that if the president does it, it isn't illegal. That's a big and ominous step down a slippery path whose consequences I don't think I have to spell out for you. Once the first fundamental check and balance is gone, others will go too. (I write knowing that some of these questions may have been answered by the time this book appears.)

Another chilling development that is not Trump's personal doing but is unique to the Trump era, with what appear to be the vast majority of the dark arts practiced in Trump's behalf, is the new role that social media played in the 2016 election. We are at a point in history on this front that's ominous and that we must recognize for what it is. For all of human history, every advance in communications technology has been good for democracy. The original printing press; the "lightning" rotary press of the 1840s; the radio; the television; Internet websites and search engines. All helped expand and diffuse knowledge, and all helped improve the quality of public debate. Not uniformly, of course; there was plenty of "fake news" (really fake, as in totally made up) in the penny press of the mid-nineteenth century. But that fake news consisted largely of outlandish stories made up for the purposes of entertaining the masses and selling papers, not with a political agenda in mind. All of these technologies came with downsides (if you're of a certain age you'll remember all the sociological hand-wringing over the "vast wasteland" of television). But on balance, all helped make the people a more informed populace. At times—the Kennedy funeral, the *Challenger* explosion, 9/11—they had a unifying effect. One can certainly argue that cable news has been a very mixed blessing, but Fox aside, even it does more to edify than to enrage.

There are good things about Twitter and Facebook. Twitter is how I (like every journalist I know) keep up with events and learn of interesting articles; on Facebook, it's a delight to argue (politely) with my old high-school friends who are conservative. And there are instances where social media has been the friend of small-*d* democrats, in closed or autocratic societies like Iran and Egypt. But paradoxically, in free societies, social media are toxic from a democracy standpoint (and in some closed societies—Facebook has come under intense and deserved criticism for allowing posters in Myanmar to use hateful language that has stoked violence against the Rohingya Muslim minority). This is so for two reasons. First of all, social media are antideliberative. They encourage and reward instantaneous, emotional reactions rather than reflection. The people who become stars of these media tend to be the people who say the most outrageous things, the most racist things, the most antidemocratic things (starting with the president, since before he was president). You're not going to amass many friends or followers quoting Gibbon on Rome. Unfortunately, the founders hoped precisely that we, or at least our leading citizens, *would* spend time discussing Gibbon on Rome (they

were all big Gibbon fans). They emphasized again and again that to survive, a democratic republic would depend on reasonable people reason-
ing together. They weren't naïve about politics and emotion; they merely
emphasized the importance of the link between calm deliberation and the
survival of democracy. Social media are pulverizing that link. The more
our political discourse is conducted on Twitter and Facebook, and on
as-yet-not-invented platforms that will move news even faster and make
Twitter and Facebook look like the Athenian Ecclesia, the more weight
will be thrown on the scale on the side of unreason. Chamath Paliha-
pitiya, who was a Facebook executive from 2007 to 2011, made waves
in 2017 when he spoke publicly about his "tremendous guilt" in having
helped grow the platform. "It literally is a point now where I think we
have created tools that are ripping apart the social fabric of how society
works. That is truly where we are," he said. "The short-term, dopamine-
driven feedback loops that we have created are destroying how society
works: no civil discourse, no cooperation, misinformation, mistruth."[21]

The second problem can be summed up in the word "Russia." As
we've seen, the potential for disinformation on these media is vast. The
U.S. intelligence community has concluded that in 2016, "the Kremlin
sought to advance its longstanding desire to undermine the U.S.-led liberal democratic order"[22]—to mess with our heads, to undermine our faith
in our institutions, and to elect Trump. These campaigns are carried out
with a subtlety and sophistication that demonstrate that someone somewhere is giving these campaigns quite a lot of thought. Of all the dozens
of articles about this I've read over the last couple years, none did more
to put my brain in a vise than the *Daily Beast*'s report on Jenna Abrams
in late 2017.[23] Abrams emerged on Twitter in 2014. At first, she tweeted
mostly about show business—making fun of Kim Kardashian and so on.
She had a sharp tongue and a saucy way of putting things and developed
an image as a "straight-talking, no-nonsense, viral-tweet-writing young
American woman," as the *Beast*'s Ben Collins and Joseph Cox put it.
Her photograph showed a woman who was young and pretty, though
definitely in an urban brainiac sort of way, with her straight, unfussed-
over hair and large glasses. Her name, even, was perfect: "Jenna" is neither too heavy-serious nor too ditzy-cutesy, and her surname obviously
marked her as Jewish, which meant liberal.

She was featured in articles in the *New York Times*, the *Washington Post*, USA Today*, and the *New York Daily News;* on BuzzFeed and BBC.com; and in many other news outlets, not just in the United States, but across the world. And then, once Jenna had achieved a certain level of notoriety and attained a critical mass of Twitter followers, around 70,000, she started tweeting about politics. Lo and behold, this young, hip, pretty, Jewish woman saw the point of Confederate monuments and had a soft spot for Donald Trump. Maybe she could convince others like her to do the same.

As you've probably guessed by now, "Jenna Abrams" does not exist. She was the invention of the Internet Research Agency, a highly informed and culturally nuanced Russian troll factory in St. Petersburg (this is one of the three Russian companies special counsel Robert Mueller indicted in early 2018). Now: Think about all the thought and planning and most of all the keen understanding of American social media that went into creating Jenna. That perfect name and face (go Google Image it), those months spent reeling in followers with Kardashian trash talk, and then boom, as the election heated up, the surprising Trumpian sympathies. And she was one of hundreds of creations, or maybe thousands.

And 2016 was just the beginning. In 2017, Russian trolls continued using social media to influence American discourse on issues like net neutrality, which (as the Russians evidently understand) is a huge concern of many liberals. Some Russian entity posted comments to the Federal Communications Commission's website from real Americans that they never in fact made—news organizations interviewed the Americans, who almost all said, "Yes, that's my name, but I didn't make that comment to the FCC, and in fact I disagree with it."[24] One can barely imagine what the Russians (and possibly others) have in mind for 2018, 2020, and beyond. What we know today is that social media are easily manipulated by dishonest people. We also know, it must be said, that conservatives are far quicker than liberals to lap this stuff up. A large study of 2016 social media consumption by three political scientists found that one in four Americans visited a fake news website in the last month of the campaign. But more tellingly it also found that "almost six in ten visits to fake news websites came from the 10% of people with the most conservative online information diets."[25] Another study from Oxford University found the same thing. Six scholars looked at thousands of tweets and Facebook posts and divided people into ten different demographic groups. They found that over a ten-day period leading up to and immediately following the 2016 election, Trump supporters—on both Twitter and Facebook—pushed more fake news than all the other nine groups combined.[26]

Facebook says it is working to prevent this. Many observers doubt that it can succeed. But even if it does, some other platform will appear to take its place, and another, and another, with no gatekeepers sorting real content from fraudulent. And the bad guys will always think up schemes that the good guys won't. Combine this reality with the rage unleashed by social media and I think it's quite fair to say that social media constitute the first advance in the history of communications technology that is actively harmful to democracy (in free societies). And it's not clear that we can do anything about it. We may finally have planted the seeds from which will grow the weeds that will strangle us.

If We Can Keep It

When we think about how to address all this in the Trump era, we need to think a lot more broadly than electoral-system reforms and whether the filibuster needs to go. We need to look at the whole society, and we need to look *to* the whole society and demand engagement and commitment to reviving our civic health from leaders in other walks of life. We need more and better and more courageous leadership from prominent people in every realm.

I think back to the Age of Consensus, and how that consensus didn't just happen but was *forged*. It was created by leaders in the corporate and business world, in organized labor, in our religious life, in our civic organizations and the nonprofit world, and in our universities. There was a lot they disagreed on; obviously, the corporate-business version of the American Dream was more conservative and individualistic than the other ones. But all of them made an attempt to say to the American people that we were one nation conceived around certain noble principles and that people had to pay heed to those principles.

We need that kind of effort now. And we have to start it by thinking not about Congress or our political system, but about our society.

A nearly ironclad rule of history: Politics changes *after* social conditions and expectations change. A clamor is raised about working conditions, a terrible shirtwaist-factory fire claims many lives, there is an outcry; only then does politics respond. That's the normal pattern. So, since politicians won't lead this effort, we need to demand something we haven't been demanding much in these recent years: We need our nonpolitical leaders to take very seriously the job of trying to pull the country together. We need them to be visionary and forward-thinking. We need them to see—and, crucially, to say, and say and say—that they will all benefit, even and especially the corporate leaders, from a less divided, and I would add less unequal, country.

First and foremost, we need to get to know one another again. Across racial and religious lines, but mostly regional ones. We have to find ways to get people (especially young people) from Vermont to go spend time in Louisiana and vice versa. And I don't mean vacations.

★

8. CREATE "FOREIGN" EXCHANGE PROGRAMS WITHIN THE UNITED STATES FOR STUDENTS

After World War I, a few groups in the United States established study-abroad programs to increase international awareness and harmony in the wake of the carnage that resulted in part from a deep lack of such awareness. Those programs were vastly expanded after World War II, with the introduction of the Fulbright scholarships and other programs. Participation peaked in the 1950s and 1960s, and they introduced millions of American students to other cultures.

Well, now we're strangers to each other across state lines. So how about public universities across the country creating voluntary exchange programs whereby students from one part of the country could spend a year in another? A UMass-Amherst student spends a year at Mississippi State, or a University of Idaho student spends a year at Hunter College in Manhattan? And so on and so on. Perhaps they could offer tuition breaks to students who volunteer to participate, and the more exotic and opposite from your normal experience your exchange choice is, the bigger break you get (and Hawaii doesn't count). States and/or Congress could not compel private universities to do this, only public ones, but one would hope that private universities would agree to do the same.

Would it change the world? No. But over the course of twenty or so years, tens of thousands of students could be introduced to a part of the country that had seemed like another planet to them. Relationships would be forged, relationships that might pay off down the road when the Yale graduate and the Clemson graduate who spent that year together in 2023 are, a quarter-century later, chairing congressional committees sharing jurisdiction on some contentious law. At least people may find some places where they agree and with any luck learn to disagree with each other in a civil register.

9. REDUCE COLLEGE TO THREE YEARS AND MAKE YEAR FOUR A SERVICE YEAR

This crisis demands a little creative thinking—reexamination of questions it wouldn't occur to people to rethink in normal times. In that spirit: Just as there's no good reason to stick with single-member districts exclusively, there's also no good reason that college needs to last four years anymore. Most of the countries of Europe have changed to three years, and a few American universities have begun to follow suit. But three years should be the norm. Colleges and universities should rethink their curricula accordingly. For one thing, tuition costs are a national emergency, and doing this would reduce them by 25 percent (actually a little more, since any student's fourth year is the most expensive because of inflation). It's true that this would decrease the number of electives and thus could create a less well-rounded student body, and that's a problem. Universities could perhaps address it with some adjustments to the curriculum. But what I propose be done with the fourth year would make up for it.

That fourth year could be a public service year, with the service performed in a part of the country that's completely alien to the student. The student should get to choose of course, but she'd have to choose a place that was a challenge to her. As to how it would work with the idea above, about studying elsewhere for one year, I suppose students could choose to do one or the other, or perhaps both.

This would be AmeriCorps on steroids, and yes, it would require ample funding. It also shouldn't be mandatory, as you can't coerce students into civic-spiritedness. But it should be made an awfully attractive option that would be difficult for many students to resist. It could be tied to a reduction in student debt, say. Again, the way to think about this idea is over the course of two decades or so, after which millions of Americans will have spent a full year in a part of the country that otherwise they may never even have driven through.

The general point is this. Higher education is supposed to respond to public needs. In the early 1900s, as colleges and universities grew, the new complexities of the modern economy and modern life demanded more college graduates; so higher-ed policy and government incentives produced them. In the 1950s, during the Cold War, it was decided that we needed more scientists and engineers; we changed curricula, and we got them. Now, we need more young people who are willing to be the next generation's civic leaders in ways that try to reduce our divisions. That's the challenge of today. Universities and colleges, and the federal government, must come up with policies that respond to that need and create such people.

★

10. FIND A WAY TO EXPAND SUCH IDEAS TO HIGH SCHOOLS . . .

Only around 40 percent of our young people finish college. So what about the other 60 percent? Well, is there any way that high schools could replicate my proposed college exchange program? It would have to be on a more modest scale, since letting kids go away from home for a full year seems too much to ask of most parents. Again, all such programs would be voluntary. But maybe states of similar sizes but very different cultural and political leanings and customs—New Jersey and Georgia, Massachusetts and Tennessee, Michigan and North Carolina—could pair up and send students to each others' states for half a year? And of course they'd have to send them to really different kinds of places; that is, the kids from Newark couldn't do their semester in Atlanta, which would be pointless. They'd need to be spread out to small towns, just as the kids from Atlanta should go to southern Jersey. City youths would see farms; Southern Baptists would meet actual living Muslims; rural youngsters might meet their first transgender person and see that he's a normal kid who deserves their sympathy.

★

11. . . . AND INTO THE WORKPLACE

There's no reason such exchange programs have to be left to the schools. Major national employers could do the same with employees who didn't yet have families and hadn't yet set down deep roots in the community. So the twenty-year-old employee of a Home Depot in Cleveland could go spend a year at the store in Dothan, Alabama. There are hundreds, or at least dozens, of businesses with a national footprint that could participate, at a relatively scant cost to the corporations (some moving expenses) that they should recognize as being worth the cost of helping to get Americans to know one another a little better again.

★

12. VASTLY EXPAND CIVICS EDUCATION

Right now, nearly every American schoolchild takes civics. But they mostly take just one year, and it's very basic. Civics education has decreased over the last quarter-century. According to the education scholars Richard D. Kahlenberg and Clifford Janey, this was no accident. American educators, they wrote in a 2016 report, "have pivoted between whether the central priority of public education should be to create skilled workers for the economy, or to educate young people for responsible citizenship." But ever since the end of the Cold War and the ascendance of the global economy in the early 1990s, "the emphasis has shifted away from preparing citizens and toward serving the needs of the marketplace."[27]

Our consumer selves knocked our citizen selves out of the classroom, too, evidently.

I'm not one to knock skills. But no one can look at what's happened to this country over the last fifteen years and deny that we need a civics education revival. And I'd say we need one of enormous proportions. Kahlenberg and Janey cite a 2003 report by the Albert Shanker Institute that recommended four prongs of civics education:

1. A "robust" history curriculum through all twelve years of schooling.
2. A "full and honest" teaching of history, which means neither glossing over the bad nor overemphasizing it.
3. An "unvarnished account" of what life is like in undemocratic societies, so that children can appreciate the difference.
4. A "cultivation of virtues" necessary to a healthy democracy.

I like all of them and say we need a healthy dose of number four in particular. I wish schools would teach some form of civics for twelve years and virtue-cultivation for a few years, say all four years of high school. Students should graduate from high school knowing the basic facts of our history and system of government, but much more. They should be made to engage deeply with our seminal democratic texts, from the Declaration of Independence and the Constitution to Lincoln's Second Inaugural Address. The journalist John Avlon, in his passionate book on George Washington's Farewell Address, reminds us that that address was taught extensively in public schools long ago and "became the subject of turn-of-the-century oratory and analysis contests in many schools."[28] We need that sort of pedagogy again. And most of all students should be taught the core responsibility of real citizenship—that our founders believed that a democratic republic could be maintained only if reasonable people reason together in good faith. That, after all, is their, and our, job as citizens: to maintain the democratic republic. The lesson may or may not take in all cases, but young people have to be taught, and not for a few weeks but over successive years, that they have a handful of responsibilities as citizens, the chief one of which is to be deliberative; to debate reasonably with those with whom they disagree.

Conservative readers may be pleased to read that the decline of civics education is one malign development in this country that I don't blame wholly on the right. While the early-nineties decision to move away from civics and more toward skills was market-driven, it was more liberal forces going back to the 1960s and even earlier that made civics education less fashionable. One trend was specific to education, according to the distinguished educator and literary critic E. D. Hirsch Jr.—a decision (not made in one place in one time, but collectively over decades) to shift from an "emphasis on initiating children into the mores of the national tribe to an emphasis on developing the nature of the individual child."[29] Another was the more general rise in antinationalist and anti-American sentiment on the broad left—first in a benign, United Nations-y kind of way ("It's a Small World After All"), and later with a harsher intensity during the Vietnam era. Hirsch is a liberal who opposed that war but nevertheless argues that the right kind of nationalism must be inculcated into schoolchildren through rigorous history and civics education so the schools can produce at least a percentage of adults who are equipped to sustain the republic. I should note that it's very unlikely that we can even agree these days on what a proper civics education is. But for now maybe it would be fine if students in Alabama learn slightly different things from students in Vermont. At least they'll both be taught to think about responsibilities of citizenship.

Would these things change the world? Maybe not. But do them all and give them time, and in a quarter-century, we'll have a critical mass of citizens a little more aware of their duties and little less susceptible to being convinced to hate people who aren't just like them. Hate and distrust always decrease when people from different groups get to know each other. Surely if we do enough things like this on a big enough scale for enough time, the ignorant haters will eventually just be outnumbered.

One great challenge the United States faces today is whether it can be simultaneously a multicultural society and one with a sense of shared national consensus. It was once a consensus society. Then it became a multicultural society. That it will remain so is a given, despite the wishes of some to reverse the tide of time. I do suspect that a tightening of immigration laws is someday coming, if Republicans continue on their present trajectory and maintain their hold on power. But even if legal immigration is someday reduced by Congress, one senses little enthusiasm, even among Republicans, for anything beyond modest reductions. In other words, we'll continue to be a diverse country. The issue today, then, is whether we can fuse consensus and diversity: Whether the United States can be a diverse society while reaching back to that earlier age to identify and broadly agree on some kind of civic consensus.

I'm not sure we can. The Age of Consensus was great in many ways; an age in which Americans put their common civic faith to the task of moving from hardship and want to creating a shared prosperity of a sort never theretofore seen in human civilization, taking time in the middle of it all to defeat fascism. But it left a lot of people out. When African-Americans and women, and later Latinos and gay men and lesbians and others, demanded to be part of the consensus, and when immigration increased dramatically, it collapsed. Maybe Jefferson Cowie is right that we achieved that consensus only because it was an overwhelmingly white nation. I'd like to think that we have it in us to be different and better today. Most of the current evidence isn't especially encouraging, given the racist ethnonationalist who sits in the White House.

★

13. INSIST ON A LEFT THAT DOESN'T CONTRIBUTE TO THE FRACTURE

The political left has contributed to the fracture as well. The left celebrates difference more than commonality, and some elements within it reject the very idea of a common civic faith, focused instead on continuing group struggles. They are not necessarily wrong to maintain that focus. A woman is still at a disadvantage to a man in this society the vast majority of the time, a black or brown person is still at a disadvantage to a white person, a gay or transgendered person is typically at a disadvantage to a straight person. And Muslim Americans in particular have a difficult, long-term battle on their hands to win an acceptance that's broad and durable enough to defeat the suspicion and hatred they face. As long as those realities remain the case, there's a fight to be waged, and you sure can't blame people for fighting it.

One can, however, critique *how* it is fought, and it's here that forces of liberalism and the left sometimes contribute to the problem. Fairly or not, history shows us that in a democratic context, the people and groups battling to win their rights, their rightful place inside the consensus, have to be morally better than the people they're fighting. They can't trade taunt for taunt or act of violence for act of violence or enraged tweet for enraged tweet. They can't engage in forms of protest that offend the mind of the uncommitted citizen. They don't win that way. They win when they appear to remain optimistic, aspirational, and not threatening to the larger community. Just days after Bull Connor turned the German Shepherds and fire hoses on the black children of Birmingham in 1963, Martin Luther King Jr. preached that people needed to work and pray together, going so far as to quote from "My Country, 'Tis of Thee." Thus did King connect his movement—at a moment when rage was amply justified—to a (then) 130-year-old song that had served as one of the country's de facto national anthems until Congress officially designated "The Star-Spangled Banner" as such in 1931.

Likewise, the activists who fought for same-sex marriage rights did so not by threatening to tear down the institution of marriage, but by insisting that they wanted to share in its protections and blessings. This was not an accident, but a conscious strategy on the part of the leaders like Evan Wolfson, who did as much as anyone to make legal same-sex marriage a reality in this country. Bigots said their real intention was the opposite. It took the public a few years to sort through this, but it did so with rather impressive speed, and large majorities have backed same-sex marriage for some time now, because its advocates framed it in such aspirational terms. And in our time, the students of Marjory Stoneman Douglas High School in Parkland, Florida, after the tragic 2018 shooting there, comported themselves with stunning dignity in the face of some vile attacks. The way they spoke for their seventeen deceased classmates, and for so many other victims of gun violence who didn't have the political power to win the kind of national attention they had, was exactly in keeping with the best traditions of American protest that we have. If that tragedy marked a turning point in the gun debate, it will be because of the skill, passion, and hope they communicated to the country in those dark days.

When any left movement fails to do this, it does three things: first, it fails its own adherents, because its movement will probably not succeed in meeting its goals; second, it contributes to the fracturing; and third, it hands ammunition to conservatives, who are ever eager to find examples of leftists behaving undemocratically (college students shutting down free speech, usually) so they can say, "Aha! See? They do it too, and they're worse!" Many liberals and leftists are just too suspicious of the idea of civic consensus to want to revive it. I see their point, sort of. We've had only one consensus in this country, and it was patriarchal and racist.

I still say that such rejection is the wrong attitude. The point is not to have no consensus. It's to have a better one. People are out there making a new consensus every day. The Parkland students are doing it. Women across the country are leading the way toward it. The response by women to this bleak political moment has been amazing—hundreds of women running for office, thousands organizing locally in ways they never have. The uprisings by teachers in red states were led by women, too—teachers are the front-line infantry in the war the right has waged on public investment, as governors slash taxes and school systems go underfunded and teachers get no raises. The #MeToo movement challenges one of the ugliest conventions of the old consensus, one in which so many men, liberal as well as conservative, were (and are) implicated. All these movements will face fearsome opposition. The natural resting state of any society is resistance to change. To alter that state requires convincing millions of people that change is worth the risk. If these movements can remain aspirational, they will succeed, and it will be their opponents who will fall outside the new consensus.

★

14. DEMAND THAT CORPORATE AND BUSINESS LEADERS COMMIT TO SOCIAL RESPONSIBILITY

All the above will take a long time. In the more immediate term, I keep thinking about who can change all this; who can help lead society out of this pit. Politicians can't, or won't, take the lead. Who else? It has to be someone, or a group of someones, who can win some modicum of trust on both sides. Religious leaders? No; the nonconservative ones will never be trusted by a critical mass of Republicans, and the conservative ones are mostly telling us what a great Christian the pussy-grabber is. Other civic leaders? No. If they're not explicitly right-wing, conservatives will be instructed by their media that they're relentlessly left-wing and told not to trust them. Athletes? After #takeaknee? We're more divided over sports than we've been since the major sports integration wars.

There's only one big category left—business and corporate leaders. Liberal readers may recoil at this suggestion, and God knows corporate leaders have given us many reasons to be deeply skeptical of their collective goals and motivations. But I think of it like this.

We're never going to end polarization. Divisions over contentious cultural issues will always exist; there are moderns, and there are antimoderns, and there always will be. However, these tensions can be reduced if we have one big thing—an economy that's delivering a general prosperity for middle-class and working-class people. When times are bad, all the other tensions rise. When times are good, though, those tensions become at least manageable. It follows, therefore, that what we need is a society that delivers general prosperity again. For nearly two decades, the system has been delivering that prosperity to only the top 5 or 10 percent. Hence, the much-discussed crisis of liberal democracy; hence, the wins for Trump and Brexit, the success of far-right parties in Germany and Italy, and the rest.

Prosperity requires investment. Investment means public expenditure —on schools, on infrastructure, on our broadband networks, on the left-behind places in rural America, which are in crisis. As William Galston of the Brookings Institution has pointed out, the great economic chasm of our time—and not just in the United States, by the way, but in Britain and throughout the European Union as well—is not between red states and blue states or North and South, but between metro areas and rural areas. When the Information Age dawned twenty years ago, the general view was that the Internet meant people could do their work from a mountaintop in Montana. And so they can, but time has proven that most innovators don't want to live on mountaintops in Montana. They want to live around people like them. It turns out, Galston notes, "that the modern, knowledge-based economy thrives on the density and diversity found in large cities."[30]

Consider these eye-opening numbers. The United States has experienced three recessions in the last two decades. An organization called the Economic Innovation Group measured how widespread the three recoveries were geographically.[31] After the early 1990s recession, the gains were broadly shared, as 71 percent of new business growth occurred in counties with 500,000 or fewer people (and within that, 32 percent in counties under 100,000). After the second recession, of the early 2000s, that 71 percent sank to 51 percent. And finally, after the Great Recession of 2008–2009, the number was 19 percent (and in counties under 100,000, literally zero). The lion's share of the growth and dynamism has moved to counties with more than 1 million people. The government has to do something to help rural people, and there is simply no way to help them without spending money on them. And of course we'd be foolish not to invest in the high-growth areas, because those are the places that will produce a faster return on investment.

So we need a program of investment, and we need leaders who can sell this program to the country. Business and corporate leaders are the only ones left who will have enough credibility with rank-and-file Republicans to help lead a societal change here, to say to Republican politicians: We don't want your low-tax, low-service paradise. We don't want a society in which we don't invest in ourselves and our future generations—in which, for example, states just keep cutting taxes while students at our public colleges and universities keep having to pay more tuition to make up the difference, and where there's zero economic opportunity in too many towns, where we do nothing to address a climate problem that 98 percent of scientists tell us imperils the planet's future, and where millions of our citizens need drug treatment but there's "no money" for it. We want the best roads and bridges and freight-rail systems and ports and canals and airports, for the purpose of helping capitalism flourish, for the purpose of moving our merchandise, and we're willing to help pay for these things, and we believe that all of us should be. And we demand a more equal society, recognizing that such a society is better for average people, and that what's better for average people is better for us—

the more people who can buy our products and educate their children adequately to become our skilled workers, the better off we the capitalist class, and we Americans, are. Also, of course, a class of leaders who are willing to make do with less themselves; willing, maybe, to live on a measly few million a year.

Is it conceivable that we can have a corporate class that will make these assertions? I don't know. Corporate behavior is often constrained by the least socially conscious among them, because the least socially conscious will often make the highest short-term profit, and everyone else has to chase behind. I guess that may never end. But these people need to think hard about where that will lead.

The pursuit of short-term profit among public corporations has been horrible for our society. This idea, that the corporation's only responsibility is to the shareholder—to maximizing profit—can be traced back to Milton Friedman and the Chicago school. In his 1962 book *Capitalism and Freedom*, Friedman called corporate social responsibility a "fundamentally subversive doctrine." He upped the ante in 1970 with a big *New York Times Magazine* piece called "The Social Responsibility of Business Is to Increase Its Profits."[32] You can imagine in the context of the times—the U.S. Chamber of Commerce so fearful about the future of capitalism that the next year it whistled up the Powell memo—how lovely was the sound of this to corporate ears. It took a while, but by the 1990s, Friedmanism was locked into place.

There has been an effort afoot ever since to dislodge this "short-termism"—to get corporations to think over the longer horizon and prize social commitments and responsibilities to community over short-term profits. For example, the Aspen Institute, a Washington think tank that has earned a nonpartisan reputation, has run its Business and Society Program for twenty years. Numerous scholars have been at work for just as long pushing ways to end this pursuit of profit above all else—for example, restructuring corporate boards so that the board members aren't so beholden to the CEO, and so that they include, say, some workers and local clergy.

Many dynamics are in place that will seek to block these reforms and support the pursuit of profit. Executives and middle managers—who read the revised, market-oriented Samuelson in business school—have spent

their entire careers pursuing short-term profit. "Activist shareholders"—
we used to be honest enough to call them corporate raiders back when
they first appeared, in the 1980s—join boards to pressure management,
often to maximize profits. Even less aggressive institutional investors are
caught in a system they're helpless to change if they want to. Pension
funds, for example, are major corporate investors. Many pension fund
managers would like to be more socially conscious. But pension funds
are broke. Pensions need yield, in a hurry.

What's the way out? The first step is for corporate leaders to step up
and speak for change. A couple have. The highest-profile one is Larry
Fink, the founder and CEO of BlackRock, which is the world's largest
investment manager. In January 2018, he sent out a letter to fellow CEOs
called "A Sense of Purpose," in which he wrote: "Society is demanding that companies, both public and private, serve a social purpose. To
prosper over time, every company must not only deliver financial performance, but also show how it makes a positive contribution to society.
Companies must benefit all of their stakeholders, including shareholders,
employees, customers, and the communities in which they operate."[33]
Fink has been associated with this view for some time—he has worked
with the Aspen Institute on these issues over the years—but this was the
boldest declaration he'd ever made. Fink's letter also mentioned "many
governments failing to prepare for the future," by which he would seem
to mean societies (like ours) that have decided that endless tax cutting is
more important than investing in the future. He's one man, but he's one
powerful man. His letter could prove to be an important moment in rein-
troducing a sense of social responsibility into the boardroom.

Around the same time, Bill McNabb, the chairman of the investment group Vanguard, urged CEOs in a letter to become a "force for
good" and to think about profit in longer time horizons and examine the
social consequences of their decisions. A *Financial Times* correspondent wrote in February 2018 that McNabb's letter shows "that [Milton]
Friedman's vision of capitalism is starting to look almost as passé as big
shoulder pads. At last week's World Economic Forum meeting in Davos,
CEOs were falling over themselves to talk about their 'corporate social
responsibility' departments."[34] I'm not sure about that passé part, but the
fact that an *FT* City correspondent was even writing such phrases marks

progress of a kind. Something is changing in corporate America. The defeat of Friedmanism is a must if we are to return to a prosperity that reaches everyone, and that's a war whose front lines will be the nation's boardrooms.

More broadly, another, more directly political problem is that corporate America has often let the Republican Party set the agenda for it rather than the other way around. This is especially true on the issue of taxes, and this must change. Some energy companies have supported a carbon tax in recent years, but because CEOs know Republicans will never consider it, they've just said it to get the PR Brownie points and have never done anything about it. Likewise, the Chamber of Commerce has for years backed a gas tax increase for infrastructure funding, but it has never pushed it. How on earth can the United States Chamber of Commerce be afraid of Grover Norquist and a bunch of politicians? They're the Chamber—they're supposed to be telling the politicians what to do! Chamber president Tom Donohue may finally have figured this out. Also in January 2018 (a big month for corporate responsibility), Donohue announced that for the first time, the Chamber will actually push Congress on a gas tax increase instead of just being for it on paper.[35] And he's not messing around: He wants a 25-cent-a-gallon increase, which would more than double the current federal tax and would yield $375 billion over a decade. That's serious money to address a serious public need. The way we used to do.

If We Can Keep It will end where it started. We are in trouble. Our political culture is broken, but it is not broken for the reasons you often read that it's broken—because "Washington" is "dysfunctional," or because politicians have no "will." No. It's broken because some people broke it. It was broken by the people who pushed an economic theory on the rest of us that has driven trillions of dollars that were once in middle-class people's pockets to a comparative few at the very top. Who refused to invest in the country anymore. Who will not even negotiate real investment. Who have been telling us for years that the market will take care of all our needs, while the market has in fact left thousands of towns and communities strafed and full of people addicted to drugs—the drugs, by the way, that that same free market is pumping out in vastly greater quantities, and for vastly greater profit, than it did twenty years ago. And who have built up a parallel media universe in which any of these commonsense assertions are dismissed as socialist, and in which anyone who doesn't endorse the thesis of Donald Trump's greatness is denounced as un-American.

They broke it. They broke it to gain power and to remake society in a way that was less communitarian, explicitly less equal, than the society we were building from 1945 to 1980. And—let me not forget this part— less democratic. I wrote earlier of Donald Trump's contempt for our institutions, our processes—put another way, for the democratic allocation of power. Many observers (me included, sometimes) have wondered why this didn't make Republicans recoil. The typical explanation has to do with their fear of his base, but I've come to believe that the simplest explanation is the best: They don't recoil because they're not especially bothered. They find him embarrassing at times, and they disagree with him here and there, but his demagogic approach doesn't really trouble them on the whole. They—not all of them, but certainly a critical mass of elected officials, operatives, and billionaires—no longer want to compete with and merely defeat liberalism on a level democratic playing field. They want to destroy it. This is why they do things like the aggressive gerrymandering, the voter suppression laws, the attempt to change how we elect senators, the blocking of Merrick Garland—all of which preceded Trump. They want to change the rules so that they never lose. And if destroying liberalism requires breaking the system—as it surely does—then so be it as far as they're concerned.

Yes, there were errors and excesses aplenty on the other side, my side, that required correction; on matters like welfare and crime, on which liberalism did surely fail (not that conservatism has succeeded: the war on drugs has been one of the great moral calamities of the last fifty years— imagine if we'd spent on treatment over all these decades what we've been spending locking up poor men caught with an ounce of weed or a gram of coke). But here's the thing: They weren't out merely to correct the errors and excesses. They used the errors and excesses as an excuse—which liberalism gave them, I admit—to import an entirely new ideology. And don't think they're finished. Ask Charles Koch how "finished" he thinks they are. If he's being honest, he'll say they're just getting their boots on.

They broke it with the thought only of winning in the moment; no concern for the long-term health of the republic. First it was some fairly mild anti-immigrant rhetoric; then it got bolder, flashier, because that's how these things progress. First it was relatively subtle racial dog-whistling; then, by degrees, a bit less so. First it was a stretching of the truth on this, on that; then, a real-live war mounted on false pretenses, complete with the accusation that those who didn't support the war were enemies of the government, of America, and of freedom itself. Each act and utterance of hatred, each lie, seemed, I suppose, defensible in the moment. But we see now what they've given us, drip by drip: a citizenry so inured to hatred and lies that is was willing to elect (even though a majority of them did not) exactly the kind of demagogue the founding fathers warned against. He is the apotheosis of the Age of Fracture.

Where do we go from here? Eventually, this Age of Fracture will end, and a fifth age will loom before us. What will we call that age? We might be able to call it the Age of Repair, if we act to repair things. And if we don't . . . I don't wish to sound melodramatic, but there is no law of the universe or heaven that says democratic republics have to last forever. They must be kept alive. Ours is dying. And a young generation is coming of age that doesn't have much faith in the American Dream, capitalism, or democracy. And based on what they've seen, why should they? All their lives, they've seen only growing inequality and increasing dysfunction.

We know what the problems are. And we know what the solutions are. We know what it will take to keep the republic. The only thing we don't know is whether the people who have the power to keep it will decide it's finally time to do so.

Acknowledgments

My great thanks to Robert Weil, who edited this book with wisdom and passion. It benefited tremendously from his enthusiasm and his suggestions. Great thanks also to Marie Pantojan, Peter Miller, and the rest of the terrific Liveright team.

Sincere thanks as always to my agent, Chris Calhoun, for his support and sound advice. My gratitude to a number of friends and associates who read all or portions of the manuscript, or who discussed some ideas with me, or simply shared some expertise: Bill Budinger, Sophia Crabbe-Field, E. J. Dionne Jr., Susan Eisenhower, Art Goldhammer, Walter Isaacson, Michael Kazin, Allen Kraut, James Ledbetter, Jane Mayer, Jim McNeill (who gave the manuscript such a close read), Jack Meserve, Miguel Padro, Ethan Porter, Joy-Ann Reid, Sam Rosenfeld, Michael Sandel, Mark Schmitt, Alix Kates Shulman, Theda Skocpol, Rob Stein, Susan Tomasky (wise older sister!), Jeffrey Toobin, and Rich Yeselson, who among other things thought up the title.

Steven P. Kelly was an incredibly conscientious and industrious research assistant; I am deeply grateful to him. My gratitude also to Margot Dionne and Gabriel Ferrante, who provided vital (and speedy!) research assistance. My friend E.J. is especially tickled that this is the Dionne family's first-ever father-daughter joint acknowledgment.

Thanks also to John Avlon and Noah Shachtman of the *Daily Beast*, my main place of employment, for their support; to Andrei Cherny and Kenneth Baer, founders of *Democracy: A Journal of Ideas*; to Clay Risen of the *New York Times*; to my friends at the *New York Review of Books*;

and, posthumously, to the wonderful Robert Silvers, whom it was such a privilege to call my friend.

Finally, my thanks to Sarah Kerr for her patience, help, and excellent suggestions; and most of all to my dear Margot Tomasky, who gets me out of bed in the morning, metaphorically and literally.

Notes

ONE: *The True History of Our Not-Very-Representative Democracy*

1. This comes from an analysis made by David Wasserman of the Cook Political Report in December 2012. The analysis is behind a subscription paywall on the Cook site, but media reports show that Wasserman found that Democratic candidates got 50.5 percent of the votes but won only 46.21 percent of the seats—partly because of the concentration of Democratic voters in urban areas, and partly because Republicans controlled many more state legislatures than Democrats, allowing them to draw districts that packed Democratic voters into a smaller number of districts.
2. See "Electoral Systems Around the World," at www.fairvote.org/research_electoralsystems_world.
3. Maurice Duverger, *Political Parties* (University Paperbacks, 1972), p. 217.
4. Ibid.
5. Max Farrand, *The Records of the Federal Convention of 1787* (Yale University Press, 1966; originally published in 1911), p. 48.
6. James Madison, *Notes of Debates in the Federal Convention of 1787* (Ohio University Press, 1985), p. 297.
7. Ibid., p. 301.
8. Andy King, *Edward I: A New King Arthur?* (Allen Lane, Penguin Random House UK, 2016), p. 33.
9. Rosemarie Zagarri, *The Politics of Size: Representation in the United States, 1776-1850* (Cornell University Press, 1987), p. 43.
10. Ibid., p. 37.
11. From Herbert J. Storing, ed., *The Complete Anti-Federalist* (University of Chicago Press, 1982), at http://teachingamericanhistory.org/library/document/brutus-iii/.
12. Zagarri, *Politics of Size*, p. 68.
13. François Furet and Mona Ozouf, eds., *A Critical Dictionary of the French Revolution*, trans. Arthur Goldhammer (Harvard University Press, 1989), p. 497.
14. Zagarri, *Politics of Size*, pp. 106–107.
15. Madison, *Notes of Debates*, p. 423.
16. Michele Rosa-Clot, "The Apportionment Act of 1842: 'An Odious Use of Authority,'" *Parliaments, Estates, and Representation* 31, no. 1 (June 2011): 37.
17. Ibid., p. 44.
18. Zagarri, *Politics of Size*, p. 140.

19. Rosa-Clot, "Apportionment Act of 1842," pp. 50–51.
20. David Canon and William Egar, "The Apportionment Act of 1842: Principle or Interest?" American Politics Workshop, UW-Madison Political Science Department, April 7, 2014, p. 4.
21. Emily Badger, "As American as Apple Pie? The Rural Vote's Disproportionate Slice of Power," *New York Times*, November 20, 2016.
22. Frederick Jackson Turner, "The Significance of the Frontier in American History," 1893, text at http://nationalhumanitiescenter.org/pds/gilded/empire/text1/turner.pdf.
23. Andrew Hacker, *Congressional Districting: The Issue of Equal Representation* (Brookings Institution, 1963), p. 2.
24. Ibid., p. 3.
25. J. Douglas Smith, *On Democracy's Doorstep: The Inside Story of How the Supreme Court Brought "One Person, One Vote" to the United States* (Hill & Wang, 2014), p. 21.
26. Ibid., p. 47.
27. Ibid., p. 4.

TWO: *We Were Always Polarized*

1. John Avlon, *Washington's Farewell: The Founding Father's Warning to Future Generations* (Simon & Schuster, 2017), p. 128.
2. Quoted in the Maryland State Archives page devoted to the history of the Maryland State House, at msa.maryland.gov/msa/mdstatehouse.
3. Wilfred E. Binkley, *American Political Parties: Their Natural History*, 4th ed. (Alfred A. Knopf, 1962), p. 5.
4. Henry Steele Commager, Samuel Eliot Morison, and William E. Leuchtenberg, *The Growth of the American Republic*, 7th ed., vol. 1 (Oxford University Press, 1980), p. 294.
5. Merrill D. Peterson, *Thomas Jefferson and the New Nation: A Biography* (Oxford University Press, 1970), p. 395.
6. Commager, Morison, and Leuchtenberg, *Growth of the American Republic*, p. 293.
7. John H. Aldrich, *Why Parties?: The Origin and Transformation of Political Parties in America* (University of Chicago Press, 1995), p. 69.
8. Commager, Morison, and Leuchtenberg, *Growth of the American Republic*, p. 297.
9. Ibid., p. 301.
10. Quoted in John Ferling, "Thomas Jefferson, Aaron Burr, and the Election of 1800," *Smithsonian*, November 1, 2004.
11. Arthur M. Schlesinger Jr., *The Age of Jackson* (Back Bay Books, 1945), p. 9.
12. William J. Cooper, *The Lost Founding Father: John Quincy Adams and the Transformation of American Politics* (Liveright, 2017), p. 246.
13. Donald B. Cole, *Martin Van Buren and the American Political System* (Eastern National, 2004; originally published by Princeton University Press, 1984), p. 16.
14. Martin Van Buren, *The Autobiography of Martin Van Buren*, ed. John Clement Fitzpatrick (Government Printing Office, 1920), p. 123.
15. Aldrich, *Why Parties?* p. 128.
16. Cole, *Martin Van Buren*, p. 151.
17. Ted Widmer, *Martin Van Buren* (Times Books, 2005), p. 56.
18. Schlesinger, *Age of Jackson*, p. 39.

19. Robert V. Remini, *Andrew Jackson* (Harper-Perennial, 1999; originally published by Twayne Publishers, 1966), p. 136.
20. Ibid.
21. Ibid.
22. "U.S. Population, 1790–2000: Always Growing," at http://www.u-s-history .com/pages/h980.html.
23. Michael F. Holt, *The Rise and Fall of the American Whig Party: Jacksonian Politics and the Onset of the Civil War* (Oxford University Press, 1999), p. 44.
24. Ibid., p. 31.
25. Jules Witcover, *Party of the People: A History of the Democrats* (Random House, 2003), p. 182.
26. Ibid.
27. Sidney Blumenthal, *Wrestling with His Angel: The Political Life of Abraham Lincoln*, vol. II, 1849–1856 (Simon & Schuster, 2017), p. 221.
28. Witcover, *Party of the People,* p. 194.
29. Holt, *Rise and Fall,* p. 957.
30. Johnson had no vice president, because there was no method for the selection of vice presidents for presidents who came to office in the way Johnson did until the 25th Amendment, adopted in 1967. Wade was president pro tempore of the Senate—then next in line for the presidency then; today, fourth in line. John Tyler, Millard Fillmore, and Chester A. Arthur also served without vice presidents.
31. Lewis L. Gould, *The Republicans: A History of the Grand Old Party* (Oxford University Press, 2014), p. 52.
32. Ibid., p. 61.
33. Heather Cox Richardson, *To Make Men Free: A History of the Republican Party* (Basic Books, 2014), p. 72.
34. Ibid., p. 118.
35. Gould, *Republicans,* p. 72.
36. Richardson, *To Make Men Free,* p. 151.
37. R. Hal Williams, *Realigning America: McKinley, Bryan, and the Remarkable Election of 1896* (University Press of Kansas, 2010), p. 61.
38. Gould, *Republicans,* p. 143.
39. Richardson, *To Make Men Free,* p. 182.
40. Witcover, *Party of the People,* p. 338.
41. Michael Tomasky, "The Boss," *New York Review of Books,* December 1, 2005.
42. Neil McMillen, *Dark Journey: Black Mississippians in the Age of Jim Crow* (University of Illinois Press, 1989), p. 43.
43. See, for example, Tara Mitchell Mielnik, "Manumission Intelligencer and Emancipator," on the website of the Tennessee Encyclopedia of History and Culture, www.tennesseeencyclopedia.net.
44. Witcover, *Party of the People,* p. 260.
45. Ibid., p. 276.
46. Michael Kazin, *A Godly Hero: The Life of William Jennings Bryan* (Anchor Books, 2007), p. xv.

THREE: *America in the Age of Consensus*

1. Roosevelt Institute, "Public Debt and Other Issues," April 28, 2010, at http:// rooseveltinstitute.org/public-debt-and-other-issues/.

2. National Bureau of Economic Research, "The Measurement and Behavior of Unemployment," 1957, at https://www.nber.org/chapters/c2644.pdf.

3. Wendy Wall, *Inventing the "American Way": The Politics of Consensus from the New Deal to the Civil Rights Movement* (Oxford University Press, 2008), p. 19.

4. Kim Phillips Fein, *Invisible Hands: The Businessmen's Crusade Against the New Deal* (W. W. Norton, 2010; originally published in 2009), p. 11.

5. Wall, *Inventing the "American Way,"* p. 15.

6. Ibid., p. 74.

7. From "100 Years of U.S. Consumer Spending: Data for the Nation, New York City, and Boston," U.S. Department of Labor, May 2006.

8. Cited in Paul Davidson, "Median Household Income Hits $59,039, Rising for 2nd Straight Year," *USA Today*, September 12, 2017.

9. Michael Morrisey, *Health Insurance*, 2nd ed. (Health Administration Press, 2013), p. 11.

10. These numbers all come from Nicholas Felton, "How Americans Spend Their Money," *New York Times*, February 10, 2008.

11. See, for example, Laura Stampler, "The Bizarre History of Women's Clothing Sizes," *Time*, October 23, 2014.

12. Krishnadev Calamur, "A Short History of 'America First,'" *The Atlantic*, January 21, 2017.

13. George F. Will, "Wendell Willkie's 1940 Nomination: When Party Establishments Mattered," *Washington Post*, June 17, 2016.

14. Michael Tomasky, "Mr. Bush, Meet Mr. Taft," *American Prospect*, November 14, 2005.

15. Harvey J. Kaye, *The Fight for the Four Freedoms: What Made FDR and the Greatest Generation Truly Great* (Simon & Schuster, 2014), p. 105.

16. Jason Maoz, "Remembering Babe Ruth's Concern for Jews During the Holocaust," *Jewish Press*, June 1, 2011.

17. Christopher J. Tassava, "The American Economy During World War II," at EH.net, a project of the Economic History Association.

18. From Reuther's online papers at Wayne State University, http://reuther100.wayne.edu/pdf/500_Planes_Speech.pdf.

19. Wall, *Inventing the "American Way,"* p. 91.

20. Michael S. Sweeney, *Secrets of Victory: The Office of Censorship and the American Press and Radio in World War II* (University of North Carolina Press, 2001), p. 109.

21. Quoted at PBS's "The War" website, at http://www.pbs.org/thewar/at_home_communication_news_censorship.htm.

22. Department of Veterans Affairs, VA Fact Sheet, "World War II Veterans by the Numbers," 2003.

23. Amy Bentley, *Eating for Victory: Food Rationing and the Politics of Domesticity* (University of Illinois Press, 1998), p. 5.

24. Ibid., p. 37.

25. Ibid., p. 35.

26. All these numbers are from the Tax Foundation, "U.S. Federal Individual Income Tax Rates History, 1862–2013," October 17, 2013.

27. Claudia Goldin and Robert A. Margo, "The Great Compression: The Wage Structure in the United States at Mid-Century," National Bureau of Economic Research, NBER Working Paper No. 3817, August 1991.

28. Wall, *Inventing the "American Way,"* p. 181.

29. Jefferson Cowie, *The Great Exception: The New Deal and the Limits of American Politics* (Princeton University Press, 2016), p. 131.

30. Richard H. Rovere, *Senator Joe McCarthy* (Harper Torchbooks, 1970), p. 3.

31. Norman Mailer, "The White Negro," in *Legacy of Dissent: Forty Years of Writing from Dissent Magazine* (Touchstone, 1994), p. 154.

32. Dwight D. Eisenhower, letter to Edgar Newton Eisenhower, November 8, 1954, at teachingamericanhistory.org.

33. John R. Thelin, *A History of American Higher Education* (Johns Hopkins University Press, 2011), p. 205.

34. Ira Shapiro, *The Last Great Senate: Courage and Statesmanship in a Time of Crisis* (Public Affairs, 2012), pp. xiii–xiv.

35. See the transcript of a Johnson-Russell telephone conversation from May 27, 1964. At https://www.mtholyoke.edu/acad/intrel/vietnam/lbjrr.htm.

F O U R : *Coming Apart*

1. Sam Rosenfeld, *The Polarizers: Postwar Architects of Our Partisan Era* (University of Chicago Press, 2017), p. 1.

2. Ibid., pp. 18–19.

3. Russell Kirk, "The Mechanical Jacobin," Russell Kirk Center for Cultural Renewal, at http://www.kirkcenter.org/detail/the-mechanical-jacobin.

4. Rick Perlstein, *Before the Storm: Barry Goldwater and the Unmaking of the American Consensus* (Nation Books, 2009), p. 15.

5. Herbert Marcuse, *One-Dimensional Man: Studies in the Ideology of Advanced Industrial Society* (Routledge, 2002), p. 10.

6. Michael O'Donnell, "How LBJ Saved the Civil Rights Act," *The Atlantic*, April 2014.

7. Cited in Thomas Byrne Edsall (with Mary D. Edsall), *Chain Reaction: The Impact of Race, Rights, and Taxes on American Politics* (W. W. Norton, 1992), p. 36.

8. Geoffrey Kabaservice, *Rule and Ruin: The Downfall of Moderation and the Destruction of the Republican Party, from Eisenhower to the Tea Party* (Oxford University Press, 2012), p. 202.

9. Jules Witcover, *Very Strange Bedfellows: The Short and Unhappy Marriage of Richard Nixon and Spiro Agnew* (Public Affairs, 2007), p. 5.

10. From 288,460 to 738,820, an increase of about 275 percent. See http://www.disastercenter.com/crime/uscrime.htm.

11. Edsall, *Chain Reaction*, p. 94.

12. See, for example, Joseph Carroll, "The Iraq-Vietnam Comparison," Gallup, June 15, 2004, at http://news.gallup.com/poll/11998/iraqvietnam-comparison.aspx.

13. Farrell found new notes written by Nixon campaign (and later White House) aide H. R. Haldeman confirming Nixon's orchestration of the "monkey-wrenching" of the peace talks while researching *Richard Nixon: The Life* (Doubleday, 2017).

14. See, for example, Nell Greenfield Boyce, "Pageant Protest Sparked Bra-Burning Myth," NPR, at https://www.npr.org/templates/story/story.php?storyId=94240375.

15. Elaine Tyler May, *America and the Pill: A History of Promise, Peril, and Liberation* (Basic Books, 2011), gives all this background; see especially chap. 1.

16. Lawrence Van Gelder, "Cardinals Shocked—Reaction Mixed," *New York Times*, January 23, 1973, p. A1.

17. Eileen Shanahan, "Equal Rights Amendment Passed by House, 345–23," *New York Times*, October 13, 1971.
18. Marjorie J. Spruill, *Divided We Stand: The Battle over Women's Rights and Family Values That Polarized American Politics* (Bloomsbury, 2017), p. 95.
19. Peter Applebome, "Jerry Falwell, Leading Religious Conservative, Dies," *New York Times*, May 15, 2007.
20. Roy Reed, "Both Sides in South Mistrust Nixon Actions on School Integration," *New York Times*, July 16, 1970.
21. Randall Balmer, "The Real Origins of the Christian Right," *Politico*, May 27, 2014.
22. Gallup, In Depth: Topics A to Z, "Abortion," at www.gallup.com.
23. See "Legal Immigration to the United States, 1820–Present," Migration Policy Institute, at https://www.migrationpolicy.org/programs/data-hub/charts/Annual-Number-of-US-Legal-Permanent-Residents.
24. David Cole, "McCarran-Walter Act Reborn?" *Washington Post*, November 18, 1990.
25. Dara Lind, "Operation Wetback, the 1950s Immigration Policy Donald Trump Loves, Explained," *Vox*, November 11, 2015.
26. All congressional votes can be found at www.govtrack.us.
27. Margaret Sands Orchowski, *The Law That Changed the Face of America: The Immigration and Nationality Act of 1965* (Rowman & Littlefield, 2015), p. 66.
28. Ibid., p. 70.
29. Andrew Kohut, Pew Research Center, Fact Tank: News in the Numbers, "50 Years Later, Americans Give Thumbs-Up to Immigration Law That Changed the Nation," February 4, 2015, at http://www.pewresearch.org/fact-tank/2015/02/04/50-years-later-americans-give-thumbs-up-to-immigration-law-that-changed-the-nation/.
30. Orchowski, *Law That Changed*, p. 49.
31. Doris Meissner, "U.S. Temporary Worker Programs: Lessons Learned," Migration Policy Institute, www.migrationpolicy.org, March 1, 2004.
32. Gallup, In Depth: Topics A to Z, "Immigration," at http://news.gallup.com/poll/1660/immigration.aspx.
33. *Economic Report of the President*, February 1968, together with the *Annual Report of the Council of Economic Advisers* (Government Printing Office).
34. From a chart assembled by the St. Louis Federal Reserve Bank, using official Census Bureau figures; can be found at http://economistsview.typepad.com/.a/6a00d83451b33869e201a5115729b5970c-popup.
35. All these global Gini numbers are from the Central Intelligence Agency's World Factbook. Not all numbers are from the same year, but all are fairly recent, within the past five years. At https://www.cia.gov/library/publications/the-world-factbook/rankorder/2172rank.html.
36. See, for example, Economic Policy Institute, "The Productivity-Pay Gap," at http://www.epi.org/productivity-pay-gap/.
37. All these inflation numbers are from http://www.inflation.eu/inflation-rates/united-states/historic-inflation/cpi-inflation-united-states.aspx.
38. These union membership numbers are from http://www.unionstats.com/.
39. Jefferson Cowie and Joseph Heathcott, *Beyond the Ruins: The Meanings of Deindustrialization* (Cornell University Press, 2003), p. 2.
40. This story is told in Judith Stein, *Pivotal Decade: How the United States Traded Factories for Finance in the Seventies* (Yale University Press, 2010), pp. 182–188.

41. See, for example, Paul Arnsberger, Melissa Ludlum, Margaret Riley, and Mark Stanton, "A History of the Tax-Exempt Sector: An SOI Perspective," in *Statistics of Income Bulletin*, Internal Revenue Service, March 2008, at https://www .irs.gov/pub/irs-soi/tehistory.pdf.

42. Paul C. Light, "Government's Greatest Achievements of the Past Half Century," December 1, 2000, at https://www.brookings.edu/research/governments-greatest-achievements-of-the-past-half-century/.

43. Lee Drutman, "How Corporate Lobbyists Conquered American Democracy," *The Atlantic*, April 20, 2015.

44. Mark Schmitt, "The Legend of the Powell Memo," *American Prospect*, April 27, 2005.

45. Alyssa Katz, *The Influence Machine: The U.S. Chamber of Commerce and the Corporate Capture of American Life* (Spiegel & Grau, 2015), p. 38.

46. Steven M. Teles, *The Rise of the Conservative Legal Movement: The Battle for Control of the Law* (Princeton University Press, 2008); see especially chap. 2.

47. Author interview with Rob Stein, October 25, 2017.

48. Matt Bai, "Wiring the Vast Left-Wing Conspiracy," *New York Times Magazine*, July 25, 2004.

F I V E : *More Consumers Than Citizens*

1. Wayne Barrett, *Trump: The Deals and the Downfall* (HarperCollins, 1992), p. 189.

2. The biographer is Harry Hurt III, and the book is *Lost Tycoon*. Quoted in Max J. Rosenthal, "The Trump Files: When Donald Destroyed Historic Art to Build Trump Tower," *Mother Jones*, July 13, 2016.

3. Jeff Guo, "Donald Trump Is More than Right: Most Americans Don't Work (But . . .)," *Washington Post*, September 29, 2015.

4. The Henry J. Kaiser Foundation, "Population Distribution by Citizenship Status," 2016, at https://www.kff.org/other/state-indicator/distribution-by-citizenship-status/?currentTimeframe=0&sortModel=%7B%22colId%22:%22 Location%22,%22sort%22:%22asc%22%7D.

5. Alexis de Tocqueville, *Democracy in America,* trans. Arthur Goldhammer (Library of America, 2004), p. 611.

6. Quoted in Albert O. Hirschman, *Shifting Involvements: Private Interest and Public Action* (Princeton University Press, 1982), p. 98.

7. Joe Nocera, *A Piece of the Action: How the Middle Class Joined the Money Class,* Simon & Schuster, 2013; originally published in 1994), p. 167.

8. https://inflationdata.com/articles/inflation-cpi-consumer-price-index-1970-1979/.

9. Robert J. Samuelson, "The Great Inflation and Its Aftermath," *Washington Post,* January 4, 2008 (excerpt from his book of the same name, Random House, 2008).

10. Nocera, *A Piece of the Action,* p. 99.

11. Ibid., p. 145.

12. Tamara Draut and Javier Silva, "Borrowing to Make Ends Meet: Credit Card Debt in the 1990s," Demos, 2003, p. 9.

13. Nocera, *A Piece of the Action,* p. 257.

14. Ibid., p. 220.

15. See, for example, William Lazonick, "To Boost Investment, End S.E.C. Rule That Spurs Stock Buybacks," *New York Times*, March 6, 2015.

16. Nick Hanauer, "Stock Buybacks Are Killing the American Economy," *The Atlantic*, February 8, 2015.

17. See Ann Crittenden, "Reaping the Big Profits from a Fat Cat," *New York Times*, August 7, 1983.

18. See Elaine X. Grant, "TWA—Death of a Legend," *St. Louis Magazine*, October 2005.

19. Lynn Stuart Parramore, " 'Greed Is Good': Top 7 Most Piggish Commencement Speeches," *Alternet,* May 26, 2013.

20. Ronald E. Yates, "Adding Up Arguments on CEO Pay," *Chicago Tribune*, March 3, 1996.

21. Amy Plitt, "$125,000 Time Warner Center Penthouse Is Now NYC's Most Expensive Non-Hotel Rental," Curbed New York, July 12, 2017.

22. Steve Fraser, *Wall Street: America's Dream Palace* (Yale University Press, 2008), p. 128.

23. For this and all inflation adjustments in this book, I used the official "CPI Inflation Calculator" of the Bureau of Labor Statistics, at https://data.bls.gov/cgi-bin/cpicalc.pl.

24. See https://www.onwallstreet.com/slideshow/wall-street-salaries-bonuses-1985-2012.

25. Alyssa Davis and Lawrence Mishel, "CEO Pay Continues to Rise as Typical Workers Are Paid Less," Economic Policy Institute paper, June 12, 2014.

26. Daniel T. Rodgers, *The Age of Fracture* (Harvard University Press, 2011), p. 41 and passim (this phrase is the title of chap. 2).

27. Stein, *Pivotal Decade*, p. 203.

28. Ibid., p. 202.

29. These tax rates are taken from "U.S. Federal Individual Income Tax Rates History, 1862–2013 (Nominal and Inflation-Adjusted Brackets), at https://taxfoundation.org/us-federal-individual-income-tax-rates-history-1913-2013-nominal-and-inflation-adjusted-brackets/.

30. An answer exists. It's called "middle-out economics," and it is the idea that investments in the middle class, not the rich, are the key to growth. That is to say, it's not an argument for *fairness*, but an argument that middle-class investments spur better *growth*. The journal I edit, *Democracy: A Journal of Ideas*, has published a number of articles promoting this idea, notably by Nick Hanauer and Eric Liu, and by David Madland. President Obama promoted the idea occasionally, but it hasn't really caught on among Democrats more widely, I suspect because Democrats aren't as interested in growth as they are in fairness.

31. Rodgers, *Fracture*, p. 76.

32. For a list of the highest-paid baseball players from 1874 to 2016, see http://sabr.org/research/mlbs-annual-salary-leaders-1874-2012.

33. For all MLB 2017 salaries, see https://www.usatoday.com/sports/mlb/salaries/2017/player/all/.

34. According to www.baseball-reference.com, Kershaw pitched 175 innings and threw 2,521 pitches in 2017, for $33 million.

35. Robert H. Frank, *Luxury Fever: Weighing the Cost of Excess* (Princeton University Press, 1999), p. 2.

36. Quoted in Robert H. Frank and Philip J. Cook, *The Winner-Take-All Society: Why the Few at the Top Get So Much More Than the Rest of Us* (Penguin Paperback, 1996), p. 41.

37. "History of Cable Television," Wisconsin Cable Communications Association, at http://www.wicable.tv/aws/WCCA/pt/sp/history.

38. The 92 billion figure is from *Business Insider*, at http://www.businessinsider .com/cable-tv-subscriber-losses-q2-chart-2017-6. The $103 figure is from Aaron Pressman, "The Average Cable TV Bill Has Hit a New All-Time Record," *Fortune*, September 23, 2016.

39. "Value of the Video Game Market in the United States from 2011 to 2020," Statista, at https://www.statista.com/statistics/246892/value-of-the-video-game-market-in-the-us/.

40. Mark Koba, "World Series Tickets for $12? . . . Yes, in 1963," CNBC.com, October 23, 2013.

41. Bill Shaikin, "Dodgers Set Post-Season Ticket Prices. World Series Seats Would Start at $166," *Los Angeles Times*, August 16, 2017.

42. All the numbers about historic Dallas Cowboys ticket prices come from a spreadsheet made by Rodney Fort, who writes a blog on the economics of sports at https://sites.google.com/site/rodswebpages/codes. The spreadsheet can be found at https://umich.app.box.com/s/41707f0b2619c0107b8b/file/256 0911917.

43. These numbers about concert ticket prices are from Meryl Gottlieb, "The 20 Music Stars People Paid the Most to See in 2016," *Business Insider*, December 10, 2016.

44. Michael J. Sandel, *What Money Can't Buy: The Moral Limits of Markets* (Farrar, Straus & Giroux, 2012), pp. 19–20.

45. See http://money.cnn.com/interactive/economy/minimum-wage-since-1938/index .html.

46. See https://tradingeconomics.com/united-states/wage-growth.

47. Michael Tomasky, "2016: The Republicans Write," *New York Review of Books*, March 19, 2015.

SIX: *From Gingrich to Trump—the System Explodes*

1. Adam Clymer, "Robert Michel Dies at 93; House G.O.P. Leader Prized Conciliation," *New York Times*, February 17, 2017.

2. Adam Lioz, "Buckley v. Valeo at 40," Demos, December 15, 2015, at http://www .demos.org/publication/buckley-v-valeo-40.

3. Campaign Finance Institute study, at http://www.cfinst.org/pdf/vital/ VitalStats_t1.pdf.

4. Andy Sullivan, "Insight: In Washington, Lawmakers' Routines Shaped by Fundraising," Reuters, June 12, 2013.

5. Lee Drutman, *The Business of America Is Lobbying: How Corporations Became Politicized and Politics Became More Corporate* (Oxford University Press, 2015), p. 60.

6. Matt Grossman and David A. Hopkins, *Asymmetric Politics: Ideological Republicans and Group Interest Democrats* (Oxford University Press, 2016), p. 286.

7. Quoted in Tim Murphy, "Your (Bonus) Daily Newt: Why Gingrich Missed Vietnam," *Mother Jones*, January 9, 2012.

8. Michael Tomasky, "Newt Gingrich, Hypocrisy Pioneer," *Daily Beast*, June 20, 2017.

9. See, for example, Rick Bragg, "Defending Smith, Stepfather Says He Also Bears Blame," *New York Times*, July 28, 1995.

10. Maureen Dowd, "G.O.P.'s Rising Star Pledges to Right Wrongs of the Left," *New York Times*, November 9, 1994.

11. Matt Storin, "Ted Kennedy and Abortion," *Notre Dame Magazine*, September 1, 2009.

12. All these numbers are from a phone interview with Kristen Day of Democrats for Life of America, conducted March 16, 2018. The group defines "pro-life" as voting in support of the Hyde Amendment, which bars the use of federal funds for most abortion services.

13. E. J. Dionne Jr., *Why the Right Went Wrong: Conservatism from Goldwater to the Tea Party and Beyond* (Simon & Schuster, 2016), p. 117.

14. "Southern Democrats Lose Clout," *CQ Almanac*, 1995, p. C-10.

15. Michael Tomasky, *Bill Clinton*, The American Presidents series (Times Books, 2017), p. 5.

16. Federal Communications Commission Reports, "In the Matter of Editorializing by Broadcast Licensees," at https://apps.fcc.gov/edocs_public/attachmatch/DOC-295673A1.pdf, p. 1258.

17. Juanita "Frankie" Clogston, "The Repeal of the Fairness Doctrine and the Irony of Talk Radio: A Story of Political Entrepreneurship, Risk, and Cover," *Journal of Policy History* 28, no. 2: p. 377.

18. Ibid., p. 383.

19. Ibid., p. 380.

20. See https://www.govtrack.us/congress/votes/100-1987/h158.

21. See https://www.govtrack.us/congress/votes/100-1987/s75.

22. Reginald Stuart, "Court Says Law Doesn't Require Broadcasting's Fairness Doctrine," *New York Times*, September 20, 1986.

23. Clogston, "Repeal of the Fairness Doctrine," p. 375.

24. Wesley Pruden, "The Democrats Search for Another Lost Cause," *Washington Times*, August 17, 2017.

25. Jim Naughton and Phil McCombs, "McLaughlin Suit Settled," *Washington Post*, December 2, 1989.

26. Sidney Blumenthal, *The Clinton Wars* (Farrar, Straus & Giroux, 2003), p. 83.

27. Tim Dickinson, "So Long, Fairness Doctrine," *Rolling Stone*, August 24, 2011.

28. Bruce Bartlett, "A Budget Deal That Did Reduce the Deficit," *Fiscal Times*, February 3, 2011.

29. Nina Easton, *Gang of Five: Leaders at the Center of the Conservative Ascendancy* (Touchstone, 2000), p. 70.

30. Economic Data from the St. Louis Federal Reserve, see https://fred.stlouisfed.org/series/FYFRGDA188S.

31. Robert Lindsey, "Howard Jarvis, 82, Tax Rebel, Is Dead," *New York Times*, August 14, 1986.

32. Michael Hiltzik, "Four Decades Later, California Experts Find that Proposition 13 Is a Boon to the Rich," *Los Angeles Times*, September 30, 2016.

33. Paul Light, *Artful Work: The Politics of Social Security Reform* (Random House, 1985), p. 187.

34. Sophie Quinton, "Reluctant States Raise Gas Taxes to Repair Roads," Pew Stateline, at http://www.pewtrusts.org/en/research-and-analysis/blogs/stateline/2017/07/26/reluctant-states-raise-gas-taxes-to-repair-roads.

35. Sam Stein, "Chuck Schumer Says No to Gas Tax Hike, Complicating Trump's Infrastructure Push," *Daily Beast*, November 23, 2017.

36. See, for example, Mark Niquette and John McCormick, "Americans Say They

Back Higher Gas Tax to Fix Crumbling Roads," Bloomberg, July 20, 2017. In that poll, a gas tax increase was supported by 55 percent of respondents and opposed by 41 percent. This is representative of the polls I looked at. Results fluctuate somewhat toward opposition when gas prices are particularly high, but generally, the American public supports an increase consistently. In this poll even 51 percent of Republicans agreed.

37. John Woolley and Gerhard Peters, "Final Presidential Job Approval Ratings," The American Presidency Project, at http://www.presidency.ucsb.edu/data/final_approval.php.

38. Ronald Brownstein, "Pulling Apart," *National Journal*, February 24, 2011.

39. Theda Skocpol, "Understanding U.S. Politics Today—and the Implications for Higher Education," PowerPoint presentation, April 8, 2018, p. 8, shared with the author.

40. Jane Mayer, *Dark Money: The Hidden History of the Billionaires Behind the Rise of the Radical Right* (Doubleday, 2016), p. 8.

41. Theda Skocpol and Alex Hertel-Fernandez, "The Koch Network and Republican Party Extremism," *Perspectives on Politics*, September 2016, pp. 689–690.

42. Matt Grossman and David A. Hopkins, *Asymmetric Politics: Ideological Republicans and Group Interest Democrats* (Oxford University Press, 2016), p. 3.

43. Ibid., pp. 51–53.

44. Ibid., p. 29.

45. Ibid., p. 37.

46. Ibid., p. 259.

47. Ronald Brownstein, "What Happens to the Democratic Party After Obama?" *The Atlantic*, January 12, 2017.

48. Sydney Schaedel, "Clinton Counties," FactCheck.org, December 9, 2016.

49. "Presidential Approval Ratings, Barack Obama," Gallup, at http://news.gallup.com/poll/116479/barack-obama-presidential-job-approval.aspx.

SEVEN: *If We Can Keep It: A Fourteen-Point Agenda to Reduce Polarization*

1. Marion Mills Miller, ed., *Great Debates in American History: States' Rights (1798–1861), Slavery (1858–1861)*, Current Literature Publishing Co., 1913, p. 164.

2. National Archives Catalog, at https://catalog.archives.gov/id/187095.

3. The age distribution of the 1940 Census is broken down by the Census Bureau at https://www.census.gov/newsroom/cspan/1940census/CSPAN_1940slides.pdf.

4. Robert Frank, "Talent and the Winner-Take-All Society," *American Prospect*, Spring 1994.

5. Christopher Ingraham, "How Doug Jones Lost in Nearly Every Congressional District but Still Won the State," *Washington Post*, December 13, 2017.

6. All these facts from David Daley, *Ratf**ked: The True Story Behind the Secret Plan to Steal America's Democracy* (Liveright, 2016), p. 23.

7. Don Beyer, "Let's Change How We Elect the House of Representatives," *Washington Post*, June 27, 2017.

8. Robert Farley, "Conservative Group Claims New Law Would Require People to Throw Away Existing Light Bulbs and Replace with More Efficient Ones," PolitiFact, May 20, 2011.

9. Cited in Stephen Macedo, "Toward a More Democratic Congress?" *Boston University Law Review* 89, no. 609 (2009): p. 613.

10. Center for Media and Democracy, "ALEC Exposed," at https://www
    .alecexposed.org/wiki/What_is_ALEC.
11. ALEC Web site, "A Restoration of the Constitutional Intent of our Found-
    ing Fathers: Repeal of the Seventeenth Amendment," at https://www.alec
    .org/article/a-restoration-of-the-constitutional-intent-of-our-founding-fathers-
    repeal-of-the-seventeenth-amendment/.
12. Quoted in Michael Tomasky, "The Specter Haunting the Senate," *New York
    Review of Books*, September 30, 2010.
13. Helpful here was the website of Nonprofit Vote, at http://www.nonprofitvote
    .org/electoral-college-compromise-never-meant-last/.
14. From the website of National Popular Vote, at https://www.nationalpopularvote
    .com/campaign-events-2016.
15. For some representative quotes, see Ryan Teague Beckwith, "Here's How Cam-
    paigns Would Work if We Abolished the Electoral College," *Time*, November
    17, 2016.
16. Jason Zengerle, "In Conversation: Barney Frank," *New York*, April 15, 2012.
17. Summer Concepcion, "David Duke: Charlottesville Rally 'Fulfills the Promises
    of Donald Trump,'" *Talking Points Memo*, August 12, 2017.
18. Denis Slattery, "Alex Jones, Roger Stone Hit Shooting Range to Prepare for
    Civil War They Say Would Break Out if Trump Is Removed," *New York Daily
    News*, December 22, 2017.
19. Richard Lyons and William Chapman, "Judiciary Committee Approves Article
    to Impeach President Nixon, 27 to 11," *Washington Post*, July 28, 1974.
20. Edward Isaac-Dovere, "John Dean: Nixon 'Might Have Survived If There'd
    Been a Fox News,'" *Politico*, January 2, 2018.
21. Amy B. Wang, "Former Facebook VP Says Social Media Is Destroying Soci-
    ety with 'Dopamine-Driven Feedback Loops,'" *Washington Post*, December 12,
    2017.
22. Quoted in Laura Rosenberger and Jamie Fly, "Shredding the Putin Playbook,"
    Democracy: A Journal of Ideas, Winter 2018, p. 52.
23. Ben Collins and Joseph Cox, "Jenna Abrams, Russia's Clown Troll Princess,
    Duped the Mainstream Media and the World," *Daily Beast*, November 2, 2017.
24. See, for example, James V. Grimaldi and Paul Overberg, "Millions of People
    Post Comments on Federal Regulations. Many Are Fake," *Wall Street Journal*,
    December 12, 2017.
25. Andrew Guess, Brendan Nyhan, and Jason Reifler, "Selective Exposure to Mis-
    information: Evidence from the Consumption of Fake News During the 2016
    U.S. Presidential Campaign," at https://www.dartmouth.edu/~nyhan/fake-
    news-2016.pdf.
26. Vidya Narayanan et al., "Polarization, Partisanship, and Junk News Consump-
    tion over Social Media in the US," February 6, 2018, at http://comprop.oii.ox.ac
    .uk/wp-content/uploads/sites/93/2018/02/Polarization-Partisanship-JunkNews
    .pdf.
27. Both quotes from Richard D. Kahlenberg and Clifford Janey, "Putting Democ-
    racy Back into Public Education," Century Foundation, November 10, 2016.
28. John Avlon, *Washington's Farewell: The Founding Father's Warning to Future
    Generations* (Simon & Schuster, 2017), p. 243.
29. E. D. Hirsch Jr., "A Sense of Belonging," *Democracy: A Journal of Ideas*, no. 44
    (Spring 2017): 65.

30. Willam A. Galston, *Anti-Pluralism: The Populist Threat to Liberal Democracy* (Yale University Press, 2018), p. 89.

31. Economic Innovation Group, *The New Map of Economic Growth and Recovery*, May 2016, p. 21.

32. Both quotes viewable at http://www.omnex.com/sustainability/csr.html.

33. Fink's full letter can be found at https://www.blackrock.com/corporate/investor-relations/larry-fink-ceo-letter.

34. Gillian Tett, "In the Vanguard: Fund Giants Urge CEOs to Be 'Force for Good,'" *Financial Times*, February 1, 2018.

35. John Wagner, "U.S. Chamber of Commerce to Push Trump, Congress to Raise the Gas Tax to Fund Infrastructure," *Washington Post*, January 16, 2018.

Bibliography

Aldrich, John H. *Why Parties? The Origin and Transformation of Political Parties in America*. University of Chicago Press, 1995.

Avlon, John. *Washington's Farewell: The Founding Father's Warning to Future Generations*. Simon & Schuster, 2017.

Bagby, Wesley M. *The Road to Normalcy: The Presidential Campaign and Election of 1920*. Johns Hopkins Press, 1962.

Barrett, Wayne. *Trump: The Deals and the Downfall*. HarperCollins, 1992.

Bentley, Amy. *Eating for Victory: Food Rationing and the Politics of Domesticity*. University of Illinois Press, 1998.

Bilder, Mary Sarah. *Madison's Hand: Revising the Constitutional Convention*. Harvard University Press, 2015.

Binkley, Wilfred E. *American Political Parties, Their Natural History*. Knopf, 1943.

Blumenthal, Sidney. *Wrestling with His Angel: The Political Life of Abraham Lincoln, Volume II, 1849–1856*. Simon & Schuster, 2017.

Borneman, Walter R. *Polk: The Man Who Transformed the Presidency and America*. Random House, 2009.

Cohen, Lizabeth. *A Consumers' Republic: The Politics of Mass Consumption in Postwar America*. Vintage, 2004.

Cole, Donald B. *Martin Van Buren and the American Political System*. Princeton University Press, 1984.

Commager, Henry Steele, Samuel Eliot Morison, and William E. Leuchtenburg. *The Growth of the American Republic, Volume I*. Oxford University Press, 1980 (orig. 1930).

Committee for Economic Development, Research and Policy Committee. *Social Responsibilities of Business Corporations*. CED, 1971.

Cooper, William J. *The Lost Founding Father: John Quincy Adams and the Transformation of American Politics*. Liveright, 2017.

Cornell, Saul. *The Other Founders: Anti-Federalism & the Dissenting Tradition in America, 1787–1828*. University of North Carolina Press, 1999.

Cowie, Jefferson. *The Great Exception: The New Deal & the Limits of American Politics*. Princeton University Press, 2016.

Daley, David. *Ratf**ked: The True Story Behind the Secret Plan to Steal America's Democracy*. Liveright, 2016.

Dichter, Ernest, *The Strategy of Desire*. Doubleday, 1960.

Dionne, E. J., Jr. *Why the Right Went Wrong: Conservatism—from Goldwater to the Tea Party and Beyond*. Simon & Schuster, 2016.

Drutman, Lee. *The Business of America: How Corporations Became Politicized and Politics Became More Corporate.* Oxford University Press, 2015.

Duverger, Maurice, *Political Parties: Their Organization and Activity in the Modern State.* Methuen, 1954.

Easton, Nina J. *Gang of Five: Leaders at the Center of the Conservative Ascendancy.* Touchstone, 2000.

Edsall, Thomas Byrne, with Mary D. Edsall. *Chain Reaction: The Impact of Race, Rights, and Taxes on American Politics.* Norton, 1991.

Eisenhower, John S. D. *Zachary Taylor.* Times Books, 2008.

Farrand, Max, ed. *The Records of the Federal Convention of 1787, Volume I.* Yale University Press, 1911.

Finkelman, Paul. *Millard Fillmore.* Times Books, 2011.

Foley, Michael. *The New Senate: Liberal Influence on a Conservative Institution, 1959–1972.* Yale University Press, 1980.

Frank, Robert H. *Falling Behind: How Rising Inequality Harms the Middle Class.* University of California Press, 2007.

———. *Luxury Fever: Weighing the Cost of Excess.* Princeton University Press, 1999.

Frank, Robert H., and Philip J. Cook. *The Winner-Take-All Society: Why the Few at the Top Get Much More Than the Rest of Us.* Free Press, 1995.

Fraser, Steve. *Wall Street: America's Dream Palace.* Yale University Press, 2008.

Freehling, William W. *The Road to Disunion, Volume II: Secessionists Triumphant, 1854–1861.* Oxford University Press, 2007.

Furet, François, and Mona Ozouf, eds. *A Critical Dictionary of the French Revolution.* Translated by Arthur Goldhammer. Harvard University Press, 1989.

Gould, Lewis L. *Four Hats in the Ring: The 1912 Election and the Birth of Modern American Politics.* University Press of Kansas, 2008.

———. *The Republicans: A History of the Grand Old Party.* Oxford University Press, 2014.

Grossman, Matt, and David A. Hopkins. *Asymmetric Politics: Ideological Republicans and Group Interest Democrats.* Oxford University Press, 2016.

Hacker, Andrew, with Robert D. Calkins. *Congressional Redistricting: The Issue of Equal Representation.* Brookings Institution, 1963.

Hirsch, E. D., Jr. *The Making of Americans: Democracy and Our Schools.* Yale University Press, 2009.

Hirschman, Albert O. *Shifting Involvements: Private Interest and Public Action.* Princeton University Press, 1982.

Holt, Michael P. *The Rise and Fall of the American Whig Party: Jacksonian Politics and the Onset of the Civil War.* Oxford University Press, 1999.

Kabaservice, Geoffrey. *Rule and Ruin: The Downfall of Moderation and the Destruction of the Republican Party, from Eisenhower to the Tea Party.* Oxford University Press, 2012.

Katz, Alyssa. *The Influence Machine: The U.S. Chamber of Commerce and the Corporate Capture of American Life.* Spiegel & Grau, 2015.

Katznelson, Ira. *Fear Itself: The New Deal and the Origins of Our Time.* Liveright, 2013.

Kaye, Harvey J. *The Fight for the Four Freedoms: What Made FDR and the Greatest Generation Truly Great.* Simon & Schuster, 2014.

Kazin, Michael. *A Godly Hero: The Life of William Jennings Bryan.* Anchor Books, 2007.

King, Andy. *Edward I: A New King Arthur?* Allen Lane, 2016.

Larson, Edward J., and Michael P. Winship. *The Constitutional Convention: A Narrative History from the Notes of James Madison.* Modern Library, 2005.

Light, Paul. *Artful Work: The Politics of Social Security Reform.* Random House, 1985.

Madison, James. *Notes of Debates in the Federal Convention of 1787, Reported by James Madison.* With an introduction by Adrienne Koch. Ohio University Press, 1966.

Martis, Kenneth C. *The Historical Atlas of Political Parties in the United States Congress, 1789–1989.* Macmillan, 1989.

Mayer, Jane. *Dark Money: The Hidden History of the Billionaires Behind the Rise of the Radical Right.* Doubleday, 2016.

McCarty, Nolan, Keith T. Poole, and Howard Rosenthal. *Polarized America: The Dance of Ideology and Unequal Riches.* MIT Press, 2006.

McMillen, Neil R. *Dark Journey: Black Mississippians in the Age of Jim Crow.* University of Illinois Press, 1989.

Mumford, Lewis. *Faith for Living.* Harcourt, Brace & Co., 1940.

Murray, Robert K. *The 103rd Ballot: The Legendary 1924 Democratic Convention That Forever Changed Politics.* Harper & Row, 1976.

Nocera, Joe. *A Piece of the Action: How the Middle Class Joined the Money Class.* Simon & Schuster, 2013.

O'Neill, Tip, with William Novak. *Man of the House: The Life and Political Memoirs of Speaker Tip O'Neill.* Random House, 1987.

Orchowski, Margaret Sands. *The Law That Changed the Face of America: The Immigration and Nationality Act of 1965.* Rowman & Littlefield, 2015.

Pells, Richard H. *The Liberal Mind in a Conservative Age: American Intellectuals in the 1940s and 1950s.* Wesleyan University Press, 1985.

Perlstein, Rick. *Before the Storm: Barry Goldwater and the Unmaking of the American Consensus.* Hill & Wang, 2001.

Peterson, Merrill D. *Thomas Jefferson & the New Nation.* Oxford University Press, 1970.

Phillips-Fein, Kim. *Invisible Hands: The Businessmen's Crusade Against the New Deal.* W. W. Norton, 2009.

Pole, J. R. *Political Representation in England & the Origins of the American Republic.* University of California Press, 1966.

Ravitch, Diane, and Joseph P. Viteritti. *Making Good Citizens: Education and Civil Society.* Yale University Press, 2001.

Remini, Robert V. *Andrew Jackson.* Perennial, 1966.

Richardson, Heather Cox. *To Make Men Free: A History of the Republican Party.* Basic Books, 2014.

Rodgers, Daniel T. *Age of Fracture.* Harvard University Press, 2011.

Rosenfeld, Sam. *The Polarizers: Postwar Architects of Our Partisan Era.* University of Chicago Press, 2018.

Rovere, Richard H. *Senator Joe McCarthy.* Harper Torchbooks, 1959.

Sandel, Michael J. *What Money Can't Buy: The Moral Limits of Markets.* Farrar, Straus & Giroux, 2012.

Schlesinger, Arthur M. Jr. *The Age of Jackson.* Little, Brown & Co., 1945.

———. *History of U.S. Political Parties, Volume I, 1789–1860, From Factions to Parties.* Chelsea House, 1973.

Seymour, Charles. *How the World Votes: The Story of Democratic Development in Elections, Volume II.* C. A. Nichols Co., 1918.

Shafer, Byron E. *The American Political Pattern: Stability and Change, 1932–2016.* University Press of Kansas, 2016.

Shapiro, Ira. *The Last Great Senate: Courage and Statesmanship in a Time of Crisis.* Public Affairs, 2012.

Smith, J. Douglas. *On Democracy's Doorstep: The Inside Story of How the Supreme Court Brought "One Person, One Vote" to the United States.* Hill & Wang, 2014.

Spruill, Marjorie J. *Divided We Stand: The Battle over Women's Rights and Family Values That Polarized American Politics.* Bloomsbury, 2017.

Stein, Judith. *Pivotal Decade: How the United States Traded Factories for Finance in the Seventies.* Yale University Press, 2010.

Storing, Herbert J., ed. *The Anti-Federalist: Writings by the Opponents of the Constitution.* Abridgements by Murray Dry. University of Chicago Press, 1981.

Sweeney, Michael S. *Secrets of Victory: The Office of Censorship and the American Press and Radio in World War II.* University of North Carolina Press, 2001.

Teles, Steven M. *The Rise of the Conservative Legal Movement: The Battle for Control of the Law.* Princeton University Press, 2008.

Thelin, John R. *A History of American Higher Education.* Johns Hopkins University Press, 2011.

Trentmann, Frank. *Empire of Things: How We Became a World of Consumers, from the Fifteenth Century to the Twenty-First.* HarperCollins, 2016.

Van Buren, Martin. *The Autobiography of Martin Van Buren.* Edited by John Clement Fitzpatrick. Government Printing Office, 1920.

Wall, Wendy L. *Inventing the American Way: The Politics of Consensus from the New Deal to the Civil Rights Movement.* Oxford University Press, 2008.

Wartzman, Rick. *The End of Loyalty: The Rise and Fall of Good Jobs in America.* Public Affairs, 2017.

Widmer, Ted. *Martin Van Buren.* Times Books, 2005.

Williams, R. Hal. *Realigning America: McKinley, Bryan, and the Remarkable Election of 1896.* University Press of Kansas, 2010.

Witcover, Jules. *Party of the People: A History of the Democrats.* Random House, 2003.

———. *Very Strange Bedfellows: The Short and Unhappy Marriage of Richard Nixon and Spiro Agnew.* Public Affairs, 2007.

Wood, Gordon S. *The Creation of the American Republic, 1776–1787.* University of North Carolina Press, 1998; orig. 1969.

Zagarri, Rosemarie. *The Politics of Size: Representation in the United States, 1776–1850.* Cornell University Press, 1987.

Index

Page numbers in *italics* refer to illustrations.

MICHAEL TOMASKY is a columnist for the *Daily Beast,* where he's written on domestic politics and international affairs since 2010. He is also a contributing opinion writer for the *New York Times* and the editor of *Democracy: A Journal of Ideas*, a quarterly journal based in Washington. He is also a regular contributor to the *New York Review of Books*, where he has written more than fifty essays and reviews since 2002. He is the former editor of the *American Prospect*. He has made numerous television appearances and is a regular guest on several radio shows.

He is the author of four books, which include *Left for Dead* (1996), about the potential future of progressive politics after the Gingrich takeover; *Hillary's Turn* (2001), about Hillary Clinton's first U.S. Senate campaign; the ebook *Yeah! Yeah! Yeah!: The Beatles and America, Then and Now* (2014), an essay on the cultural impact of the Beatles on the occasion of the fiftieth anniversary of their arrival in the United States; and the 2017 release *Bill Clinton*, a short political biography of the former president as part of the American Presidents series conceived by Arthur M. Schlesinger Jr. and edited by Princeton historian Sean Wilentz.

He was born and raised in Morgantown, West Virginia, the son of a trial lawyer and a schoolteacher. He received his undergraduate degree in journalism from West Virginia University and his master's in politics from New York University.

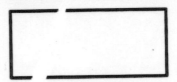
DATE DUE

This item is Due on
or before Date shown.

FEB – – 2019